D0812642

'This book should be on the reading list of every new parent who is struggling with the complexities of raising boys in a world where technological culture intrudes ever more insistently and irresistibly into family life' *Juno Magazine*

'As Sue Palmer says, it will be the small actions of parents and other responsible adults who will make the greatest difference, enabling the next generation of young men to grow up bright, balanced, resilient and ready for the challenges of the 21st century' *Families First* (Mothers' Union)

'A major new insight into the difficulties of raising boys, and how parents can help their sons fulfil their potential'

Lovereading.co.uk

'Informative and inspirational . . . Based on the latest research from around the world, *21st Century Boys* provides parents and teachers with a clear pathway to bringing up boys' *Green Parent*

'It has invaluable advice on opening up conversations about school or anything else, and helping children talk through problems' *Sainsbury's Magazine*

'Practical advice for parents is evident in each chapter and offered in a very non-patronizing "common sense" style. There are amusing and very realistic case studies and helpful chapter summaries, which allow the reader to recap, think, dwell and reflect. A great read for anyone and everyone'

Eye (Early Years Educator)

TOXIC CHILDHOOD

'Excellent book . . . practical, sensible and eminently attainable advice on how to detoxify childhood' *Independent*

'A fascinating account of the problems facing kids today . . . contains solid parenting advice on subjects ranging from diet to childcare' *Sainsbury's Magazine*

'A brilliant book, *Toxic Childhood*, demonstrating how deprived children bear the brunt of rapid social change, and the knock-on effect this has on Britain's streets, schools and crime rate'
The Week

'Absolutely essential reading for anyone who has, or who works with, children. It's like Eric Schlosser (author of the exposé *Fast Food Nation*) for parenting' Lovereading.co.uk

'One of the most talked about books on the market . . . teems with perceptive observations and sound advice' *Family Bulletin*

'One of the most inspirational books I have ever read . . . a must-read for all parents' The Coffee House, netmums.com

'More and more of us have begun to wonder, with real anxiety, just what it is that has gone so horribly wrong with childhood. How can we face the future with confidence if we lose faith in the way most of the children around us are raised? In this book, Sue Palmer tackles a range of areas and issues that affect growing bodies and minds. Bravely, she gives us the unvarnished, and often startling, facts. More cheeringly, she then offers us ways to think afresh about a host of matters to do with young people, their health, their upbringing and their education, which we would – both as individuals and as a community – be very foolish indeed to either ignore or dismiss'
Anne Fine, author and former Children's Laureate

Sue Palmer is a writer, speaker and broadcaster on the subject of child development and education in the modern world. After 15 years as a nationally respected authority on literacy teaching, in 2006 she published Toxic Childhood, which helped spark a national debate on the nature of contemporary childhood. She regularly comments on childhood issues in the national press and media, and is listed among London's most influential educationists by the Evening Standard. She lives in Scotland, where in 2009 she was described in the Scotsman as one of the country's 'new radical thinkers'.

BY SUE PALMER

Toxic Childhood
Detoxing Childhood
21st Century Boys

21ST CENTURY BOYS

SUE PALMER

An Orion paperback

First published in Great Britain in 2009
by Orion
This paperback edition published in 2010
by Orion Books Ltd,
Orion House, 5 Upper St Martin's Lane,
London WC2H 9EA

An Hachette UK company

1 3 5 7 9 10 8 6 4 2

ISBN 978-1-4091-0338-7

Printed and bound in Great Britain by Clays Ltd, St Ives plc

The Orion Publishing Group's policy is to use papers that
are natural, renewable and recyclable products and
made from wood grown in sustainable forests. The logging
and manufacturing processes are expected to conform to
the environmental regulations of the country of origin.

Every effort has been made to fulfil requirements with regard
to reproducing copyright material.
The author and publisher will be glad to rectify any omissions

ACKNOWLEDGEMENTS

Specific acknowledgements for help, ideas, information and insights while I was writing 21st Century Boys are due to: Shaun Bailey, Ros Bayley, Nigel Baker, John and Enid Bald, Professor Simon Baron-Cohen, Virginia Beardshaw, Pablo Benedetto, Steve Biddulph, Sir Richard Bowlby, Tessa and Paul Bradley, Ernie Brennan, Beth Brinton, Lynn Broadbent, Sandy Campbell, Professor Guy Claxton, Paul Cooper, Carol Craig, Dave Crowley, Margaret Edgington, Cordelia Fine, Anna Firth and colleagues at Promoting Parenting, Dr Connie Fozzard, Alan Gibbons, Melanie Gill, Tim Gill, Sally Goddard Blythe, Sian Griffiths, Alex Hall, Pam Hall, Gerry Hassan, Elizabeth Haylett Clark, Diane Hofkins, Professor Peter Hobson, Dr Richard House, Adam Hughes, Bob Hughes, Jill Jenkins, Eddie Jones, Ian Jukes, John Kellerher, Grant Knight, Dr Sebastian Kraemer, Professor Richard Layard, Warren Mansell, Ian Marshall, Dr Paul Martin, Ed Mayo, Alison Mitchell, Carey Morning, John Murray, Dr Agnes Nairn, Lucinda Neall, Melvyn Owen, Dr John Raven, Finton O'Regan, Graeme Paton, Georgina Pensri, Anna Raeburn, Dr Rachel Ragg, Sarah Rees-Elford, Chloe Ruthven, Alan Sinclair, Andrew Steel-Dodd, Dan Sutch, Dr Sami Timimi, Sam Walford, Gary Wilson, Dr Jennifer Wright and Dr Chris Yapp.

Thanks also to the hundreds of parents, teachers and other professionals who've told me things during my travels around the UK, to the teachers who arranged for me to interview boys at their schools and, of course, to the boys themselves and the scores of other random young men I've accosted and interrogated over the last three years. They were all very kind to an apparently mad old woman.

And very special thanks to my researcher Aidan Simpson, my agent Luigi Bonomi and my editor at Orion, Daniel Bunyard.

CONTENTS

MEET THE BOYS

Why a man-made world is making
boys' lives toxic ...
and how we can raise boys fit to meet the
challenges of a new century

Meet **Dylan**. Five years old and in a state of perpetual motion. Happiest when outdoors – running, tumbling, climbing, fighting. Indoors he squirms and jostles, limbs flailing all over the place. According to his mum, he only ever seems at peace in front of the TV (although perhaps peace is the wrong word – more a sort of zombie-like trance). According to his teacher, Dylan is a real handful, always getting into fights and mischief and already having problems in class: she worries for his future. And she's finding more and more little lads with Dylan-like behaviour arrive in her class every year.

Perhaps you'd rather meet **Ozzy**. Eight-and-a-half, going on 30. He'll engage you in very serious conversation, and would love to show you his remarkable collection of fossils. Ozzy's parents hope he'll eventually make it to Cambridge, but realise that his immediate problem is to find some way of relating to his classmates. They're worried that the relentless teasing might soon turn into something worse. Ozzy's teacher, on the other hand, isn't so sure it's all the other kids' fault. She too finds Ozzy extremely annoying: if a subject takes his fancy, he'll work like a Trojan, but if it doesn't, he's a menace and can be very disruptive ...

You'd probably prefer to avoid **Leo**. He's 14 and really pissed off with school. He just about coped at primary, but since starting secondary it's been downhill all the way. He's now such a handful that his teachers are secretly grateful when he bunks off, but his mum is terrified. Leo is hanging out with a very disreputable-looking crowd and she fears he might be taking drugs. He's definitely smoking and drinking, messing around with girls he calls 'bitches' and 'hos', and out on the streets with his new mates till all hours. The police have been round a few times, and told her she has to keep him under control. But what can she do? – he's bigger than her now ...

Still, you're unlikely to bump into **Kevin**, 16. He disappeared into his black-painted bedroom many moons ago and nobody's seen much of him since. His parents hear the door slam as he leaves for school, then again when he returns – but apart from brief encounters for the exchange of food and washing, they've given up trying to communicate. He's supposed to be revising for his GCSEs, but he might be hacking into the White House computer for all they know, or racking up a nightly death toll on Grand Theft Auto IV. Kevin's always been a bit difficult to talk to ... and far too keen on computer games. Now his parents fear he's given up on this world and taken up virtual residence somewhere else.

Boys have always been boys – restless, impulsive, excitable; obsessive, aggressive, inscrutable – but in an overcrowded, overheated, 21st century world their boyishness seems to be more of a problem. These four are fairly extreme examples, of course, but many parents I meet see echoes of behaviour from one or more of them in their own sons – not to mention their son's friends, and the boys they see out on the streets and in the malls. So maybe we need to talk about Kevin, Leo, Ozzy and Dylan ...

Do we need to talk about boys?

During the last few years, there's been what newspapers call a 'moral panic' about childhood – every day seems to bring more stories of disturbed children or disaffected teenagers. A couple of years ago UNICEF reported that, on a range of measures of well-being, British children were the unhappiest in the developed world, while a think tank found that the UK had the worst behaved teenagers in Europe – at, or near the top of, the poll for drug abuse, binge drinking, under-age sex and youth crime.

None of this came as a surprise to British teachers, who'd noticed a steady deterioration in children's behaviour and capacity to settle at school over at least two decades. It was their concern that led me – as a literacy specialist – to spend three years interviewing experts from a range of disciplines to find out what was going on. In *Toxic Childhood*, published shortly before the official reports began to appear, I collated research showing how junk food, poor sleeping patterns, a screen-based sedentary lifestyle, the wrong sort of childcare and educational experiences, family fragmentation and the effects of consumer culture can affect children's development. Many youngsters now suffer from a combination of these factors – a dangerous cocktail that's bound to have an effect. So as well as fuelling childhood obesity, 'toxic childhood syndrome' damages the brains of a growing number of children.

As I ferreted about among the statistics, it became depressingly obvious that boys were particularly affected. In terms of school work, they'd begun to lag behind girls in the 1980s, gone into free fall in the 1990s and – although government threw money and initiatives at them for over ten years – are still languishing in their sisters' shadow. Girls now out-perform boys in every subject of the curriculum except maths and science, with almost 70% going on to university or college, as opposed to around 50% of boys. Considering that, less than a century ago, the chances of a girl even being allowed near a university were negligible, this is a remarkable reversal of fortunes.

Part of the reason is boys' greater chance of suffering from one of the 'developmental disorders', rarely heard of 30 years ago, but now affecting around one in ten children. These include ADHD (attention deficit hyperactivity disorder) and dyspraxia (problems with physical co-ordination), both four times more likely to affect boys than girls, and Asperger Syndrome (a form of autism which causes problems with social relationships) which is nine times as common in males. Academics are at the moment locked in dispute over whether more boys than girls are dyslexic but – whatever the finer points of their argument – they're at least twice as likely as girls to have problems with reading at school.

Boys come out worst in terms of mental health too. The British Medical Association reported in 2006 that boys in the five to ten age group were twice as likely as girls to have an emotional, behavioural or mental health problem, while among 10- to 15-year-olds 11% of boys had diagnosable conditions, as opposed to 8% of girls. They also found that young men in the 15 to 24 age range were the group most at risk of committing suicide. Indeed, in this age group suicide is the second most common cause of death.

So yes, I think we should recognise that all is by no means well with children and young people in contemporary Britain, and that boys in particular are getting a pretty raw deal. What's more, if boys aren't reasonably civilised, confident and able to exercise self-control by the time they reach their teens, they can become a problem for society: four out of five criminal offences are committed by males. In the words of psychologist Sami Timimi, who has written widely on the subject: *The big difference is that boys externalise their problems and it comes out as bad behaviour*

– girls tend to internalise it, as sadness. Boys' issues are therefore issues for others, not just themselves.'

There have always been disaffected young men – scamps, scoundrels, hooligans and 'juvenile delinquents' litter the pages of social history – but the fact that youth crime has always been with us doesn't excuse it. As we learn more about the workings of the human mind, it should be possible to make life and learning easier for boys, so they grow up balanced, happy and able to make their own contribution to society. But at present, more and more 21st century boys seem to fall victim to the toxicity of modern childhood. And if we close our eyes to the problem, hoping it'll go away, these lost boys' plight will become an ever greater threat, not just to themselves but to society as a whole.

This is the first of two books about bringing up children in a 21st century world, one about boys and one about girls. The decision to treat the sexes separately doesn't mean I believe that one is more equal than the other. As a thoroughly 20th century woman, I'm as committed to gender equality as it's possible to be. But 60 years of personal experience and wide research into gender and child development have convinced me that there are essential differences between boys and girls. And if we refuse to acknowledge them, we damage the prospects of all children – indeed, perhaps of our species as a whole.

The role of nature

Why should a 21st century lifestyle be particularly damaging for boys? The evidence suggests it's to do with fundamental truths about human nature – and the growing discrepancy between instinctive male behaviour and the demands of modern life. According to evolutionary biologists, major gender traits relate back to our remote past, when the responsibility for keeping the species alive was divided up between males and females. Females, who were usually pregnant or looking after small children, stayed behind at camp, keeping the home fires burning and nurturing the next generation. The job of the male was to protect and provide, fending off dangers and roaming the local terrain in the quest for food.

The sorts of masculine behaviour required for stalking, pursuing and killing wild animals are very different from the feminine virtues needed for raising infants and getting along with one's fellow campers. Natural selection therefore meant that over the millennia, male and female developed gender traits fitting them for their particular roles, and these traits are hard-wired into our psyches at birth. There's now a huge mass of statistical data generated throughout the world – such as psychometric tests, educational assessments, crime statistics and a plethora of social surveys – that link convincingly with the evolutionists' case.

For instance, males are proven to be more violent than females, as would be required for fending off attackers and hunting down prey. They're also better at 'visuospatial tasks' such as judging distances and 'three-dimensional mental trans-formations', which means imagining how objects look from dif-ferent angles or as they move through space. These skills would be useful when making one's way around the hunting grounds, working out how to turn natural objects into tools and weapons, or visualising the trajectory of a spear slicing through the air. And men are far more likely than women to be risk-takers, which would come in useful when throwing themselves head-long into the chase or closing in for the kill.

They're also extremely competitive – necessary not only for hunting, but for mating with the most attractive females, thus passing on one's successful genes to the next generation. Evo-lutionists reckon this competitiveness underpins the male pre-occupation with rank and status, from church hierarchies to football league tables. It probably also accounts for men's preference for status (as measured by their rank at work but also money, fast cars and other trappings of success) over per-sonal relationships and family. Women, on the other hand, tend in surveys to give more balanced weighting to status and relationships.

It makes sense that relationships would be more important to females, since their main function was to bear and rear children while getting along with the other mothers. They'd also find the human potential for language helpful for smoothing social interactions and passing on knowledge to their young, so it's no surprise that conversation comes more naturally to women. For hunters, more inclined to action, the main use of language would be warnings, commands or brisk discussions of strategy, so men are constitutionally nowhere near as inclined to chat.

From Stone Age to city limits

If every little boy is born with the brain of a Stone Age hunter, and his natural inclination is to be active, run about outdoors, take risks, compete ... and win, he's going to come up against obvious problems in our uptight, urban 21st century world. 2008 was the year when the global balance tipped in terms of human habitation: around the world more people now live in cities than elsewhere, so there's far less space for most boys to run about. In an increasingly risk-averse society, there's also less opportunity to throw oneself headlong into any physical activity and opportunities to compete physically are increasingly regulated.

Little wonder that poor young Dylan, full of pent-up male energy and designed by nature for a free-range existence, causes problems for his mother and teachers. He's desperate to run and scramble in the great outdoors – but lack of space, too much traffic and adult fears about a range of real and perceived dangers mean he's being battery-reared indoors for most of the day.

He also needs ways of dealing with his instinctive need to compete and fight. In the past, boys sorted this out through play of various kinds. But in a world where childcare is increasingly institutionalised, play-fighting and other rowdy, boyish activities are frowned upon. And now he's at school, the only accepted way to compete is through schoolwork. Since he can't even sit still at his desk for five minutes, let alone make progress in reading and writing, he's not going to win much status there.

And then there's Leo – an older, stronger, untamed Dylan who's finally escaped back into the wild. As a 21st century boy who has never found a socially acceptable way of channelling his energy, he's drifted into a range of socially unacceptable behaviours. He can't achieve at school, so he either plays up or bunks off. Out on the streets, he's discovered a tribal subculture in which impulsive, antisocial activity can bring status and success. And now that his male drive for action, risk-taking and dominance has been topped up by a fierce surge of adolescent hormones, Leo has regressed right back to the Stone Age.

Stone Age teenagers would at this point be initiated into the tribe to join the other men in the hunt. But a tribe of disaffected lads on a 21st century housing estate has nothing to hunt but drugs, drink and trouble. Their male role models – rappers, macho movie stars and older gang members – preach that, with enough muscle on your side, you can take what you want, when you want it (including those 'bitches and whores'). And if that means the life of man returns to being nasty, brutish and short ... well, too bad. For Leo there doesn't seem much else to look forward to.

The natural impulses of these two boys are in direct conflict with the mainstream 21st century culture they live in. Dylan's still just a little boy, but his teacher's rightly worried – unless we acknowledge his problems, find ways for him to work off excess energy and help him settle down at school, he could turn into a Leo. And Leo's behaviour may soon become a threat to the law-abiding majority – teenage gang culture has become increasingly violent of recent years, with stabbings and shootings dominating the headlines.

At present society applies short-term solutions. If Dylan runs out of control in the classroom, we diagnose ADHD and give him Ritalin, a psychotropic drug to calm him down – in 2007, almost half a million prescriptions were doled out in the UK. When Leo oversteps the mark, we issue an ASBO – if he still won't toe the line, he'll end up in the criminal justice system, and if there's room in the overflowing prisons, we might lock him up for a while.

These are both sticking-plaster solutions that ignore the underlying issues. If we want these boys and millions like them to contribute to society rather than threaten it, we have to find ways of helping them adjust to life in an increasingly urban culture. That means acknowledging that they can't be battery-raised.

Systems, status and success

But Dylan and Leo are only half of the problem. There's another sort of boyish behaviour that's always been around but may be becoming more problematical, for the boys themselves and, in the long run, for society. Fossil-loving Ozzy and computer-loving Kevin don't so far seem to fit as neatly as Dylan and Leo into the evolutionary jigsaw.

Neither looks like a natural action man – it's hard to imagine Ozzy yomping around the neolithic hunting ground, and Kevin seems more like a solitary stalker than a functioning member of the tribe. Since both of them seem more academically inclined than our first two examples, you'd expect them to be thriving in a culture that lays great store by education. But neither is a balanced, happy boy.

A further strand in the evolutionary argument, put forward by Cambridge psychologist Simon Baron-Cohen, might explain their problems. He's identified two types of human thought and behaviour, which he believes are related to gender. In his book *The Essential Difference: Men, Women and the Extreme Male Brain* he suggests that men are more likely to be 'systemisers' (S-type thinkers), while women are more inclined to be 'empathisers' (E-type thinkers). Systemisers are driven to understand and build various types of systems, ranging from the mechanical or natural to systems of abstract ideas such as mathematics or music. Empathisers, on the other hand, are interested in human beings, how their minds work, how they feel, and how they interact with one another in terms of relationships.

The two ways of thinking aren't in any way mutually exclusive – indeed, all human beings need to be able to do both, as they're both necessary for survival. We have to systemise our understanding of the world, to bring order to the immense amount of information we absorb every day, and to gain increasing control over our environment. But as social animals, dependent on each other to keep our world turning, we must also be aware of – and responsive to – each other's needs and feelings.

However, Baron-Cohen argues that men, with their long-term interest in tools, weapons and strategies for using them, are more likely to incline towards S-type systemising, while females, after countless millennia collaborating over the care of children, have more natural capacity for E-type empathising. Large-scale surveys of adults' thinking skills do indeed show that while most people are proficient in both S- and E-type thinking, males are more inclined to systemising while women score higher on tests of empathy.

Baron-Cohen acknowledges that social expectations of gender roles are bound to affect men's and women's behaviour. However, his team at Cambridge has also conducted two ingenious experiments strongly suggesting that this 'essential difference' is actually written into our DNA (see pages 28 and 34).

The ability to systemise underpins the capacity for rational thought, so in terms of cultural evolution it's been an incredibly useful skill. For instance, a Stone Age systemiser with forensic powers of observation and analysis could use his brainpower (along with his fellow tribesmen's brawn) to dominate the hunting grounds. Ever since, given our species' ability to pass on knowledge through the generations, the insights of talented systemisers, combined with competitiveness, yearning for status, and willingness to take risks, have been the major force behind human progress. Tools and technologies, models and machines, cities and civilisations, empires and economies – are all based on the principles of S-type thought. So it's not surprising that talented S-type males through the ages have acquired high status, or that parents should encourage this strength in their sons.

Too much of a good thing?

The problem is that brain backed up by brawn is not enough to drive human progress. S-type systemisers may devise machines and institutions, but E-type empathy underpins the collaborative effort needed to build and operate them for the long-term good. In the same way, civil society depends on E-type thinking: unless citizens can take each other's point of view into account, the social fabric of life will unravel.

Indeed, when the drive for systems, status and success is allowed to accelerate without the counterbalance of an E-type brake, it can threaten the survival of the species and possibly the planet. Most of us would agree that wholly systemised solutions to human problems, such as those devised by Hitler, Mao Tse Tung and Pol Pot, are fundamentally flawed. And as man's systemising ability increases, the tools he devises – such as DDT and nuclear weapons – may usher in as many problems as they do solutions.

Just as the species needs empathy to survive, so do individuals. The relationships underpinning all positive human endeavour are personal, emotional and social. Without empathy to balance it, the ability to systemise can become a liability. This is poor Ozzy's problem: he can systemise for Britain, but he can't work out how other people think. So although he knows everything there is to know about fossils, he hasn't the faintest idea what's going on in the minds of the people around him. He rubs everyone up the wrong way: so his teacher thinks he's arrogant and defiant, his classmates consider him a complete oddball, and he's a gift to playground bullies. From Ozzy's point of view, the social world of school is by turns baffling and terrifying. Little wonder he prefers the company of fossils.

In fact, Ozzy is dangerously close to what Baron-Cohen calls the 'extreme male brain'. This is his term for autistic children, locked in a world of non-communication, with no ability to empathise at all. In autism's milder variant, Asperger Syndrome, children can speak and learn (and some have high systemising ability in particular areas) but still have little or no idea of what makes other people tick.

Over the last 20 or 30 years, an increasing number of children, particularly boys, have been burdened with 'an extreme male brain'. Autism – especially Asperger Syndrome – is hugely on the increase. Baron-Cohen notes a tenfold rise in diagnoses in the UK over the last 30 years, with current estimates ranging from 1 in 200 to 1 in 58. He puts this wide range of estimates down to variations in methods of diagnosis. But while there's clearly a biological basis for the condition – and many Asperger sufferers are undoubtedly locked by birth into social isolation – I suspect, and argue throughout this book, that changes in lifestyles and attitudes may be exacerbating the problem. In days gone by, a boy like Ozzy might have achieved – through constant unavoidable human interaction – a good enough level of social competence to pass muster.

Then there's Kevin, locked in his personal black hole. His natural drive to systemise has led him to an obsessive interest in computer games, and thus to growing social isolation. For a boy who finds the cut and thrust of real life a tad too threatening, gaming is a simple way to satisfy the masculine quest for action, risk and conquest. When you have endless onscreen worlds to conquer in the privacy of your own room, why bother with the real one?

A natural systemiser is always at risk of getting carried away. And, indeed, the obsessive behaviour this inspires occasionally brings great success: musicians or sportsmen who practise remorselessly may become world-beaters; scientists or engineers who can't stop worrying at a problem may eventually make a ground-breaking discovery; genius is famously 99% perspiration. But most people aren't geniuses.

In Kevin's case, his obsession is essentially passive and non-productive, distracting him from both schoolwork and normal social interaction. The more he withdraws into his virtual world, the less successful he's likely to be in the real one. There may also be other long-term effects: in a living, breathing, social animal like a human being, we don't yet know the psychological and social consequences of choosing to live one's life through an avatar.

Nature and nurture

However, although these 21st century problems seem to be on the increase, the vast majority of boys are still on track. Human beings are remarkably adaptable, and through the centuries we have managed to accommodate our Stone Age brains to the requirements of a vast range of cultural environments.

That's one of the reasons that, as a species, we've been so successful. Being born with a sparsely formed brain means children can be moulded by nurture to survive and thrive in their own particular physical environment and culture. This is why babies born with the same brain structure may end up wearing fur coats or loin cloths, speaking Chinese or Hindi, living in long huts or high-rise flats, or thrilling to the music of a string quartet or a didgeridoo.

The really good news is that, unless something is seriously awry with brain structure, there are tried and tested ways of raising well-balanced boys that seem consistent across cultures, and can work just as well in 21st century Britain. So ...

Meet **Adam**. After our uncomfortable introduction to Dylan, Ozzy, Leo and Kevin, you'll find it remarkably easy – he'll proffer a hand, look you straight in the eye and grin as he says 'Hello'. Your only problem will be pinning him down – what with cricket, band practice (he plays keyboard), working on the bike with his dad and playing computer games with his mates. He somehow also manages to fit in his schoolwork, and to do pretty well. His last school report calls him 'a good all-rounder' (Adam claims he'd be a 'brilliant all-rounder' if they'd teach him something worth learning) and predicts he'll achieve the grades needed for university.

Of course, Adam is not perfect. His parents say he has the usual teenage moods and whinges, and got into his fair share of scrapes as a child. But he doesn't stay down for long, can gruffly apologise if he's in the wrong, and always tries to learn from mistakes. It helps that he has, as his mates point out, a wicked sense of humour.

Adam's parents are quietly proud of their son and he's quietly grateful to them. Though really looking forward to leaving home next year, he knows they've worked hard to give him a happy childhood. They spent time with him, sharing their interests and teaching skills like cooking and how to fix things, but they also gave him plenty of freedom to play out with his mates. Even when he hit their bad books, they usually tried to listen to his point of view – but that didn't make them a pushover: there were always firm boundaries for behaviour and big trouble if he crossed them. Now he's older they trust him to make his own decisions, and he wouldn't want to let them down.

When you ask Adam how he feels about being a 21st century boy, he says 'Great!', and you know by the look in his eye that he means it. You also know that, whatever challenges the future brings, he's ready for them.

I've met many boys like Adam as I researched this book. And it's fascinating how little they differ from boys I met 30 years ago, during my time as a teacher, and the boys one meets in literature from across the centuries. The world may have changed immeasurably over recent decades, but the boys haven't. They're still born the same squirming bundles of human promise that they always were and, given the right sort of nurture, are just as likely to grow up bright, balanced and raring to go.

In our species, nurture counts for a lot – which is why a boy's parents, friends, teachers and local community are so important to the way he eventually turns out. Between them, they have to help this prototype hunter rein in his aggression and find productive ways to channel his competitive and risk-taking instincts. Their influence can encourage his natural drive to systemise, while ensuring it's balanced by the capacity to empathise. Nowadays this means developing good language and people skills. Neither of these comes as naturally to most boys as they do to girls, but in an overcrowded, urban culture the strong, silent type is way past his sell-by date.

However, like any natural organism, the human brain develops according to a biological timetable, not at the whim of other human beings or the behest of systems. Nurturing a child involves being attuned to where he is, and providing the sort of input that will help rather than hinder his development. Brain growth is also governed by emotion: insecure or unhappy children are inclined to learn the wrong sorts of lessons. So rearing a son – particularly in the first seven or so years, before he develops the capacity for rational thought – requires deep sensitivity on the part of the nurturer. Perhaps this is why human females have, over the millennia, developed a particular talent for empathy?

The basic recipe Adam's parents found is the same as that recommended by countless mothers and fathers I've met over the years, and appears to be much the same across time and cultures. It begins by giving a boy love, time, talk and freedom to explore. While necessary throughout childhood, these are particularly essential for healthy brain development in the first three years. As he grows older, he needs to play, especially with other children, and for boys this must include opportunities for lots of physical, active, outdoor play. Then, although it's important not to push boys into formal education before they're ready, he'll need the 3Rs. Even in a multimedia world, reading and writing are now human must-haves – the acquisition of literacy skills leads to more rational, civilised behaviour as well as access to humanity's accumulated store of S-type wisdom.

But there's another R boys need to learn from their earliest years, upon which success in the educational system is based: respect. Respect for others, respect for social rules and – very importantly – self-respect. This involves a careful balancing act on behalf of parents and teachers. On the one hand, to nurture self-respect they have to be 'warm', taking their charges' feelings and opinions into account. On the other, since boys are born to take risks and test boundaries, they have to be firm. If the adults in their lives can achieve the right balance of warmth with firmness, boys will accept the discipline they need to learn. The external discipline provided by parents, teachers and other responsible adults can then turn into self-discipline, which boys need to acquire the knowledge, skills and values to survive and thrive in adult life.

None of this is rocket science. Neither has it proved, in the past, particularly taxing: countless parents – working alongside their sons' teachers and others in their community – have found themselves 'good enough' to carry it through. Indeed, if we want to see the fruits of their labours, we need only to look around us. The steady march of human progress through the centuries, leading to the Age of Enlightenment and the spread of democratic ideals, are testament to generations of parents who've nurtured their sons into bright, balanced, thoughtful men.

In fact, they helped them become so civilised and thoughtful that, at the end of the last century, the human quest for scientific understanding and social justice helped overturn the 'natural' order of things, and blew apart traditional gender roles.

The S/E balancing act

And here, very probably, is one major cause of 21st century child-rearing problems. In terms of social history, this change in traditional male and female behaviour has been little short of seismic, and has had a profound influence on the way we rear our young.

Since the beginning of time, women were trapped by biology into their domestic role as nurturers while men were out, moving, shaking and transforming the world. Suddenly – with the advance of science (contraception, labour-saving devices, electronic media) and in an age of reason (universal suffrage, equality, human rights) – women's domestic shackles crumbled away. Not surprisingly, they seized the chance to escape from domestic drudgery and join in with the moving and shaking.

Since all human beings are capable of S-type thought – and since the education system is designed to deliver it – women had no problem acquiring the skills needed in a 21st century workplace. They were also happy to embrace the masculine values of status and success. Indeed, after countless millennia of low status 'women's work', they relished the opportunity to show what they could achieve, and to earn some material rewards. So women entered the economic fray on men's terms.

The trouble is – as pointed out earlier – systems, status and success aren't enough to guarantee human progress. While women were locked into their domestic role, one of the few rewards open to them was a loving relationship with their children. So throughout history they valued their talent for E-type thinking and passed it on by example. But when women moved out of the home and into the workplace, they – and everyone else – suddenly ceased to value the traditional female talent for caring.

This devaluing of E-type skills has blinded 21st century society to many ancient truths about childcare (indeed, about care in general). In the space of two or three decades, we seem to have forgotten the importance of love, time and talk in the early years of childhood, of allowing children freedom to explore and play, and of balancing warmth with firmness to ensure they are well disciplined and able to learn. In over-valuing systems as opposed to empathy, we've also been blinded to the significance of trust in human relationships. This has had an effect on many aspects of our lives, including education.

It doesn't help that the momentous shift in gender roles coincided with two other sociocultural revolutions. First came the rapid development of the ultimate systemising tool – computers. Within a matter of decades, digital technology has transformed the lives of everyone on the planet, not least through the influence of the electronic media. Second, there was the triumph of consumer capitalism as the main driver of human progress. The relentless quest for economic growth focused everyone's attention on material wealth at the expense of personal relationships.

It's not surprising that, in this highly systemised environment, parents began to look for system-driven, technological, commodified solutions to the challenges of child-rearing. Nor should we be surprised that governments and businesses constantly try to provide them. But turning a baby into a fully rounded human being isn't something you can systemise. It still involves the intensely personal human input described in the last section. E-type thinking is grounded in the here and now, in face-to-face contact between real live human beings. The reason Adam looks you straight in the eye is that, from the moment he was born, people have been looking him in the eye and responding to him as a person.

If we want to raise more boys like Adam – boys with the emotional resilience and social competence to rise (alongside their sisters) to the challenges of the 21st century and continue (alongside their sisters) to take the human race onward and upward – we have to recalibrate the balance of S- and E-type thinking in our society. It's not enough for men and women to regard each other as equals. Both sexes have to value the E-type skills that women traditionally passed on in the home, and recognise the E-type ways men have built on these skills to civilise boys through the ages. We have to accept that empathy, emotional engagement and eye contact matter just as much to human progress as systems, status and success.

There's no doubt that the 21st century will be challenging. As I write, the global village is confronting a worldwide financial crisis, climate change, food and fuel shortages, the possibility of pandemics and other alarming scenarios. These challenges are by no means insuperable – now that computers have extended our systemising powers far beyond our own mental capacity, there's immense potential for rapid scientific advance. In his book *The Meaning of the 21st Century* the futurologist James Martin describes today's children as the 'transition generation', who must guide that advance for the good or ill of the planet and the species.

Today's adults are responsible for raising this transition generation, so when research suggests all is not well with our children's mental health, it's definitely time to stop and consider what we might be doing wrong. And if, as the statistics suggest, the male of the species is faring less well than the female, perhaps we should start by talking about boys.

How are we to raise our young men in a culture that's evolved so far beyond their biological nature? How can we give them the skills they'll need in the future while respecting developmental needs that stem from mankind's distant past? How can we make sense of age-old concepts such as *mothering*, *play* and *discipline* in a unisex, quick-fix consumer culture?

This book is not a call for women to return to domestic

servitude or adults to forswear the many benefits of modern technology. Progress means going forward, not harking back – but it's perfectly possible to learn from the past without having to live in it. To recalibrate society's S/E balance we have to accept the limitations of S-type material values, and recognise the importance throughout human history of E-type personal contact and care.

While researching and writing 21st Century Boys, I kept remembering the words of economist Richard Layard when I interviewed him about 'toxic childhood'. As one of Britain's foremost economists, he believes that hypercompetitive consumerism is now eroding social capital, the glue that holds communities together. I asked what we need to do to get society back on track, and his off-the-cuff reply was:

'We just have to change the relative prestige accorded to smart-arsed behaviour and that accorded to kindness.'

Chapter summary

The introduction explores why it's worth considering boys' development – as distinct from girls' – within a specifically 21st century context. Research suggests British children are the unhappiest in Europe and that boys are falling behind girls educationally, are more at risk from developmental and mental health disorders and more likely to become involved in crime in their teens.

It suggests that the reason many boys find it difficult to adapt to the demands of 21st century life relates to their evolutionary inheritance. For some, the restrictions of a sedentary, urban lifestyle may cause problems in focusing attention and controlling behaviour, leading to disadvantage in the education system. For others, a male tendency to S-type (systemising) over E-type (empathising) thinking may increase educational attainment, while leading to problems with emotional and social development.

These problems are by no means insoluble, but tackling them depends on 'warm but firm' child-rearing tactics, with personal involvement by parents and other responsible adults in boys' lives. During several decades of rapid social and cultural change, the E-type skills required for this approach have been devalued.

Getting boys back on track

The message of this book is that bringing up children is a hugely important social enterprise – and it's not just the responsibility of parents. While mothers and fathers are clearly on the front line in terms of their sons' physical and mental health, they have, in the past, been personally supported by their families and communities. But in a complex 21st century culture, professionally manned and screen-based systems have often taken the place of personal, relationship-based support. The emergence of 'toxic childhood syndrome' suggests that these systems are not good enough. Bringing up children in the 21st century still requires E-type personal involvement. S-type institutions can clearly support the enterprise but they'll never be an adequate substitute, even (perhaps especially) for the 'cleverest' children – see Chapter 10 (Born winners). Because of the biological 'fragility' described in Chapter 1, boys are likely to suffer more than girls from a dearth of E-type understanding and kindness within their society.

So each chapter of *21st Century Boys* ends with a few suggested starting points for rebalancing our attitude to child-rearing – not just for parents, but for the other adults whose lives impinge on them and their children, and for the policy-makers whose decisions influence us all.

What can parents do?

Parents' part in ensuring a healthy S/E balance to ensure their sons' physical and mental health is really pretty basic. First, they have to provide the obvious ingredients of nutritious food, a safe warm home and plenty of sleep and exercise. Next, there are the ingredients that underpin boys' social and emotional needs so they grow up able to survive and thrive in a modern technological society. These can be counted on the fingers of one hand:

LOVE   LANGUAGE   DISCIPLINE   PLAY   LITERACY

Of these ingredients, love – the first and foremost – is parents' major responsibility: everything else flows from that. The next three are still largely up to the family, but responsibility is shared with the rest of the community. The final ingredient can these days usually be handed over to schoolteachers, but since its foundations rest in the preceding four, parents still play an important part.

There's no perfect recipe – parents can only ever hope to be 'good enough' – but given a reasonable dollop of the key ingredients, the vast majority of boys should acquire the human qualities they need to become confident, caring, responsible citizens. As boys grow older, parents, working with teachers and other responsible adults, have to do everything possible to develop the personal qualities they need to keep them on track. There are five of these to watch for too:

| Physical fitness | Emotional resilience | Social competence | Intellectual curiosity | Creative potential |

What can the rest of us do?

One of the greatest social evils of recent decades – earnestly debated as I write by the Joseph Rowntree Foundation (www.jrf.org/socialevils/defaultf) – is the fragmentation of our local communities. There are many reasons for this social disintegration, but several are specifically identified as factors driving 21st century boys off the rails:

- Encouragement of individual citizens by commercial and marketing forces to pursue 'self-realisation' through consumption rather than relationships with others in the community. Marketers now aim their messages at very specific groups of consumers making them ever less aware and tolerant of those outside their immediate social group (see Chapters 3, 7 and 9).
- The professionalisation of social support means specific social groups are increasingly viewed as discrete units, provided for by specialist departments (e.g. Children's Services) or organisations (e.g. Age Concern). There's therefore probably less contact today between different members of the community – including different generations – than ever before (see Chapters 1, 2, 6 and 9). This development is recognised by policy-makers, who regularly trot out mantras about 'social inclusion' and 'cohesion', but their systemised solutions tend to make the problem worse rather than better (see Chapter 10).
- A generalised climate of risk aversion has eroded trust between individuals and increased dependence on 'health-and-safety' regulations. Among other evils, this has left the old frightened of the young (Chapters 6 and 10) and – as far as children are concerned – it's made everyone irrationally distrustful of men (Chapter 9).

In terms of child-rearing, the ill-effects of social breakdown seem worse in the UK than other countries – we may now be the least child-friendly society in the world. Turning the situation round involves a change of mind-set in every sector of the adult world, e.g.

- For businesses and marketers it means accepting that long-term economic success depends upon social responsibility, especially to children.
- For professionals it involves recognising the limits of sys-temised support, and helping parents and other members of the community take more personal responsibility for chil-dren's welfare.
- For all of us, it means challenging our excessively risk-averse health-and-safety culture, replacing fear with tolerance and assuming other people are trustworthy unless there's good evidence to the contrary.

Basically, we all have to stop putting such store by smart-arsed S-type solutions and values and accord more prestige to per-sonal relationships and human kindness.

What can politicians do?

Just as everyone has to share responsibility for the community in which we live, politicians must accept that, in today's sophisticated global culture, one man's irresponsible behaviour can affect the destiny of the whole species. This has been graphically illustrated by the financial and economic crisis that hit the world in 2008. The better we get at systemising, the more profound the effects of individual irresponsibility can be. Environmental campaigners have, of course, been arguing this case for decades – but perhaps the near destruction of the world economy will help focus politicians' minds for the future.

If we're to create a brave new 'transition generation', able to cope with 21st century interconnectedness, policy-makers need to recognise the importance of what happens at the beginning of human beings' lives (see also Chapter 10). This involves accepting the limitations of systems: the transmission of E-type understanding to the next generation relies on the *personal* input of real-life adults. The political challenge is to devise systems that can support the personal contribution of parents, families, teachers and communities to boys' (and girls') long-term mental well-being.

Recent governments have focused heavily on systemisation and accountability. The resulting health-and-safety legislation, child protection procedures, and statutory regulation of childcare (including, in England, the Early Years Foundation Stage) have created a mass of red tape that deskills and disempowers individual parents and other adults and adds to the problem. On the other hand, there's been little attempt to restrain the market forces that have helped skew social attitudes, throwing family life out of balance. To rebalance our society, the excesses of consumer capitalism must be reined in. In the words of social campaigner Richard Reeves, we need a family-friendly economy, not economy-friendly families.

Chapter 1

THE FRAGILE MALE

Why baby boys need mothering more than ever ...
and why modern mothers need support

So is it nature, nurture or culture that leads so many of our boys towards ADHD, Asperger Syndrome, ASBOs and avatars? As with most human phenomena, it's probably a complicated, personal cocktail of all three. But as far as nature's concerned, there's increasing evidence that boys are more fragile than girls from the very outset.

'It's as if boys have a flaw line of biological weakness from the word go,' says consultant psychiatrist Sebastian Kraemer, who has made a study of 'the fragile male'. This biological weakness shows itself long before babies are born. Kraemer estimates that around 120 male embryos are conceived for every 100 females but they are from the outset more vulnerable. More male embryos are lost through miscarriage in the early weeks of pregnancy than females, and thereafter 'the male foetus is at greater risk of death or damage from all the obstetric catastrophes that can happen before birth'. By the time those embryos have got through nine months in the womb, the ratio is only 105 male per 100 female live births. The remainder, having weathered more natural catastrophes, have a greater risk of problems in later life.

In a world accustomed for millennia to viewing females as 'the weaker sex', male fragility comes as something of a surprise. Might men and boys not be as constitutionally tough as they've always wanted us to think they are?

What are little boys made of?

A boy-child's DNA is handed down by his parents. His mum and dad both have their own personal DNA, found in each cell of their bodies in the form of 46 chromosomes, arranged in 23 pairs. In 22 of these, the chromosomes are essentially identical (half derived from grandma, half from grandpa) and look, under the most powerful of microscopes, like two chummy little X shapes. But in dad the 23rd pair is different.

This is the pair that influences sexual characteristics. While the mother's 23rd pair is another two Xs, the father's consists of one X and one Y. This male Y chromosome is, in the words of a distinguished (female) obstetrician, '*an X chromosome with a little bit missing*'.

Each parent hands on half their personal DNA to their offspring, so every mother's egg contains one of her X sex chromosomes and every father's sperm has either an X or a Y (half of an XY). When an egg and sperm fuse, it's the sperm that determines the baby's sex. During reproduction, an equal number of the father's X and Y sperm set out on the great competitive journey to fertilise the egg. But Y sperm swim faster than X sperm (perhaps because they're slightly lighter?), which may account for that 120:100 ratio of male to female embryos.

So it's not slugs, snails and puppy dogs' tails that determine the nature of a boy-child, but a string of DNA in which the final chromosome is lighter and leaner than the female version. Smart-arsed feminists enjoy the 'little bit missing' joke and refer snidely to men as 'the products of a damaged gene', and mischievous male biologists encourage them by pointing out that the Y chromosome has shrunk in size over the millennia, and is gradually 'fading away'. According to geneticist Steve Jones, author of *Y: The Descent of Men*, every second of every day the world's women produce 400 eggs between them, while men produce 200,000,000,000,000,000,000 sperm. This profligacy has gradually eroded the Y chromosome, which is now 'a mere remnant of a once mighty structure' and destined eventually to disappear altogether. Fortunately for the human race, male extinction is still a few million years away. In the meantime, in the challenge to create each new human being, those feisty little Y sperm are out there in the lead from the start, racing headlong into the great unknown.

Must try harder

Once the Y sperm makes it to the egg, things go quiet for a while – every fertilised embryo starts off as sexually neutral. However, at around eight weeks the Y chromosome triggers the formation of male sex organs, which start producing the male hormone testosterone. From then on, hormones combine with other genetic factors to affect the development of the soon-to-be-baby-boy's body and brain.

X-fertilised embryos take it easier – ovaries don't begin to form for another couple of weeks. Very occasionally, if a faulty Y chromosome fails to trigger male changes on time, ovaries begin to form in that foetus too. Biologists have therefore concluded that female anatomy is our species' default mode, occurring more naturally than male sexual characteristics.

So, right from the beginning, the male of the species has to put in that little bit more developmental effort than the female in order to stay on track. As Sebastian Kraemer points out, '*Males are attempting something extra all through life.*' Females, on the other hand, with their XX chromosome, '*are endowed with what is in effect an extra Duracell battery*'. If one X is faulty or damaged in some way, they have a spare and since many brain-related genes are located on the X, females have an insurance policy against certain neurological traits.

It may also be that male embryos and foetuses find survival in the womb more challenging because they're less in tune with their mother's metabolism. As hostess to any developing child, a mother is in effect harbouring an alien body. Her immune system is more likely to reject an interloper full of male hormones than one sharing her own female hormonal make-up. So advice to pregnant women about eating healthily, eschewing cigarettes and alcohol, and avoiding inessential medication has even more resonance if they are carrying boys. A study of mothers who took cocaine during pregnancy showed long-term ill-effects in terms of their sons' development, but not of daughters).

This image of a fragile male, struggling to survive in a potentially hostile environment and forced to make more of an effort than his laid-back sister, is a very new one. Indeed, until the scientific advances of the 20th century, there was no reason even to suspect it. Most fragile male (and female) foetuses were in the past obliterated by nature. A baby that suffered prenatal damage was seldom born alive, and more often than not premature arrivals also perished.

With vast improvements in medical science over the 20th century, many more children survive those perilous first nine months and the trauma of birth, so it's not surprising that more are born with disabilities of some kind. Physical problems are usually immediately apparent, but learning difficulties are not usually noticeable till later childhood. And given this newly discovered male fragility, there's a far greater chance of those difficulties affecting boys rather than girls.

Strong, silent … and slow

The prenatal development of male foetuses has further long-term implications. Simon Baron-Cohen, whose theory about S- and E-type brains was outlined in the introduction, believes that many boys' lack of interest in people and how their minds work begins the minute the Y chromosome triggers the release of testosterone. All foetuses – like all babies, children and adults – have both male and female hormones in their bloodstreams, but in boy foetuses testosterone levels are usually much higher than in girls.

Baron-Cohen measured the levels of testosterone in amniotic fluid taken from pregnant women during medical tests in the early stages of pregnancy (this testosterone comes from the foetus). A year or so later, he contacted the mothers concerned and asked to meet their offspring, who were now toddlers. He found that the higher the level of testosterone these children had before birth, the less communicative they were in early childhood, making less eye contact and speaking fewer words than children who'd had low foetal testosterone. We'll see in succeeding chapters how these natural characteristics may act alongside nurture to affect emotional, social and cognitive development.

It's also been suggested that foetal testosterone speeds the growth of the right hemisphere of the brain (the side that specialises in spatial relationships – which would, of course, have been helpful on the hunting grounds) and slows down development of the left hemisphere (housing the main language areas – helpful for socialising back at camp). While there's still huge debate about this in scientific circles, it can't be denied that, by the time they're born, girls have better connections between the two sides of the brain than boys. The corpus callosum, a bundle of nerve fibres linking the left and right hemispheres, is thicker in the brains of female newborns than males.

Newborn boys' brains are actually heavier than girls' – there are around 9% more grey cells in the cerebrum, the part at the front of the brain where higher mental functions are centred. And there's some statistical evidence that, as well as being prone to more learning difficulties, the male sex produces more brilliant male scientists. (This evidence is hotly contested by at least one brilliant female scientist.) However, while there seems to be a relationship between brain size and intelligence among males, size doesn't seem as significant in females, who appear to get along fine with their slightly smaller cerebra. Maybe the greater ability to make links across the two hemispheres allows girls to make more 'balanced' use of the grey matter?

Foetal testosterone also sets up the male body for greater

muscle development and higher bone density than a female, preparing a boy to be physically stronger (pound for pound), and with a natural advantage in terms of muscle growth and repair. It makes another bit of brain tissue swell too: the hypothalamus – the area that regulates sexual behaviour. Once that baby boy reaches maturity, his more proactive role in conception means he's primed by nature to think about sex much more often than his girlfriend does.

But despite the potential to grow beefier than the female in the future, general development in the womb is slower. One indication of this was noted by psychology professor Peter Hepper. He found that at four months males and females make about the same number of movements with their mouths, but a few weeks later the females have raced ahead of the males – the neural connections between the brain and the mouth seem more mature. It's tempting to conclude that, even in the womb, girls practise to be the more talkative sex.

Not so big and bouncy?

By the time they're born, this developmental gender gap has become quite noticeable, with boys lagging several weeks behind girls in a range of ways. For instance, immediately after birth girls are more likely to respond to sounds, scents and light, suggesting their senses are better developed. Boys are described as more 'emotionally reactive' than girls and researchers note that boy babies display more 'distress and demands for contact' than their female counterparts. This immaturity could be the reason that, even with all today's medical miracles, premature baby boys are less likely to survive than girls – in terms of actual maturity, they're much *more* premature.

With less well-developed senses, boys may also be less sensitive to parents' attempts to comfort and communicate with them through smiles and songs. In experiments where parents hummed to premature babies, girls benefited from the experience whereas boys did not. And the developmental differences noted by Simon Baron-Cohen could make the problem worse. Since their brains were bathed in testosterone in the womb, boys may be less inclined to make eye contact than girls, thus making it more difficult for parents to engage with their sons. Research collated by the Gurian Institute in the USA suggests that by the time they're four weeks old, boys make half as much eye contact as girls.

However, in a world programmed through countless millennia to assume that males are the stronger sex, boy babies – far from being considered fragile – are usually viewed as sturdier and more competent than their sisters. When assessing their newborn infants, parents use words like 'big' and 'strong' in relation to boys far more often than girls. Researchers record these comments even when there's no measurable difference in weight and strength among the babies concerned, so it's obviously a case of wishful thinking: 'The masculine ideal is big and strong,' think the parents, 'therefore our perfect baby must already be on the way to fulfilling that ideal.'

This misconception (along with other atavistic fears relating to gender) leads some parents to believe that too many cuddles might do their baby boys long-term damage. There's a widespread fear of 'spoiling' them, a fear so deep-seated that it's spawned a special derogatory word: *mollycoddle*. So, despite boys' immaturity, fretfulness and sensitivity they may well get less loving time and attention even in the early months of life than their sisters. After all, a baby girl – basking in the epithets 'sweet' and 'little' – is positively asking to be cosseted and cuddled, isn't she ... ?

Knowing me, knowing you

It's pretty obvious that, in the early months of life, *all* children need to be 'mollycoddled'. They are at this point helpless little bundles of instinct, and it's up to their parents to keep them alive: fed, watered, clean, comfortable and safe from harm. But as well as these obvious physical needs, tiny babies also have profound emotional needs. They may be physically helpless but the emotional and primitive survival centres of their brains are fully functioning, and they desperately need to know that someone is there to care for them at all times. So they're programmed to become 'attached' to this someone (usually their mother) from birth – by sight, sound, touch, smell and taste.

Psychologists believe the quality of this attachment in the early months and years has repercussions throughout the whole of our lives. Babies who are securely attached – meaning they feel utterly confident in the loving attention of their adult carers – are at a lifelong advantage. They're likely to thrive at school, and to find it easier to make and maintain relationships throughout adulthood. Above all, they have a greater chance of developing emotional resilience – the inner strength and self-confidence to cope with whatever slings and arrows fortune may have in store. So at the beginning of life, the best way to build up the emotional, social and cognitive defences of a fragile male baby is a good dose of mother love.

Since a mother is physically close to her baby from the outset, she is the natural 'primary attachment figure'. Hormones associated with giving birth and suckling an infant also provide a head start for mum in bonding with her offspring. But looking after a tiny baby is physically and psychologically draining, and for a mum to keep on top of his interminable (and often tediously repetitive) needs, she herself needs ongoing support and rewards.

Support from her partner, other family members or others in the community is vitally important, and with luck some of these supporters will gradually become 'secondary attachment figures', to whom the baby will also learn to turn. But a mother also needs the support of the baby himself. Right from the beginning, the bonding process between mother and child is reciprocal. The baby's gaze rewards the mother. If she can gaze lovingly at her infant and feel that he's gazing lovingly back, she's much more likely to be a contented committed attachment figure.

Developmental psychologist Colwyn Trevarthen describes how eye contact between parents and their babies leads into a 'dance of communication'. When adults hold their tiny infants and look into their eyes, they seem programmed for certain behaviour: exaggerated facial expressions, rhythmic rocking movements, sing-song baby talk or nursery rhymes and songs. Babies, on the other hand, are hard wired to imitate what adults do (if you put your tongue out at a newborn infant, it'll put its tongue back out at you) so they gradually start copying the parental example.

The Royal College of Paediatrics and Child Health borrows Trevarthen's image when it describes attachment as a 'reciprocal relationship', developing into 'attentive parenting in which children and parents follow each other's rhythms, rather like dancers'.

The dance of communication

However, Trevarthen has noticed that the first steps in the communicatory dance appear to be slightly different for girls and boys. While new mothers soon start singing and crooning to daughters, they often spend more time making faces at their sons. This could be the result of social expectations – adults may assume girls are more interested in language and song – or it could be that it's actually easier to engage a baby girl's attention. Since they're generally more mature at birth than boys, they may be more competent to hold the parental gaze and attend to the sound of the human voice. This backs up the ancient wisdom of old wives that 'girls are easier than boys'.

Another experiment by Baron-Cohen's team at Cambridge has suggested that baby boys are less interested in looking at people's faces. They tested children in their first week of life, when social influences could scarcely affect behaviour, by placing images on either side of their cots and counting the number of times the infants turned to look at them. The choice was between a friendly human face (Jennifer) and a mobile on which Jennifer's features had been rearranged to look like a machine ('The Alien'). Baby girls showed a clear preference for the face, baby boys for the alien. So it's highly possible that mothers through the ages have resorted to gurning in a desperate attempt to attract their sons' attention.

If boys, because of the effects of high foetal testosterone, are slightly less well equipped to join in the dance of communication, there are implications for attachment. A baby who cries a lot because of an immature nervous system, and who's constitutionally disinclined to reward adults with early eye contact (and the other copycat behaviours that follow), will need his mother to work harder. She'll have to summon up *more* mother love to tune into her son's feelings. And if she's tired, anxious or low-spirited, it won't be easy to keep up the cheery face-making and baby talk.

There's no doubt it's harder to get boys going. Scientists studying babies in the first three months of life found girls' skills in making eye contact and attending to their parents' faces increased fourfold, while in boys facial-gazing skills didn't increase at all. Another group found six-month-old girls streets ahead in the imitation stakes. By this time, they were much more likely than boys to widen their eyes and lift their eyebrows when greeting new arrivals. Researchers describe girls as more 'interested and sociable' and boys as 'more excitable', less easy to soothe and settle.

Similarly, children whose parents spend lots of time talking and singing to them are more likely to develop good language skills, with all the attendant personal, social and cognitive advantages (see Chapter 2). But as Trevarthen pointed out, mothers are more likely to talk and sing to girls than boys. And psychologists Gwendolyn Stevens and Sheldon Gardner found that this continues throughout the first six months: among the babies they studied the girls got more talk and song, the boys more physical contact. More worryingly, Stevens and Gardner found that, at six months, some mothers give up the unequal struggle. From then on, they not only continue to talk and sing more to their daughters than their sons, but they also give them more cuddles.

This could well be the genesis of all those strong, silent men throughout the centuries. And perhaps it didn't matter too much in the past if many men were unempathetic and uncommunicative – their working lives depended on strength and/or systemising skills, and they left the caring, sharing stuff to the womenfolk. But in a crowded 21st century world where work is generally indoor, upfront and personal, everyone needs people skills. Which means 21st century baby boys need attentive mothering more than ever before.

Fragile parents

Unfortunately, this is where the march of systemised progress throws a further spanner in the works. Another unintended side effect of the tumultuous cultural changes of recent decades is that adults are on the whole far less well prepared for parenthood than our grandparents. So natural, enjoyable interaction with little babies may not come as easily to modern adults as it did to previous generations. And despite our material wealth, new parents may also often be less well supported on a personal level. This can significantly affect their mental state, especially if a baby is apparently antisocial, distressed and demanding.

In the days when child-rearing was 'women's work', most new mothers already had some experience of babies. As they grew up, they'd probably helped with siblings or other children in the local area. Then, when their own babies were born, they were usually surrounded by an extended family and other women in the wider community who provided adult company and helped out if any problems arose. This is still the case in developing countries, where the women of a community observe various routines and rituals, coming together to support a new mother in the weeks after the birth.

But in a contemporary technological culture, parents – male and female – seldom have much personal experience of babies before bringing their own home from the hospital. They may also be several generations away from an extended family and the female lore that saw their own parents through. What's more, if they've moved away from the place they grew up, their main social contacts are probably from the world of work – not likely to be much use for support or advice. While professional help is available in acute circumstances, the cost of providing ongoing personal advice and support for all new parents is considered prohibitive.

Many new mothers (and others caring for small babies) thus find themselves spending the greater part of their lives with little adult company, and with no one to turn to if they're not sure what to do. A 2007 report found young mothers spent only 90 minutes a day with adults other than their partners – it was the 'loneliest time of their lives'. Even when all goes well, looking after a small baby is a hugely demanding but not wildly entertaining task, and for adults used to the busy social life of a workplace this solitary servitude can be deeply destabilising. If problems arise, tackling them alone is doubly stressful. And women who've learned to value themselves in terms of their status in the workplace can find it difficult to cope with relegation to the low-status role of 'mother'.

Between 10 and 15% of mothers are eventually diagnosed with postnatal depression, but according to the Royal College of Paediatrics and Child Health as many again probably go undiagnosed because they don't realise that their feelings of guilt and helplessness are a recognised clinical condition. There are many other parents and carers who, although they never reach the stage of feeling helpless, find the demands of childcare render them tired and low-spirited. And when human beings feel down, depressed or despondent, they don't find it easy to smile, sing, make silly faces or engage in baby talk.

It's therefore not surprising that research shows the mothers of baby boys are more likely to suffer from postnatal depression than the mothers of girls, or that male babies are more affected by their mothers' depression. The dance of communication is a two-way process, and a miserable mum would find engaging with a less naturally sociable infant much more difficult. Research also shows that depressed mothers are less able to read their babies' feelings, seem 'out of sync' with them, and have a tendency to look away. Unable to communicate with her son, it's not surprising if a fragile mother chooses to direct her gaze elsewhere.

The technology trap

At this point another aspect of modern life enters the fray. Twenty-first century adults have an unprecedented range of things to gaze at – TV, email, social networking sites, blogs, MSN ... If we aren't careful, it's easy to spend hours engrossed in virtual communication which – once one's gone into systemised thought mode – is far less demanding than face-to-face encounters. So it's not surprising if harassed parents and other carers, particularly those for whom low spirits have made real human contact difficult, are attracted to electronic communication or entertainment. And when you're watching a TV programme, answering your emails or plugged into an iPod, you can't give personal attention to a baby.

Not only can modern technology distract adults from attending to the dance of communication, it can also distract babies. Before the arrival of video and all-day TV about 30 years ago, there was only one way for a mother to comfort her fractious baby son. She had to pick him up, give him a cuddle, look him in the eyes and try to communicate with him – the dance of communication was a downright necessity. Nowadays, however, even tiny infants can be hypnotised by the colour, movement and sound effects of screen-based entertainment. With an electronic babysitter blinking in the corner of the living room, a welter of children's channels on offer every minute of the day (including dedicated baby channels), and a range of DVDs offering to turn one's child into an Einstein, Mozart or Michelangelo, any parent who's not in a dancing mood can easily sit this one out.

In a technological world, this doesn't at first seem too worrying a development. After all, 21st century children are growing up in a high-tech, screen-based world – surely it's good for them to learn their way around it from an early age? And can't TV and DVD – granting access to a whole world of images – entertain and educate a baby far better than a humble mother, stuck in the dreary domestic here and now? As for all those lullabies and nursery rhymes, surely professional recordings would be much more enjoyable than mum's amateur rendition? The answer, in terms of their baby's development is, emphatically, no.

A baby boy in the first year or so of life is much closer to his Stone Age past than his 21st century future. His brain is designed to learn through first-hand experiences (see pages 53–58), not disembodied sounds and shapes on a flat screen. He also needs genuine, personal interaction, as Trevarthen demonstrated in a study where babies and mothers interacted over a video link. When the link was in real time, so that mother and child responded to each other's images on screen as in real life, the babies were hooked. But when the babies were shown a recording of their mothers – meaning mum's gestures weren't responsive to her child in real time – they became distressed.

Through the rituals of attachment – eye contact, physical closeness, body language, song – parent and child gradually become attuned to each other's emotions, and the baby gradually learns what it is to be human. But a baby boy who'd rather stare at an alien mobile than a friendly face (see page 35) isn't naturally all that interested in learning these human skills. With his hunter's visuo-spatial skills and his drive to systemise he's much more likely to be fascinated by flickering patterns on a brightly lit screen. Given half a chance, he'll attune himself to screens rather than people.

For many years, the American Academy of Pediatrics has recommended that children under two shouldn't watch TV at all. There was no research to back up this recommendation – just a gut reaction on the part of doctors who knew something about child development. Indeed, it's only in the last few years that research into the effects of technology on children's brains in the first few years of life has begun to trickle through. Studies have now appeared linking early television-watching to those male-dominated disorders, ADHD and autism. As argued in later chapters, I suspect the technology trap may also be related to many speech and language difficulties and to dyslexia. In 2008, the French government concluded the evidence is strong enough to ban French channels from airing TV programmes aimed at children under three and insist cable channels display a health warning.

This is not to claim that developmental disorders are *caused* by screen-based entertainment. There's copious evidence that these conditions are genetic in origin, and there are probably a multitude of other contributing factors in the case of each individual sufferer. Human conditions are never simple. But if a boy has a predisposition towards a developmental condition (and they seem to be around four times more likely in boys than girls), tuning him into screens from an early age isn't going to help.

If nature has made boys more fragile than girls, the nurture we offer should compensate for this from the moment of conception. The mother's role is crucial in countering male fragility. First, she has the responsibility of protecting her son's development in the womb by taking care of her body during pregnancy. Then, as the most likely primary attachment figure, it's she who must engage him from the moment of birth in the dance of communication.

Yet 21st century mothers are probably less well prepared for the realities of motherhood than those of previous generations and can expect less practical support from their families or other women in their community. Instead, they're often misled by popular misconceptions that boys are damaged by too much attention, and surrounded by technological distractions that can easily come between them and their sons. Baby boys are thus in danger of fixating from their earliest months not on a loving human face but on a flashing screen. As Sebastian Kraemer puts it, from the moment of birth our cultural attitude to boys adds *'social insult to biological weaknesses'.*

Chapter summary

This chapter summarises the research suggesting that boys are at a biological disadvantage in comparison with girls from soon after conception, leading to slightly delayed development and a greater potential for difficulties in communication with an attachment figure. This possible impairment of the mother-child relationship may be exacerbated by societal fears of 'molly-coddling' boys, by the lack of support for mothers in contemporary society, and by the ubiquity of screen-based technology (which may be particularly attractive for a 'systemising' male).

Tackling 'male fragility'

What can parents do?

- With such a wealth of guidance for mothers-to-be these days, it's difficult to know where to start. In fact, it's easy to be over-faced and, eventually, totally confused.
- Stick to a few authoritative sources, starting with your doctor

and local health services. These websites are likely to give up-to-date advice:

> National Health Service: www.nhs.uk/Pregnancy
> Food Standards Agency: www.eatwell.gov.uk/agesandstages/pregnancy
> BBC parenting website: www.bbc.co.uk/parenting/having_a_baby

If you're interested in the science behind the advice, try *What Babies and Children Really Need* by Sally Goddard Blythe (Hawthorn Press).

- Treat commercially produced information with caution. With the best will in the world, commercial concerns can't avoid self-interest and advice may focus on aspects of 'lifestyle' rather than the real-life needs of parents and children.
- Don't let material concerns take precedence over human, personal ones. Babies don't care about lifestyles – they just want love. And new parents need human support far more than material 'must-haves'. Read Chapters 2 and 3 about what babies need in the first thousand days, and don't waste too much time and money on expensive nursery decoration and equipment.
- Instead, spend time and effort in the months before your baby's born in building a personal support system. Make contact with people in your immediate neighbourhood, with whom you can develop friendships and exchange support in the months and years to come:
  - meet other prospective parents through organisations like the National Childbirth Trust: www.nct.org.uk (I've met many mothers who say the friends they made on an NCT course saw them through the next 18 years!)
  - while still child-free and mobile, check out your local area for places new parents can meet up (e.g. your local health centre, library, Citizen's Advice Bureau, community centre,

children's centre and so on). You may be able to track down this information on the web, but it's far more helpful in the long run to familiarise yourself with your locality in real life

- supplement your travels by using websites (e.g. www.netmums. com and www.fatherhoodinstitute.org) to find local ante-natal courses and ideas for parent 'meet-ups'

- make an effort to get to know your neighbours – stay-at-home mums, retired people and others not out at work may value a bit of chat or company, and they could turn into a tower of experienced strength in years to come

- learn to ask for and accept help from the people around you. A society that sees such requests as a sign of weakness is one in which trust and reciprocity break down. Parents-to-be often attract kindness, so enjoy it – a smile and thanks are usually reward enough, but if being helped makes you feel like a passenger, vow to pay both individuals and the com-munity back at a later date.

- Once your baby's born, don't try to be perfect. Mothers need to focus on their own and their baby's well-being; fathers and other family members on supporting them. Surroundings need only be as clean and tidy as necessary to maintain well-being and once children have moved into your life, a home that looks like something out of a magazine means you've probably got your priorities wrong. (See Chapter 1 and 'Dylan's Story'.)

- If you think you might be depressed, check out this useful leaflet for information and advice: http://www.understand-ingchildhood.net/documents/03UCPND01.pdf. But if you just feel beset and bewildered, it may be more helpful to talk to a real person. Home Start (www.home-start.org.uk) is an ex-cellent organisation that puts new parents in touch with people who've been there before.

- Keep 'the dance of communication' in the centre of the

process. Take time getting to know your son and learning the steps of two-way attunement. Don't worry about getting it wrong: this dance is unique to you and your baby. (See also Chapters 2 and 3.)

- Of the five 'must-haves' quoted on page 22, the most important in the early weeks is LOVE. For the scientific evidence for this claim, read *Why Love Matters* by Sue Gerhardt (Routledge).

What can the rest of us do?

Smart-arses through the ages have preached the doctrine of looking after number one. In their cynical, materialistic value system, altruism is for fools, social conscience is for losers, and it makes sense to exploit others before they exploit you. Hence their scorn for 'do-gooders' and 'bleeding hearts', and their tendency to assume that absolutely *everybody* is – like them – on the make.

For the sake of society as a whole, we have to challenge these attitudes, which are now widespread in society. The communities that support us all at a personal level are based on collaboration, tolerance and mutual support. It's in everyone's interest that children are reared to respect this community ethos, so it's in everyone's interest to support parents in rearing them.

- Fortunately, kindness and consideration to pregnant women, new mothers and tiny babies still comes pretty naturally to most of us. Every adult can help extend this kindness, not only by consciously practising it themselves, but by valuing and applauding it in others.
- Some of the most intolerant adults, as far as new parents and babies are concerned, are young, single and/or childless working people who simply have no idea of the realities of caring for a baby. Since many media and marketing

professionals fall into this group, their attitudes are often reflected onscreen and help perpetuate a 'smart-arsed' culture. It would help enormously if broadcasters and businesses paid as much attention to developing 'a child-friendly ethos' as to tackling sexism, racism and other acknowledged social evils within their institutions.

- Sadly, older people are also growing increasingly intolerant. With greater geographical mobility, many grandparents live far from their grandchildren, and are unable to see them as often as they'd like. So perhaps, as the baby boomer generation moves into retirement, the message should be 'If you can't be with the babies you love, love the ones you're with.' Men and women who've already raised their own families (and who know all the pitfalls) are an amazing resource for a young parent, and volunteering with an organisation like Homestart (www.home-start.org.uk), which matches new parents up with older experienced 'mentors', is a great way of using all that experience.

- Parents-to-be and new parents come into contact with professionals such as doctors, midwives and health visitors, but in today's complex and over-stretched system these contacts are usually far from personal. Many communities also now have Children's Centres where parents can consult professionals from social work and educational backgrounds, but again they may have little time to forge personal relationships. A key function of all these agencies should be to help create informal parent networks (the sort of thing recommended in the 'parents box' above), by providing:
  - simple ways of forging personal contacts
  - inviting premises for meetings and *real-life* chat-rooms
  - ways of promoting contacts within the community and between the generations.

- Helping new parents forge personal support systems is one

way for professionals to take increasing pressure off the systems they serve. Another is by passing on information. Regular talks and discussion groups led by health visitors, speech and language therapists, nutritionists, sleep experts, and so on could demystify parenthood, as well as providing something for people to chat about.

- But the best way to provide all adults for the social and emotional reality of child-rearing would be to use the secondary education system. If schools were to provide a short course in child development – informed by up-to-date neuroscience – for students around the age of 16, they'd ensure a universal baseline of knowledge for all future members of a community.

What can politicians do?

The change of mind-set required to reforge communities and ensure a better deal for the children of the future is to a large extent up to the electorate. It requires 'bottom-up' action from people in the community – the sort of thing suggested in the 'What can parents do?' and 'What can the rest of us do?' boxes throughout this book. But this won't happen without the 'top-down' influence of law-makers and opinion-formers.

The best way to draw attention to the importance of the early months of childhood is to support parents in caring for their children, such as:

- Political and financial encouragement for parents to look after their children at home, at least for the first thousand days (see Chapter 1).
- Extra *personal* support from the very beginning for at-risk children (see Chapter 10).
- Support for local systems that develop 'self-help' solutions

like those described above, as opposed to deskilling parents and other adults by professionalising and/or regulating care. This means avoiding over-generalised regulatory control (for instance, excessive bureaucratic intervention into the care of all children outside the home, such as that behind the Early Years Foundation Stage legislation in England). It also means ensuring that budgets for Children's Centres, Sure Start and so on are not so tightly controlled from the centre that it's impossible to respond to specific local needs at a local level.

- Financial support and promotion of charities – not just national charities, but small local ones – that help a community help itself. This requires devolving some financial control to local government, and encouraging them to support promising local initiatives.
- Support for educational campaigns to inform all young people of the realities of child-rearing before they become parents, including a child-development course in secondary schools.
- Vetting and, if necessary, regulation of media and market forces that target prospective and new parents (e.g. banning baby TV channels, as has been done in France).
- Public information campaigns pointing out that what happens to children has long-term implications for us all – especially in the case of boys, who tend to 'externalise' their problems – and thus raising the status of parents and others who care for young children.

FOUR FRAGILE MALES

How much might genetic fragility account for the problems of the four boys we met on page 1? Let's rewind to the weeks after their birth.

Dylan's parents have waited a long time for their baby, because they wanted to provide a decent home and lifestyle before children came along, so they're well prepared. And since Mandy's a staff nurse, she was up to date with all health issues during pregnancy. The birth went well, and even though Dylan can be 'fussy', his doting mother is used to awkward patients and his dad helps out at night. They seem the perfect family: they have a new home on a new estate, with an inside like something out of a magazine, Dylan is bright-eyed and beautifully turned out, while Mandy is a very yummy 30-year-old mum, and planning to take at least 18 months off work. As her husband Craig leaves for work in the morning, he feels it's worth the long hours and stress it costs him to maintain their 21st century lifestyle.

But under her carefully applied make-up, Mandy has begun to feel slightly less confident than she looks. After ten years as an efficient professional, the waves of emotion that hit her when Dylan wails are unsettling, and it's harder than she thought to keep on top of everything. She misses the routine orderliness of work, and that sense of calm control when you're sitting behind the ward computer ...

Ozzy's mum Sarah is the picture of happiness. She too knew exactly what to expect, having read all the books about pregnancy and early childcare, including two she commissioned herself, as editorial director of a large publishing firm. Her solicitor husband Josh keeps up to date with child-rearing too, but prefers to get his information off the web. They already have one eight-year-old daughter, from Josh's first marriage. She and Sarah hit it off from the beginning, and she's doing very well at school and is thrilled with her new little brother, so their family seems complete.

Ozzy is clearly very bright, staring and reaching for everything, and Sarah loves taking him out in the sling, pointing out the sights in the park. He's such a good baby, already sleeping five hours a night, which Josh maintains is due to the 'low-frequency sound' CD he streams into the nursery and Sarah reckons is because of all the Mozart Ozzy's heard since he was an embryo.

She hadn't been sure how long to stay at home, but Ozzy is turning out very self-sufficient. When the agency sent a Portuguese nanny for interview, he was perfectly happy to be handed over and nursed – and obviously a professional can look after him far better than Sarah. Being hopeless at domestic stuff, she's decided to return to the office part-time at the start of next month.

Leo's mother Cary always loved children. In fact, she wanted to train as a nursery nurse but instead took an office job, because it paid better and she was seeing her boyfriend Mike through college. Soon after he qualified she fell pregnant, and although they hadn't meant it to happen so soon, they were both excited at the prospect of being parents. Pregnancy was tough – giving up smoking and drinking ruined Cary's social life – but her mates at work kept her going, and Mike was very supportive.

Then Leo was born, more than a fortnight premature, and had to spend 48 hours in an incubator. Cary and Mike were beside themselves with worry, and desperate to get him back to the flat – but now they have, it's turned into a nightmare. He's a demanding baby, won't feed properly, won't sleep, keeps crying all the time … Cary's feeling exhausted and isolated – health visitors call occasionally, but she's terrified they'll think she's doing something wrong. Mike's exhausted too, from the lack of sleep, but at least he gets away to work during the day. It isn't what they expected at all …

On the other hand, **Kevin's parents** are delighted with their infant son. They already have two boys, both now at school, so although it's a shock to the system to have a baby in the house again, they know from experience that things will settle down. Stephanie reckons his was the easiest of the three births – 'Must be getting the hang of it' – and is enjoying having a new baby to spoil.

She's been a full-time mum for ten years now, and has been using her spare time as the kids got older to study for an Open University degree in information technology – she's due to graduate next year. She'd been planning to start her own business, but will probably put it off now till Kevin's a little older. She and James (who's deputy head of a primary school) aren't sure what they think about sending children to nursery, even though everyone seems to do it these days. But at the moment, everything's on hold and Kevin is the apple of everyone's eye. Even – when they can tear themselves away from the PlayStation – his big brothers.

So there they are, four much-wanted, much-loved baby boys. All have healthy parents, mothers who took care during pregnancy, safe warm homes and – compared with children in the past – an enviable level of material comfort. Medical science brought them all safely through birth, even little Leo who may have perished in the past. Apart from his current problems (presumably the result of immaturity) and Dylan's 'fussiness' none of them seems particularly fragile ... yet.

Chapter 2

A MIND OF HIS OWN

How 'mother love' helps boys grow up
bright and balanced ...
and how modern life can dumb them down

Fragile or not, male or not, all babies need 'mothering'. But it needn't be a mother that does it. It could be a father, grandparent, nanny or anyone else prepared to devote themselves body and soul to looking after a tiny infant. Mothers have three natural advantages that particularly fit them for the task: a close blood tie, a bodyful of maternal hormones and a natural female inclination to empathy. Since, even today, the 'primary carer' for most babies is their mother, I'll stick to the traditional terminology.

The relationship between mothers and sons is recognised as an intense and very special one, celebrated in countless pictures of the Madonna and Child. Thanks to Freud and various 20th century novelists, we're only too aware of the long-term damage if a boy becomes too fixated on his Madonna figure ... not to mention the damage to his mother and her marriage. She therefore has to tread the fine line between adoring her infant son and turning him into her own personal Messiah, or herself into a mere handmaiden of the Lord.

The natural corrective factor is, of course, a father. The male of the species is not only the most obvious source of support for his female partner, but also nature's choice as a secondary attachment figure for their son. While mother love (whoever supplies it) is the natural starting point for raising a balanced boy, 'father love' (whoever supplies it) is just as essential. No matter how these ingredients are provided in a 21st century family, research findings won't allow us to ignore their significance in turning out happy, successful young men.

The lust to learn

In the beginning is attachment. There are many reasons for parents to work hard at tuning themselves into their baby's needs. From their own point of view, a responsive relationship can help make domestic life run more smoothly, as they learn to understand their offspring and thus gently guide him into the rhythms of the adult world. And from the son's point of view, he can begin to use his limited range of communication to let his adult carers know how he feels about life.

This starts, of course, with pressing physical needs, such as food, nappy changes, temperature control and so on. Twenty-first century boys are on to a winner here, since our society places great emphasis on keeping children physically clean, healthy and safe. But he also has pressing cognitive needs, and the way his parents respond to these will underpin his attitude to learning throughout life. Perhaps this is why secure attachment is associated with academic success.

The drive to learn, and the means of learning, is hardwired into every infant's brain. Some cognitive psychologists describe babies and toddlers as behaving like mini-scientists, naturally equipped to find out about their world by engaging with it in an experimental way. However, since each infant scientist is born physically helpless, in the early stages he needs a faithful personal assistant to help him conduct these first-hand experiments. The more responsive that assistant is, the more the little scientist will be able to indulge his lust to learn. A securely attached baby, with a loving adult finely attuned to his needs, is at a huge advantage. In the words of the distinguished developmental psychologist Urie Bronfenbrenner, '*Someone's got to be crazy about that kid. That's number one. First, last and always.*'

Every mini-scientist is programmed for two series of investigations. The first is a study of the physical world he lives in – what the items around him look, sound, smell, feel and taste like, what they're for, how they work and how they relate to each other. The second is the study of human behaviour – as a social animal, he also needs to know how people work: how they think, why they act as they do, and the implications for his survival in a social world.

Interestingly, these two quests correspond with the two modes of thought described by Simon Baron-Cohen: S-type systemising and E-type empathising (see page 9). We've already seen that Baron-Cohen's research suggests baby boys are more naturally inclined to S- than E-type investigations, but he's happy to concur with other scientists that – given adequate opportunities to learn – gender differences are very small. The developmental psychologist Elizabeth Spelke points out that *'Infants don't divide up the labour of understanding the world with males focusing on mechanics and females focusing on emotions. Male and female infants are both interested in objects and people, and they learn about both.'*

As long as nature is allowed to take its course, this is almost certainly true. Which is just as well for boys – in a highly populated, urban world, they need to grow up understanding the mechanics not just of things but of other people's minds and feelings.

S-type learning: the material world

As far as S-type investigation of the physical world is concerned, most parents would probably agree that boys need little encouragement. Indeed, the main task of a responsible and responsive adult is to ensure they don't actually kill themselves (or anyone else) in the process. Parents have to tread a fine line between facilitating their offspring's experimental enquiries and keeping him safe.

To begin with, babies can only investigate the items that grown-ups put in range of their eyes, ears, hands and mouths; but baby boys tend to be very voluble in expressing their desires, so mothers are usually left in no doubt about what their sons wish to investigate. Once able to sit up, crawl, and eventually walk, children are more able to call the shots themselves, which makes their minders' task more challenging. But, generally, adults accept that boys have a questing spirit, and usually allow them a fair amount of leeway.

This is just as well, because baby boys are fragile, and if adults thwart their investigative efforts too often, they may eventually lose interest and stop wanting to learn. On the other hand, the infant scientist with a sensitive assistant can make remarkable progress. By six months he knows enough about the objects in his environment to categorise them mentally in a systematic way. He also begins to suss out a few physical rules – for instance, by eight months he clocks that just because something disappears from sight, it's not necessarily gone for good: peek-aboo!

By the second year of life his drive to systemise rules has usually led to a deep interest in mechanics – most boys by now show considerable interest in clocks and watches, keys and locks, levers and switches. By 18 months he's started testing objects systematically to find out how they work, for instance by constantly throwing household items into the loo to investigate the action of water on different materials. He's also discovered cause and effect, and is using things he finds lying around as simple tools. (Being male, of course, he may be particularly interested in using them as weapons.)

It's a remarkable scientific feat. In less than two years – given that his adult helpers allow enough rein – the natural drive within every boy's Stone Age brain takes him to a top-ranking position among the primates. Indeed, he's now ready to leave the great apes far behind because from the moment of birth he's been engaged in another immense systemising task: steadily collecting data about his native language (otherwise known as the 'mother tongue'). By listening to his mother as she talks and sings, he's systematised the sounds and meanings of her words, and usually some time in his second year begins experimenting with them himself.

Once a scientist has gained control of a language system, he has access to all the thoughts and experience in the heads of the adults around him. Questions like 'What that?' mean he can constantly refine his categorisation of objects, and sometime during his third year he discovers the ultimate questioning word: 'Why?' So now he can use language as well as hands-on experience to investigate, speculate, explore and, given an interested audience, communicate his findings. However, keeping that audience interested relies, to some extent, on success in the second great investigative quest.

E-type learning: the social world

It's in this second mission – to find out about *people* and how they work – that the commitment and patience of a boy scientist's assistant are crucial. In addition to all her other duties, his mother is also her infant scientist's major human specimen. It's upon her behaviour, and that of other adults within his radar, that he'll base his deductions about how people tick. And the lessons they teach will be encoded into the internal wiring of his brain, so he'll carry them with him for the rest of his life.

It's a momentous responsibility. However, before it can begin, a newborn son must be encouraged to look into his mother's eyes – which accounts for all those women through the generations desperately distorting their faces to look like aliens in order to attract a tiny scientist's attention. For once this contact is made, a mother can model human sounds, gestures and expressions for him to copy and, through constant meaningful exchanges, he'll gradually learn the ropes of human interaction. He'll learn how gesture, body language and facial expression are used to convey people's feelings and intentions. He'll also start to recognise the speech sounds of his native language and the key words that define his world.

All this interaction also helps towards another momentous discovery. The infant scientist slowly begins to realise that his faithful assistant and he are two different people: they might be attached, but they're also separate. Within a year or so, he's so socially aware that he recognises that other people have their own, separate points of view, and has sussed out how their words, faces and body language can help him 'read their minds'.

This also leads to the wondrous discovery that he himself has a point of view – a mind of his own – and can use his growing knowledge about social science to communicate it. Awareness of one's own and others' thoughts and feelings is a major factor in human development, as significant (and happening at around the same age) as tool use. 'Mind-mindedness' – the quality that above all distinguishes us from other animals – is a hot topic among neuroscientists and philosophers.

At around the age of two, the infant scientist's 'theory of mind' leads him to another significant stage in his quest to understand. Now that he's gaining in physical and mental independence (and feeling pretty good about it) he embarks on a series of experiments to discover exactly what he can get away with, and how far he'll have to cave in to the will of others. This is the point when a lovable toddler suddenly turns from Dr Jekyll into Mr Hyde. He'll do something he knows is forbidden ... but rather than concentrating, as he used to, on the object he's mishandling, he stares straight into his mother's eyes.

The terrible two-year-old is now using his beloved human specimen to find out how people react when he breaks the rules. He needs to see the expression on his mother's face, to hear her tone of voice, and to discover whether she actually means what she says ... It's an exercise in boundary testing – and status-driven, risk-taking young males often need to do quite a lot of it.

It can also be a terrible shock to an empathetic mum who's just given up two years of her life demonstrating civilised behaviour to her son. Where did he learn such *defiance*?

The parental balancing act

The way parents (particularly the primary attachment figure) treat their son in the first few years is hugely important in terms of his future character. On the one hand, it's vital to be *warm*, empathetic and responsive to ensure he feels safe and securely attached. On the other it's just as important to be *firm*, not only to ensure his safety and the rest of the family's sanity, but – as he grows older – to establish and maintain his concepts of acceptable social behaviour in the world beyond the family.

The balancing act is particularly difficult because reading a baby's mind isn't easy, and just as you feel you're making progress, something new crops up: small children's needs keep changing. To begin with, the new parents must learn to interpret all those terrifying cries, and find ways of responding that keep their son happy, healthy and gurgling (while at the same time taking into account their own need for more than three hours sleep a night). What's more, all babies are different, so what works for one may not work for another. It's all part of the ancient dance of communication.

As time goes on and parents gradually tune into their son's particular needs and nature, they find themselves confronted with another dilemma: his drive to find out about the world versus their drive to keep him safe. The more mobile a boy becomes, the more problems arise for parents. Psychologist Cordelia Fine describes the conflict in all its painful reality:

> *My son, 13 months old, is crying as if his heart will break. He sobs with his entire body, and I know that in a few seconds he will assume what my husband and I call 'The Tragedy Pose'. Sure enough, soon he collapses onto the floor and flops forward so that his*

forehead hits the carpet. I am holding in my hand the accomplice
to the act that has obliterated all joy from my son's existence. This
object and I, between us, have left no other course available to my
young child but to give himself over completely to unmitigated,
carpet-drenching grief. I struggle painfully but successfully with
the urge to ruin his character for ever by returning to him this item
upon which, clearly, his happiness depends. It is a ballpoint pen.

A sense of humour is helpful, because such cool maternal wisdom is hard to maintain. Apart from the constant need to make
decisions ('Which is more important: his desire to investigate
the potential of a ballpoint pen, or the possible damage he could
do with it?'), there's the shared – and very real – pain of his distress. The usual parental dance steps on such occasions are (1)
loving sympathy and lots of cuddles and/or (2) distracting his
attention towards an alternative exciting investigation. As Dr
Fine points out, recanting is out of the question: once a decision
is made, it's essential to stick with it because consistency is, in
the long run, reassuring for a boy. And fair rules, humanely applied, are an essential element of a secure stable home.

Another problem for 21st century parents is the boredom and
irritation of constant repetition. Once a particular activity takes
his fancy – such as putting objects down the toilet – he can become locked in an endless Groundhog Day loop, no matter how
often one intervenes. He is, of course, a scientist on a mission,
needing repeated experiments in the search for patterns and,
through his passionate attachment to the quest, laying down
his own patterns of neural connections in the brain. If his passion is for an unacceptable activity (and blocked loos are no
joke), there are likely to be displays of carpet-drenching grief
until that particular 'thread of thinking' dies away. On the other
hand, if you can work out what it is that's caught his interest, it
might be possible to provide an alternative experimental model
– a bucket of water outdoors and a selection of stuff you don't
mind getting wet?

It's when boys move into the terrible twos, and Dr Jekyll turns into Mr Hyde, that setting and maintaining boundaries becomes much more emotionally charged. Mothers throughout the ages have struggled with feelings of rejection when their carefully reared Messiah falls from grace. But the more they've engaged him, right from the beginning, in empathetic communication, the sooner he's likely to understand that the 'warm but firm' approach is for his benefit as well as for the grown-ups.

How to thwart a scientist

Unless there's some severe neurological defect, the lust to learn is present in every child's brain. And since boys are primed by nature to be particularly active and inquisitive, catering for their investigations can prove deeply wearing for 'faithful assistants', especially when there's little day-by-day support from close family or the local community. For many exhausted mothers in the 21st century, the only available source of comfort and advice may be TV chat shows or web-based social networking sites.

While these undoubtedly offer a lifeline, there are considerable dangers. For a start, the electronic media is financed largely by commerce, so marketing influences are everywhere, and consumerism paints its own picture of successful mother–child relationships. Images of perfect babies interacting joyfully with serene mums in their spotless, ideal homes contrast starkly with the reality of childcare, and can feed unhelpful aspirations. A mum convinced by market forces that motherhood is about keeping her child safe from all known germs is likely to become excessively risk averse and to limit scientific enquiry. So is one who's constantly balancing her offspring's drive to explore with her own yearning to maintain a beautiful, ideal home.

There's also the problem that a mother glued to a computer or TV screen isn't able to keep an eye on her son's activities. So in order to feed her need for human contact, his movements must be restricted. Children inevitably have to be penned up for some of the time – adults can't be constantly on watch – but in the past maternal support systems (grandparents, aunts, older siblings, other neighbourhood mothers and their families) were present in the here and now. Real-life human support is not only more personal but means more eyes to share supervision, which is why it's essential for today's parents to build up real-life, rather than virtual networks of support. It's easy to let a baby or toddler play around your feet while having a cup of tea with a real person, but not when your eyes are focused on a screen.

Meeting up with real human beings is also more likely to get mother and child out and about. Again though, there are 21st century problems. If most journeys are by car, babies and toddlers spend the outing strapped into car seats; walking in city streets, they are probably for safety's sake strapped into buggies. As life has become increasingly urban, traffic has expanded to fill the given space, and adults have shied away from the discomfort of inclement weather and the messiness of the natural world. The result is that opportunities for small children to experience or explore their outdoor environment have gradually receded.

The problem is that, if we restrict the movement and exploratory instincts of very young children too much, we risk destroying their spirit of scientific enquiry. In the famous 'smart rat' experiments of the 1980s, researchers found that rats raised in a boring environment became steadily more apathetic and lowbrow, while those reared in stimulating conditions grew up bright-eyed and curious. The everyday world that adults take for granted (indoors and out) is, for an apprentice human being who's experiencing everything for the first time, an intensely stimulating environment.

However, instead of first-hand, active experiences, we increasingly offer children second-hand, passive ones, keeping them safe indoors staring at screens. As Marion Cleves Diamond, the 'smart rat' researcher, once pointed out at a conference about children's TV, the dull sedentary rats didn't get any smarter if they watched other rats running around having fun.

'It is important to interact with the objects,' she said, 'to explore, to investigate, both physically and mentally.' By encouraging passive viewing rather than active investigation in the first couple of years, there is a serious danger of thwarting boys' passion to learn.

How to dumb a scientist down

Just as restricting access to the physical world can make a scientist dull, lack of social engagement can also make him dumb. A talent for language is a winning ticket in the lottery of life. It's a key survival skill, allowing a boy to communicate his needs, explore and express his understanding, and work together with other people. He also needs language to learn, especially as he moves through the education system and the curriculum becomes increasingly abstract. So it's not surprising that difficulty with language, in both the spoken and written form, is a significant handicap.

As might be expected in the less conversational, more fragile sex, language problems are more prevalent among boys. Boys are generally slower to talk than girls, and three times as likely to suffer from a speech and language disorder. But unless there is a neurological glitch, they should be just as well equipped as their sisters to pick up their native tongue eventually. Little children learn language just as they learn other human lessons: their brain is primed for it, nature interacts with nurture, which interacts with culture. In the words of America's top cognitive psychologists, *We know a lot to begin with; we learn much more; other people unconsciously teach us.*

Through singing and talking to him, the adults who care for a baby provide data for his systemising brain. Over the first year or so of life, he catalogues the sounds of his native tongue (there are 44 to identify and practise in English) and works out the meaning of the words. The unconscious teaching of his faithful adult assistants provides a context for these meanings, so language grows out of loving attention, emotional engagement and day-to-day social chit-chat.

Here then is another reason for parents to persevere in singing, talking and interacting with an infant son, and to eschew the lure of the TV or computer screen. In the earliest months their sing-song, nonsensical 'baby talk' and the old songs like 'Dance to Your Daddy' or 'Bye Baby Bunting' are perfect for introducing the language sounds, and their rhythms help attune their son's ears to the cadences of speech. The more often he hears a song or rhyme, the more it helps tune him into the language, so there's no need for parents to worry if their nursery repertoire is limited.

Like all instinctive learning, ability declines as time goes on. At birth a baby has the potential to learn any language on earth, but as his ears attune to his mother tongue, he loses the ability to discriminate other speech sounds. This is why adult Chinese people find it so difficult to pronounce 'r': it doesn't exist in their language, they didn't hear it in early childhood, so they can no longer register the sound. So a boy's very early language experiences may affect his ability to read and write in a few years time – if he's not had sufficient experience of language to make fine discriminations between sounds like 'b' and 'p', he'll probably have trouble with phonics (see pages 143 and 156).

Many parents buy DVDs of nursery rhymes, thinking children will enjoy the variety and visual effects, but as explained earlier, repetition is critical for growing brains and the emphasis here is on *sound*. A child staring at a familiar face, rather than rapidly moving visual images, is more likely to focus on the sounds of the rhymes. Boys, who may be less well equipped than girls to discriminate specific language sounds, need as much repetition as a loving adult can provide while still staying this side of sanity – so a parent's limited repertoire is more powerful than the variety of a DVD. Indeed, there's now research evidence that, under the age of sixteen months, 'educational' DVDs can suppress language development rather than promote it.

A dance to the music of time

Attachment and communication skills are profoundly inter-
related. Indeed, the very first step in the dance of communication – eye contact – continues to be hugely important as time
goes on. The developmental psychopathologist Peter Hobson
believes that once parent and child are used to tuning into each
other, the dance turns into a triangular arrangement, with the
child at one corner, the parent at the other and the rest of the
world at the third. By looking at each other, out at the world,
and back at each other again, parent and child connect emotionally over a shared experience and understanding.

For instance, the child looks at a dog and cries 'Da!'; mother
looks to see where he's looking – *'Yes, it's a doggy. Isn't he lovely?'*
Or mother spots a dog, points and says *'Look at the doggy, George!'*;
child follows gaze and laughs – 'Da! Da!' – and mother and child
smile back at each other, complicit in their shared experience.
This type of interaction, repeated countless times, is how the child
learns words. Over many such experiences, he associates the word
'doggy' with a particular sort of creature, and refines his control
over the muscles of his mouth so he can say it for himself. (Incidentally, his mother's intuitive use of the 'babyish' term *'doggy'*
helps him hear the *g* – not always obvious when we say *'dog'*.)

It goes without saying that mother and child must be facing
each other for this exchange, so if the child's in a pushchair it
should face towards the parent. Another unintended conse-
quence of human progress is that, as more parents wanted light-
weight pushchairs that could be folded up to put in the car, the
traditional parent-facing design was changed. Manufacturers
found that for safety and convenience of folding, the cheapest
design was one where the baby faced away from his parent.
About 30 years ago, pushchairs turned outwards practically
overnight. It's only recently, after concerted campaigning by language experts, that reasonably priced, parent-facing chairs have
become available again.

As a growing boy gradually assembles the building blocks of language and struggles to use it for himself, his mother's responsiveness nudges him forward. By seeking the meaning in his words, she helps him see how to make sense.

'Doggy out!'

'Has the doggy gone out?'

'Out! Out! Tch tch!'

'Oh, was the doggy naughty? Did Daddy send him out? Oh dear.'

'Daddy out. Daddy out. Doggy tch tch!'

Through these real-life contexts, parent and child tune into each other's use of language, and gradually the child develops command of his mother tongue.

Peter Hobson argues that this triangular dance to the music of time is also hugely important to the development of human thought, underpinning the 'mind-mindedness' described on page 57. Like Simon Baron-Cohen, he has studied the clinical roots of autism, and found that children who don't get opportunities to engage in this way with loving adults often develop autistic-like behaviour. He cites the Rumanian orphans, brought up from birth with very little human contact as they lay untended in their cots, and children who cannot make eye contact because they are born blind.

These are extreme examples, of course, and in both cases it has been proved that such 'acquired autism' can be overcome to some extent by later loving attention (although the more time that passes, the less successful this tends to be). But Hobson's observations clearly support the case for personal early care and the significance of real-life first-hand interaction. Indeed, he states categorically that 'For adults to speak to babies and toddlers should be regarded as a civic duty of the greatest importance.' And his reason? 'What gives us the capacity to think is the quality of a baby's exchanges with other people over the first 18 months of life.'

Who cares?

It is one of life's little ironies that, just as neuroscience has confirmed the huge importance of attachment in early learning, the
people who once selflessly took on the role of faithful assistants
to each generation of infant scientists are no longer available to
do the job. Women, released from their traditional roles as help-
mates and home-makers, have now left home in their millions
to join men in the workplace.

It's not been easy for them. Many have found themselves
dreadfully torn between the competing demands of work and
childcare – even Madonna once got quite tearful about it in a television interview. On the one hand, there's the huge cultural pull
of economic freedom and self-realisation, the ultimate prize of
success and status in a man's world after millennia of unsung
martyrdom. On the other, there's the deep biological urge to
nurture one's offspring.

Now that, after several decades of equal opportunities, some
of the shine has gone off the world of work, the majority of
women surveyed on the subject say they'd prefer the childcare
option. But work, as often as not, still wins the day. The British
economy has now adjusted to women's independence, and the
cost of living has gone up to take account of their earnings. Taking several years off the career ladder and/or losing several years'
pay is a luxury many mothers no longer feel they can afford. In
the space of a couple of decades, a huge daycare industry has
grown up to fill the childcare gap. And much of that industry
consists of institutional care.

There is a world of difference between personal loving attention in a familiar domestic environment and the sort of care that
can be provided by a day nursery for children under three. Unless staff ratios are extremely high, there's little chance of much
one-on-one attention, and no one is likely to be as attuned to a
particular infant's wavelength as his own dedicated carer. Each
little scientist is competing for attention with a lot of other

scientists, also engaged on the frantic search for knowledge but all at slightly different stages in the proceedings.

What's more, in the UK where many private nurseries are run on a shoestring, staff are often low paid and poorly qualified, and there may be a worryingly high turnover. To ensure a baseline of 'good practice', the English government has introduced a legal framework of accountability procedures, which means nursery workers are kept busy with bureaucracy and box-ticking. This eats into the time available for personal interaction with the children, and lowers morale, leading to more staff absences and problems with turnover.

Official reports have repeatedly assured parents that nursery care doesn't damage children's chances of success at school – indeed, in the case of children from poorer backgrounds, it may even improve school performance, at least in the short term. But scores on school tests are not the only measure of well-being in early childhood. Indeed, focusing on the academic at this stage seems rather to miss the point: long-term academic success, like long-term emotional resilience and social competence, is rooted in a young child's sense that he is loved and secure. There has so far been little research into the emotional effects of institutionalised early care, but what there is gives cause for concern.

Government researchers have noticed a '*small but significant difference in a large group of children*' for whom daycare led to '*withdrawn, compliant or sad*' behaviour or to higher levels of aggression. This suggests that the children concerned are under stress, and recent projects measuring levels of cortisol (the stress hormone) in their brains during and after the nursery day confirm this. Even in some children who are quietly well behaved and causing no concern to staff, hormone levels indicate more stress than a small human brain should have to cope with, and these levels remain high even after the child has gone home. Children whose brains have been marinated in cortisol at an impressionable age are at a higher risk of emotional and social problems as the years go by.

More and more authorities on early childcare are now speaking out on the subject. The internationally respected psychologist Steve Biddulph, whose book *Raising Boys* has been a *vade mecum* for parents and teachers for over a decade, recently published *Raising Babies: Should Under Threes go to Nursery?*. In it, he warns parents and politicians that we're in danger of rearing '*a colder, sadder, more stressed and aggressive generation of children*' and that '*quality nursery care for young children doesn't exist. It is a fantasy of the glossy magazines.*'

The power of the personal

Technological distraction and institutional care are both products of a systems-based culture. To provide the best start in life for a boy, his parents have to provide the personal care he needs in a way that fits with a 21st century lifestyle. They may be able to juggle their lives to look after him themselves, by job-sharing, flexitime or working from home, or by one taking time away from work for domestic duties. Or they might find someone else to become an extra 'attachment figure' – perhaps another family member, a trusted childminder, or a work colleague who'd like to share both job and child-rearing responsibilities. Once it's established that the best sort of care is personal, there are a wide range of possible solutions.

But adults need person-to-person contacts too, and everyone caring for a small child needs a support system, to avoid the mental meltdown of isolation and the possibility of falling into the technology trap. We take great pains in our systemised society to prepare women for the physical aspects of pregnancy and childbirth, but very few to help with their social and emotional needs after the birth.

In a 21st century world, this social face of child-rearing has practically disappeared. For both men and women, social life has gravitated over the last 30 years away from the domestic sphere to the workplace, reflecting women's move into men's traditional domain. It's also become increasingly competitive, with everyone very aware of how others might judge them (is my house spotless enough? am I a sufficiently yummy mummy?).

It's becoming clear that in order to reinstate traditional feminine strengths (whether demonstrated by men or women), we have to develop a more collaborative, less judgemental social life around the raising of children. In 2007, the National Childbirth Trust, which had previously concentrated mainly on preparing mothers and fathers for childbirth, extended its scope to include supporting parents, and helping them support each other, in the months and years after the birth. It would be relatively easy for locally based organisations – children's centres, maternity units, local health centres and so on – to put prospective and new parents in touch with each other to create social support groups.

This would have advantages not only for adults but for their offspring. Although boys don't usually show an interest in playing with other children until into their third year, they benefit from social mixing right from the start. It builds up immunity to childhood illnesses, gives a stimulus for new activities, and provides their scientific enquiring minds with more data on the human condition, including the very difficult concept of 'sharing', which takes most boys a long time to acquire. In the days of large families and close communities, this happened naturally. And, as will be argued in Chapter 4, in the long run the male of the species may learn as much about empathy from each other as from their adult caring community.

In a world where new parents often live some geographical distance from their own family, it should also be possible to put them in touch with experienced older mothers and fathers, who could offer informal advice, reassurance and – perhaps – occasional babysitting. Child-rearing wisdom has traditionally been handed down through the female line, and cross-generational contacts between both genders are desperately needed in 21st century communities (see Chapter 6). In a fragmented modern world, it's difficult for young parents to make informal non-professional contacts with other mothers and surrogate grand-parents – but it shouldn't be beyond the combined power of the web and local children's services to match people of similar profiles who'd have a good chance of hitting it off and forging long-term relationships.

It's also likely that the more trusted lieutenants his primary attachment figure can acquire, the better for a boy. While in the early months he needs to cleave to one or two beloved adults, he gradually needs to expand his social circle as a hedge against 'separation anxiety'. The downside of attachment is, of course, the dread of loss. For a child who hasn't yet developed the capacity to reason or imagine the future, separation from a beloved adult always carries the threat of total abandonment. The worst period for this tends to be between about six and nine months and boys often seem to suffer particular pain. Indeed, there's evidence that unresolved separation anxiety in young boys can cause long-term psychological damage.

This is another occasion when a bit of mollycoddling pays off: if his 'faithful assistant' feels sufficiently strong to cope with his clinginess and soothe away his fears, and during any short absences other familiar adults can care for him in a familiar domestic sphere, a worried boy's sense of security grows and, gradually, he comes to terms with short separations. Then as time goes on, he'll find it easier to attach to other adults, and be happy for them to take over when his key attachment figures aren't available. Even then, however, research suggests that more than a few hours a day away from the beloved mollycoddlers isn't a particularly good idea until children are two or perhaps even three.

One thousand days. That's roughly how long it takes for a new-born baby, muling and puking in his mother's arms, to be miraculously transformed into a walking, talking little boy, bursting to break out of domesticity and into the wider world.

If all's gone well in those thousand days, he'll have moved far beyond his native Stone Age heritage. He'll have a growing understanding not only of the natural world and the fundamentals of human nature but also of his own technological age, and he'll have more than 500 words to help him learn more and tell excitedly about his findings. But it depends – particularly in the first 18 months – on *personal* care. In a society obsessed with systemised solutions, we've forgotten the significance of love in raising happy balanced children. It's led us to accept practices which – in a healthy, wealthy society, after more than 50 years of peace and prosperity – are frankly shameful.

I spotted an example recently when, walking my dog in the local park, I overtook three young nursery workers who were chatting animatedly among themselves. Each of them, like me, held a leather lead, but while I had just one dog on the end of mine, their leads divided into three strands, each attached to the waist of a tiny child. The tethered toddlers were safe, of course, and were getting some necessary exercise. But, as they milled about bumping into each other, they were learning nothing but bewilderment and confusion. Their parents were presumably out at work, earning the nursery fees that entitled their offspring to less personal attention than my family dog.

Something is seriously wrong with a society that accepts this as inevitable. As one harassed mother recently told a nursery worker as she handed over her toddler, '*I don't have time to bring up my son.*' If boys are to receive the high-quality personal attention they need at the start of their lives, we have to find 21st century ways of tipping the domestic balance away from systems and institutions and back to personal interaction and parental collaboration. Because without the love, learning and language that comes from personal care, boys are more likely than girls to grow 'colder, sadder, more stressed and more aggressive' with every passing year.

Chapter summary

Chapter 2 looked at evidence from developmental psychology about the vast amount of natural learning in the first couple of years of a child's life, and the importance during this period of an 'attachment figure' to provide one-on-one constant loving care. Not only does the mother (or mother substitute) have to be well enough attuned to her son to exert warm-but-firm control of his S-type investigation of the material world; she also acts as a model of consistent, compassionate behaviour to inform his E-type investigation of the human world. These S- and E-type roles overlap as she provides the linguistic data her son needs to learn his mother tongue.

The significance of attachment in these processes cannot be over-emphasised. If the child is thwarted in his natural desire to learn, it may affect his capacity for learning in the future. What's more, in recent decades many parents have been convinced that institutionalised care is an acceptable substitute for the personal involvement of an attachment figure. This chapter argued that systemised solutions of this kind cannot replace 'the power of the personal', just as screen-based contacts cannot support mothers as well as real-life ones.

Helping a boy develop a mind of his own

What can parents do?

- First of all, make sure you're adequately supported yourself. Being a faithful assistant to a small boy is an exhausting task, and can often feel deeply unrewarding. You need to discuss your attitudes to childcare with your partner before becoming a parent, and make sure you're fully informed about the responsibilities and possible ways forward in a 21st century society (my book *Toxic Childhood* was an attempt to systemise this information).

- You also need lots of other adult company to help see you through, so if you've managed to build a support system as recommended on page 69, cherish it. If not, start building one *now*, e.g.:
  - attend a 'new parent' course, such as the ones run by the National Childbirth Trust (www.nct.org.uk)
  - seek support through one of the agencies listed on page 42
  - try making contacts through the web, e.g. Netmums or MAMA (Meet A Mum – www.mama.co.uk), but don't spend too much time there: arrange to meet up in real life.

- To ensure your scientist isn't thwarted in his quest to discover the material world, give him as much physical freedom as possible. Early learning depends upon movement, and your son needs to touch, taste, smell, see, hear, and feel the world around him. Modern homes tend not to be baby-friendly, so you'll have to balance your lifestyle needs with his need for scientific investigation.

- But remember that – though it may be less immediately attractive to him – your son also has to learn about the social world. Make sure that when you're feeding, comforting or entertaining him, he can *see* your face and *hear* your voice. This means ensuring that your sling or pushchair allows him to focus on your eyes and face and keeping background noise to an absolute minimum. See advice on the website www.talktoyourbaby.org.uk.

- Don't let your son be distracted from either of his quests by TV or other technological entertainment. Until he's around three, the fewer screen-based activities in a boy's life the better. If possible, avoid them altogether. From the moment he's born, use the age old entertainments of:
  - face-making and baby talk (don't be embarrassed – he's a baby after all)
  - songs and rhymes (sing them yourself, the same ones over and

over again – eventually he'll start to recognise them and one
day he'll join in!)

- stories (tell or read simple stories repeatedly and use your face
  to demonstrate the characters' emotions – even though a baby
  doesn't understand the story, with plenty of repetition, he'll
  start to recognise the rhythms of language and facial expressions; one day it'll translate into understanding)
- the more *you* entertain your son, the more responsive he'll be
  to you. But if you delegate entertainment to the electronic
  media, he'll learn to respond to that instead.

- Get him outdoors as much as you can.
- Try to travel by foot rather than car, since this allows time to communicate about your surroundings. When he's in the pushchair,
  talk to him about what's going on around you. As he gets older
  he'll probably twist and turn to see around him, but unless he's
  able to make eye contact with you, the levels of noise in our outdoor modern world means communication will probably fall on
  deaf ears.
- Let him explore the outdoors too (wearing suitable clothes – see
  Chapter 3). Sand, mud, grass, rocks, leaves and water are all
  fascinating to young children. As he investigates them, talk
  about what he's doing. If possible, give him opportunities to
  meet animals (always balancing the requirements of the RSPCA
  and NSPCC).
- As he gets older, find safe spaces where he can run, climb and
  tumble – these movements usually come much more easily to
  boys than sitting still. Keep him from damaging himself, but
  remember that being dirty isn't life-threatening.
- When indoors, let him watch you go about your everyday
  activities.
- Talk about what you're doing. The humdrum and ordinary to
  adults is new and interesting to babies, and as your son gets
  older, routine and ritual are deeply reassuring. Make up your

own rhymes and songs about household chores and to celebrate 'punctuation marks' in the day. (See also Chapter 3, for suggestions about mealtime and bedtime routines.) As he gets older, let him 'help'.

- Once he's mobile and starts tearing your home apart, look for ways of avoiding having to say 'No!' too often. Rearrange your living area so it's as child-proof as possible (remembering always that these days will pass). When you do have to say 'No!' say it warmly but firmly, and stick to your guns. Distraction often helps.

- Collect objects that are interesting to investigate but unlikely to damage or poison him – wooden spoons, plastic containers and lids, different sorts of fabric and boxes, crackly wrapping paper, old shoes, gloves, hats and so on. And watch him when he's on the loose – what sort of things fascinate him and why? Can you provide other interesting examples? As well as keeping him busy, these items often make effective distractors.

- Don't waste a fortune on expensive toys. Select a few sturdy tried-and-tested children's favourites (building blocks, bathtime toys, cuddlies, board books, etc.) to supplement your 'interesting objects' collection. The best children's play comes from their own creative use of whatever's to hand.

- Take him shopping, and so on, but balance his need to explore and communicate with consideration for other adults. Parents need the support of the community in rearing healthy boys, so it's important to keep them onside. If his behaviour in an adult environment is disturbing others, always apologise and remove him immediately.

- If you aren't able to care for your son yourself – and some mothers simply *aren't* maternal (especially those who've been educated out of their E-type instincts), look for someone else who'd be prepared to take on the role of faithful assistant. But expect to pay for good quality care in money just as you'd pay in time if you did it yourself. And be sure you really *do* want to hand him over – if you're jealous of your surrogate mum, it's not going to do anyone any good (see Chapters 5 and 6 of *Toxic Childhood*).

- For mothers who've mislaid their maternal instincts somewhere in the education system, it can help to learn more about cognitive psychology – knowing what to look out for makes caring for a small baby intellectually as well as emotionally satisfying. Try *The Scientist in the Crib* by Gopnik, Meltzoff and Kuhl. Or download the up-to-date summaries of neuroscientific knowledge compiled at Harvard University on www.developingchild. net.
- If you choose (or have no alternative) to use institutionalised childcare in the first few years, look for one-on-one loving care. The problems of institutionalised care are described on page 67. If you want to know more, read Steve Biddulph's 2007 book *Raising Babies* (Harper Thorsons). The alternative is to find a good childminder whom you can get to know and trust: see National Childminding Association on www.nmca.org.uk (or Scottish Childminding Association: www.childminding.org).
- In helping a boy form a mind of his own, all five of the 'must-haves' on page 22 are important, but in the first couple of years the next most important ingredient after LOVE is LANGUAGE. If you're at any point worried about your son's language development, consult www.talkingpoint.org.uk, which is run by the speech and language charity, I CAN.

What can the rest of us do?

- While few people would deny the importance of a formal education system in creating responsible citizens, not many yet recognise the similar importance of children's early child-

hood experiences. To ensure 21st century boys are fully prepared for both S- and E-type thought, all the adults in their
community have to change their attitude to early childhood
and traditional 'women's work'. This change of mind-set involves:

- really valuing the contribution to society of 'full-time'
  mothers (and fathers) who choose to care for their own
  children during the first few years of their lives, often at
  considerable personal cost in terms of lost earnings
- recognising the important social role of childminders and
  other full-time carers, who act as surrogate parents for the
  children of those adults who return to work
- accepting that caring full-time for a small infant is hugely
  demanding work, particularly as the systemising skills that
  come easily to 21st century adults are very little help and, as
  yet, there is no recognised 'training' for the development of
  E-type skills.

- Changing the communal mind on such an issue shouldn't be
  too difficult – most women, at least, are halfway there. And
  when a few opinion-formers in a community change their
  minds (and change their behaviour accordingly), they tend to
  carry others with them. Doctors, teachers, religious leaders,
  local newspaper editors and so on can, by their words and actions, give status to people in their local area who care for small
  children.

- In the global electronic community, popular broadcasters, screen-
  writers and public figures could do the same on a national scale.
  Female opinion-formers in particular could help undo the damage
  of the last half-century by publicly recognising the importance of
  the E-type strengths women have nurtured through the millennia,
  rather than allowing themselves to be trapped in a 'patriarchal'
  paradigm, valuing material success and worldly status over human
  relationships.

- One small change in everyone's behaviour would start the ball rolling. As Professor Peter Hobson says, '*For adults to speak to babies and toddlers should be regarded as a civic duty of the greatest importance.*' If all responsible adults were to assume this civic duty tomorrow, they would:
  - demonstrate interest in the child and respect for the parents' task
  - help bring both parents and children back into the centre of their community (instead, as at present, feeling increasingly marginalised – see Chapter 6)
  - according to Hobson, help to improve the child's thinking capacity as a future citizen
  - raise the prestige of human kindness, and thus chip away at the supremacy of smart-arses who value only cynicism and worldly success.
- If you're an older resident with time to spare, this way of making contact with a young family could prove advantageous to you both. Over time, as you consolidate the relationship, the parents may be grateful for support (a spot of babysitting?) or advice, and you might gain from the friendship of younger, fitter neighbours (often very good at moving heavy objects about). If you're male, you may have even more to offer to a small male neighbour, as a grandfather-figure. As the boy grows up, you could become another important 'responsible adult' in his life.

What can politicians do?

Changing the national culture to value traditional female work as highly as we currently value the long-established male variety would – in the long run – require political action, such as:

- educational programmes and public information campaigns as suggested on pages 45–46

- revising the attitude to economic growth to create a family-friendly economy, with more emphasis on the importance of relationships and less on economic growth. (This would, incidentally, sit very comfortably alongside environment-friendly policies.)
- abandoning the drive to persuade women to return to work when their babies are small (see the arguments in the paper on http://www.fulltimemothers.org/submissions/ConsCC0207.doc)
- perhaps paying mothers to stay at home for the first three years, as is done in some Nordic countries
- reviewing, revising and reducing to the status of advice current legislation on early childcare outside the home in England (the Early Years Foundation Stage) which attempts to systemise early childcare
- expanding one-on-one childcare provision, especially high-quality childminding, and finding appropriate ways to prepare, accredit and inspect childminders – while remembering that personal care in a domestic setting is *very* different from the institutional variety
- ensuring that qualified childminders are paid fairly for their work.

All this requires recognition that childcare is different from, but just as important as, education. High-systemising politicians and academics often have a lot of trouble getting their heads around this one. But if policy on early childhood is driven by educational goals rather than the importance of children's natural learning (including social, emotional and linguistic development), it is likely to completely miss the point.

Chapter 3

GOOD HABITS AND BAD INFLUENCES

How big business undermines parents' authority and confidence ... and the effects on boys' health and well-being

If some parents no longer have time to bring up their sons, there are plenty of other adults in our contemporary global village keen to lend a hand. Among them are politicians – mentioned in the last chapter and due to make further appearances in chapters to come – who believe government-controlled childcare and education can make up for lack of parental time and attention. This chapter, however, is devoted to another deeply interested group: the marketers whose job it is to sell more and more stuff, and whose direct influence over children grows greater every year.

In a multimedia world, technology is part of daily life. Children need to know their way around it, and to keep up with the rapid pace of developments – as part of the digital generation, they're likely to depend on the electronic media throughout their working and domestic lives. Shielding one's son from its influence would not only be impossible but against his long-term interests. Many parents, however, are increasingly uneasy about the extent to which marketing drives the media and the effect this has on their offspring.

Until the 1990s, advertising aimed at children was a relatively low-key affair, as they weren't seen as big spenders. But when the arrival of all-day children's TV stations coincided with the rise of the dual income family, marketers realised the potential of 'guilt money' and 'pester power'. Children have since been bombarded with marketing messages – and at an increasingly early age.

The child is father of the man

For most of human history, the first few years of a boy's life were of interest only to the humble womenfolk who looked after him. The amazing transformation that occurred during his first thousand days went unremarked by all but his immediate family. Even religious leaders who recognised the value of 'catching them young' waited until children were old enough to engage in conversation. And it didn't occur to the 19th century politicians who introduced universal education that the experiences of a child's preschool years could possibly be relevant to its outcome.

Adults have, of course, little or no recollection of their own early years – what happens to us before the age of about three or four isn't recorded in ways that can be consciously accessed, so the experiences of very early childhood are like the foundations of a building: out of sight and out of mind. They may underpin the whole structure of our lives, but they're so well buried that we're not aware of it. So until very recently the minutiae of little children's lives were left entirely in the hands of low-status women.

It's only in the last few decades, as neuroscience shone its light ever deeper into the human brain, that S-type thinkers have taken notice. They now know that, while genes determine our nature to a remarkable extent, a boy's genetic potential is triggered, for good or ill, by experience – particularly the experience of the first few years. The child is indeed father of the man.

Good mothers have known throughout the ages that early nurture matters. They saw that, during a boy's first months and years, they could really make a difference in moulding the man he would eventually become. As described in Chapter 2, this is when he can develop habits of mind, such as self-confidence, curiosity and the ability to get along with other people, that stay with him lifelong. But it's also when the people who care for him encourage basic habits of behaviour, such as sleeping, exercise and eating habits that will inform his lifestyle as an adult. If these are integrated into the very foundations of his being, there's a good chance they'll remain the default mode into which he unconsciously slips in years to come.

Mothers, of course, are keen to do the best for their children. Their natural impulse is to equip their sons with habits of mind and behaviour that will help them lead happy, successful lives. But when talented systemisers recognised the importance of early childhood their impulses were less altruistic. In no time at all, babies and toddlers were seen as economic units that could be exploited for financial gain.

James McNeal, guru of marketing to children, recognised in the 1990s that, '*at six months of age, the same age they're imitating sounds like mama, babies are forming mental images of corporate logos and mascots*'. Soon all marketers knew that, given careful corporate attention, by two-and-a-half '*they are able to associate items in their world with specific brand names. For example, when they think about juice, they don't just think juice ... they think company!*' As the president of Kids R Us put it, '*If you own this child at an early age, you own this child for years to come. Companies are saying, "Hey, I want to own the kid younger and younger."*'

Nature, nurture and culture

Parents have always known instinctively about two major learning devices that work for young children. The first is the instinct that kicks off the dance of communication: imitation. Babies copy the facial expressions, body movements and vocal sounds that they see and hear. Then as they grow older, they instinctively want to copy adult behaviour, which helps them become more physically competent and independent. This is why – although mothers have always taken the lioness's share of early nurture – fathers' involvement is just as vital: the examples of masculine behaviour they provide for their sons can set lifelong patterns.

The second learning device is repetition. As mentioned in Chapter 2, this is how deep-seated neural networks in the brain are laid down and consolidated. The more often a boy experiences an action or sequence of actions, the more likely he is to learn them. So setting up good habits of behaviour for one's son is all about providing the right models for him to imitate and repeating the right sorts of experiences again and again. This is why regularity and routine are so important in childhood – regular meals, family rituals and bedtime routines programme the brain and body, and boys (perhaps because of their strong systemising instinct) seem to find this sort of regularity particularly reassuring.

So the aim of any caring parent's nurturing regime must be to use imitation and repetition to set up a default mode of behaviour that encourages a healthy, successful lifestyle. In the modern world, this would include a taste for fresh natural food as opposed to processed junk, and healthy sleep and exercise patterns as opposed to 24-hour living and addiction to sedentary, screen-based entertainment.

Between nature and nurture, it shouldn't be too difficult to achieve these things. A boy born with a Stone Age brain should be naturally inclined to eat natural food, to seek the sort of healthy outdoor life befitting a hunter and to sleep as much as his brain and body require, especially during the hours of darkness. But it's never been just a question of nurture and nature. Human culture always influences the way parents raise their sons.

The huge problem for modern parents is that today's culture is not only extraordinarily all-pervasive, but in many ways is in direct conflict with the habits and values associated with the default mode I've described. The siren voices whispering that junk food, junk play and late-night entertainment are more fun than a 'healthy lifestyle' are now beamed day and night into their homes. Avoiding them would mean cutting off the whole family from the global electronic village and its many benefits.

Even if parents feel sufficiently strong-minded to do so, the underpinning values of those siren voices are probably embedded to some extent in their own psyches, and those of the adults their son will meet. As lifelong inhabitants of the global village, today's adults have all been bombarded with the message that consumption brings happiness and – even if reason and experience suggest setting sensible limits – it's difficult to resist lifelong conditioning. Human beings also associate love with the giving of gifts and the offer of choice, and marketers have skilfully drawn this into the consumerist message.

Making your son eat up his greens, taking him out into the unpredictable natural world, maintaining routines for eating and sleeping that may be deeply inconvenient – all these seem pretty unattractive in the light of the blandishments of the marketers. What's more, time and attention – the main ingredients of old-fashioned nurture, and the key to regularity, routine and ritual – are the very things most contemporary parents can least spare. In the nature–nurture–culture triangle, our S-type culture has now evolved so far beyond our biological nature that it's seriously inhibiting parents' potential to nurture their sons.

The electronic cradle

These problems in child-rearing have been mounting for centuries. We now live in a world so removed from the Stone Age that a baby's nature clashes with his cultural surroundings from the moment he enters the world. In a clinical, high-tech delivery room, he's immediately assailed with electric light, mechanical sound effects and the rapid pace of hospital life (it seems likely that, with their generally less mature sensory systems, baby boys find the transition from the womb even more traumatic than girls). When he goes home there's the roar and smell of traffic outdoors, and indoors the constant cacophony of TV and other electronic equipment. The room in which a baby boy is put to sleep is probably neither completely dark nor particularly quiet. What's more, in most modern western cultures he's expected from a very early age to sleep apart from his beloved attachment figure.

Not surprisingly, many parents now have trouble persuading their sons into sleeping patterns that fulfil their own natural needs and those of the rest of the family. This has knock-on effects on everyone's state of mind, not least the baby, who – if he doesn't develop sensible sleep habits – may be in for long-term problems. Babies need a long night-time sleep and several naps during the day. If they don't get these, they're more likely, as they grow older, to show 'non-adaptable' or hyperactive behaviour. Surveys in the US have found sleeping problems in around half of preschool children, and these difficulties have been related to ADHD and other developmental conditions common in boys.

The obvious course of action – recommended by all sleep specialists – is to simulate natural conditions from the very start by reducing light and noise, and ensuring a gradual wind-down to bedtime. Many parents are, however, lured into increasing the cultural distractions, because little boys who are difficult to soothe can often be quietened by switching on an electronic babysitter. Since using TV or DVD to soothe a tired child and perhaps lull him to sleep doesn't seem as harmful as using it to distract him from wakeful activity, many parents fall into this particular technology trap with an easy conscience.

Middle-class mothers interviewed by business journalist Susan Gregory Thomas were frank about their use of *Baby Einstein* videos as a comforter ('*He loves it, and it lets me take a shower*' – '*We were all raised on TV, after all … and we didn't turn out to be completely brain dead.*') And mums I've met are happy to admit that a favourite video such as *Thomas the Tank Engine* or *Bob the Builder* often performs the miracle that no amount of parental rocking or lullabies can. Unfortunately, however, once Thomas or Bob has taken on the role of boy-soother, it may be difficult to wean him back to more human bedtime rituals. The movement of a TV into one's son's bedroom is the next obvious move.

In recent UK surveys, a startling 40% of children under four years old were found to have a TV and other electronic equipment in their bedrooms. This has happened despite scientific warnings over the last decade of links between TV-watching and sleep problems in school-age children, and the knock-on effect for healthy sleeping patterns throughout life. Just as the concerned voices of nutritionists weren't heard until evidence of childhood obesity was incontrovertible, those of paediatricians and sleep specialists currently fall on deaf ears.

Meanwhile, little boys who can retire whenever they wish into technology-rich personal space will continue to tune into screens rather than people, so that media and marketing men continue to have unsupervised access to their minds. They can provide examples of behaviour for boys to imitate, and constant repetition of messages they want them to absorb. Not surprisingly, research links bedroom TV to the familiar 21st century story of poor eating habits, a couch-potato lifestyle and obesity.

They are what (and how) we feed them

Like most aspects of 'toxic childhood syndrome', the obesity explosion has hit boys worse than girls. UK government scientists now reckon that, on current trends, half of all boys between six and ten years old will be obese by the year 2050, with horrific long-term effects in terms of health hazards. Boys are generally less concerned than girls about physical appearance and, as natural risk-takers, more likely to resist behavioural guidelines. They are thus much easier for marketers to target with 'unhealthy' messages.

But 21st century influences on eating habits may begin even

before a child is born. Research suggests that his mother's diet during pregnancy influences her baby's tastes, so if she gorges at McDonald's, he'll be born with a yearning to feed on burgers and fries – another good reason for expectant mothers to eat healthily. Parental choice continues to affect a child's tastebuds in the early weeks and months of life. Despite the scientific advice that 'breast is best', the ready availability of formula milk means that a mum who finds breastfeeding difficult or unappealing has an instantly accessible man-made alternative. Skilfully marketed baby brands allow parents to wean children directly on to processed food. And parents who want to show love by giving their son 'treats' often introduce sweet drinks such as juice at an early stage, even though babies are perfectly happy with milk or water if they've never tasted anything else.

As soon as a boy is able to focus on a screen, marketers have him in their sights. Marketing is now based on a 'cradle-to-grave' policy and, as guru James McNeal has pointed out, '*We have living proof of the long-lasting quality of early brand loyalties in the cradle-to-grave marketing at McDonald's, and how well it works... we start taking children in for their first and second birthdays, and on and on, and eventually they have a great deal of preference for that brand.*' A recent study showed the simple power of this policy: preschoolers offered a choice of foods in plain packaging or Mc-Donald's wrappers claimed that carrots, milk and apple juice tasted better when the familiar golden arches were printed on the pack. '*You see a McDonald's label and children start salivating,*' said child psychologist Diane Levin, while the study's author claimed that children's perception of taste was 'physically altered by the branding'.

Psychologists have now established a blueprint for initiating young consumers into brand awareness, beginning with a child-friendly character: '*We know that kids point at characters, that's why we use them. That's why cereal companies use them,*' one marketing executive explained. '*They don't know what the product is, but they*

point to *Tony the Tiger and Mickey Mouse.*' In the past, foodstuffs
could be linked to popular characters from books or cartoons,
but the obesity scare made licence owners unwilling to associate
their creations with unhealthy food. So manufacturers create
their own characters to target tots, according to the psychologists' recipe: bright colours because young children don't register subtle tones, high sing-song voices to mirror parental baby
talk and '*for very young kids, every character you use has to be roundish,
with big eyes, the theory being that young children prefer round because
round is safe, pointy is dangerous*'.

'Pointy' is very dangerous indeed if you're a parent trying to
negotiate your way round a supermarket with your baby or toddler in tow. Marketers are desperate to get children pointing at
characters as early as possible, as pester power is a powerful
selling mechanism for foodstuffs. A combination of misplaced
love (that deeply ingrained wish to give 'treats' and choice) and
the desire to complete the shopping trip without embarrassing
tantrums makes parents particularly vulnerable on these occasions. In one recent US consumer report, 100% of parents of
two- to five-year-olds said that their children had a major influence on food and snack purchases. And a British government
survey noted that family food purchases are hugely influenced
by packaging and cartoon characters that '*generate recognition, fa-
miliarity and even affection amongst children*'.

Early allegiance to popular brands of snacks and fizzy drinks
also helps boys develop a taste for key ingredients – sugar, salt,
additives and fats – which once established is very difficult to
break. Marketers want to establish the tastes (and 'affection' for
the brand) as early as possible, because after the age of two or
so, children are often increasingly reluctant to try new dishes.
So parents who can keep their sons out of the junk-food jungle
for the first thousand days should be able to establish healthy
rather than unhealthy tastes, so that natural childhood pickiness
then works in their favour rather than against them. It's well
worth the effort, as research has now shown that poor diet at

the age of three is linked to poor school performance between the ages of six and twelve.

Similarly, if parents can establish regular mealtimes and table manners before their son is three or four, these habits are likely to stay with him lifelong. This is the age when the drive to imitate grown-up behaviour is at its strongest – before playground culture takes a hold – so if parents demonstrate how to use knives and forks, their son will copy them. If, on the other hand, they leave him to watch marketers' repeated demonstrations of the joys of finger food, this is likely to become his long-term default model, and burgers, chips, pizzas, pastries and sweets will be even more appealing.

The relentless rise of 'toy consumption'

One reason that licence holders for much-loved fictional characters no longer associate themselves with dodgy foodstuffs is that they can make much more money elsewhere. Second only to pester power in the marketers' list of child-based targets is 'guilt money'. Parents worried that their crazy work–life balance leaves precious little time to be with their sons are only too ready to throw money at the problem. All that remains is to create merchandise that boys want to consume – and to capture the consumers as young as possible.

This means linking them to characters with boy appeal. Jocelyn Stevens, the media executive who created the Bob the Builder series, described his role thus: '*My job is to come up with the gentle, lovely, wonderful preschool programming so that the company can then go out and do all the marketing and branding, then sell the toys and the DVDs and so on...* ' What Stevens is doing is helping children become 'attached' to Bob in the same way they would attach to a real-life person, associating him with safety and happiness. The boy-friendly ingredients of tool use, basic mechanics and male status ('*Can he fix it? Yes he can!*') help cement the relationship.

Children have, of course, always become attached to favourite toys or other special objects and used them as comforters. What's different here – the product of a 'smart-arsed' S-type culture – is the commercial exploitation of a deep human need in children under three years old. As the president of another children's TV station puts it, *'We're not only looking for ratings, but how to get into kids' psyches on a day-to-day basis.'* Add to this the established wisdom of James McNeal – *'Kids are the most unsophisticated of all consumers. They have the least and therefore want the most. Consequently, they are in a perfect position to be taken'* – and you have a recipe for the commercial manipulation of very young minds.

Of course, TV stations need to bring in revenue. Even public service broadcasters such as *Children's Television Workshop* who produce *Sesame Street* need money to stay in business – and a popular character like Elmo, appearing on board books, bedding, mobiles, lamps, bath accessories, baby shoes, clothing, bottles, teething rings, dummies, playpens, etc. etc., certainly brings it in. But in order to keep earning in the teeth of ever greater competition, they have to plumb ever deeper into kids' psyches. And when the rewards are very great – the Teletubbies brought the BBC £169 million in four years – even public service broadcasters sometimes lose track of what public service is all about.

According to investigative reporter Eric Clark, author of *The Real Toy Story*, marketing of toys and other merchandise to the under-threes is now a ruthless multi-billion-dollar business, with scant regard for the customers' real needs. Indeed, by emphasising 'toy consumption' as opposed to genuine play, it may be doing them considerable long-term damage (see Chapter 4). But the role played by the media in promoting this consumption is worrying in its own right. As Clark says, *'The line between selling and entertainment is blurred to the point of near invisibility.'* Not only does a favourite character from a film or TV show appear on endless merchandise, it also leads the child to a website and perhaps to a computer game, where there's more potential to develop brand allegiance, and thus encourage the quest for more merchandise to consume.

Boys, who need no encouragement to cleave to screen-based entertainment, are easily drawn into this unholy alliance between technology and consumerism. If parents aren't careful (and especially if they aren't around), their son's relationship with Elmo, Bob the Builder or Fireman Sam could rival his relationship with them. Their own role could then dwindle to being little more than the providers of the cash that feeds his consumerist fervour.

Handing over control of a little boy's mind to media and marketing executives has a number of consequences. First of all, since their main concern is to make money, they may well lead him towards obesity, couch potatodom or learning difficulties if it's to their immediate financial advantage. Second, the boy will take progressively less notice of those who really do care about his welfare, and while it's reasonably easy for parents to control the behaviour of a three- or four-year-old, the older he grows the more of a challenge behaviour management will become. Third, his chances of long-term mental well-being are greatly reduced.

Colwyn Trevarthern, the developmental psychologist, argues that initiating children into this sort of media-driven toy consumption '*is tantamount to neglect. There is a sense of poverty in these activities compared to those that develop the natural creativity of children.*' Real play, which doesn't require any special equipment, comes naturally if children are allowed reasonable freedom to explore and engage with the world about them. For this they need the loving presence and watchful eye of a real-life attachment figure. Not some big-eyed, brightly coloured screen idol.

Anything that gets the kids to read, huh?

Literacy matters. If a boy's to make it at school and in life, he must be able to read. And these days all parents know that the sooner children can be interested in books the better. So literacy matters to marketers too – link your character to literacy, and you'll reel in not just the boy but his doting parents. Marketers have noticed that the only books that sell in supermarkets (by far the most profitable outlet) are those featuring a recognisable character from TV or film. The baby or toddler points at the face on the cover, the parent is delighted at this apparent interest in literature and the sale is clinched.

Thomas the Tank Engine was a natural for this marketing strategy. The combination of big round wide-eyed face and mechanical body fascinates little boys. Having been around for over 60 years, Thomas is well loved by several generations of literate males, assuring him of success in the middle-class market, and a TV serialisation in the 1980s widened his appeal. So no one was surprised that his relaunch as a multimedia star on the eve of the new millennium generated millions. As the president of the company said to justify the growing profits, '*Anything that gets the kids to read, huh?*'

However, a visit to the Thomas and Friends website suggests that reading is the last thing on marketers' minds. A Thomas fan can sleep in a Thomas bed, under a Thomas duvet, watching Thomas DVDs to help him drop off. His family can take him on a Thomas day out, he can play free Thomas games on the website, buy endless Thomas toys and collectibles (and carry them in a special Thomas carry-case), wear a Thomas watch, learn to swim with a Thomas towel, ride a bike wearing a Thomas helmet, or tell the time on a Thomas watch. There are a few books for sale, but they're difficult to find.

Immersion in this sort of Thomas paraphernalia may feed a boy's consumerist impulses, but it's not likely to turn him into a reader. But then, neither are the many 'educational' products for the under-threes, such as *Teach Your Child to Read* workbooks, computer games and website activities. As an independent literacy specialist, I've watched 'educational' materials for the very young proliferate over the last ten years – indeed, in the early days I actually wrote some. But there's no independent evidence that this stuff improves children's performance in the long run.

Trust me, I'm a literacy expert. As described in Chapter 4, there are many important 'pre-reading' activities, but none of them involve picking up a pencil, moving a mouse or staring wide-eyed at flash cards. One significant way parents can help is by talking and singing to their son from the moment he's born (see Chapter 2, '*How to dumb a scientist down*'). Another is to tell him stories and read him books. Like every other important parent–child interaction, this involves time, personal attention and endless patience. It may also involve building up a *small* personal library of picture books, because repetition is of the essence and, with any luck, your son will soon have favourite stories that he wants to hear again and again. The more often he hears the same story, the more likely he is to start joining in and 'reading' along with you, a significant stage in moving from spoken to written language. But he's unlikely to start reading himself until he's five or six, so don't panic and don't push him. The early years are, yet again, about imitation and repetition.

Ingenious technological alternatives to the parental voice may keep a boy busy for a while fiddling with the bells and whistles, but they're unlikely to teach him to read. The enormous success of *LeapFrog* products – the books that read themselves – is testimony to parents' concern about reading and their faith in technology. But technology is a feeble substitute for a warm, breathing adult.

Money can't buy me love

'Trust me, I'm a literacy expert.' Nowadays there seem to be legions of scientists and specialists doling out advice about children. How can parents know which ones to trust? Over the last decade, I've interviewed many world-famous experts on aspects of childhood, from fields as varied as nutrition, neuroscience, linguistics and psychopathology. What always strikes me about the research findings they describe is that the key ingredients in raising a happy, balanced child are not things you can buy in the shops. With the obvious exceptions of basic material needs, like fresh food and warm clothing, everything they recommend is free: love, talk, song, play. As far as small children are concerned, the experts to trust are the ones who advise keeping it simple and getting back, as far as possible, to a natural approach.

However, since the economic growth that drives our consumerist technological society depends on the generation of money, this message isn't particularly easy to spread in a 21st century global village. 'Love', 'talk', 'song' and 'play' are all four-letter words as far as big business is concerned, and big business controls the electronic media through which experts broadcast their findings to parents, so it can be tricky to get non-commercial messages across.

Nutritionists, for instance, find themselves up against the media savvy of the food industry. In contrast with the slick, colourful appeal of junk-food ads, their advice to eat fresh food takes on a distinct aroma of wet blanket. Similarly, a child psychologist rambling on about the importance of imaginative play doesn't grab the attention half as effectively as an all-singing, all-dancing advert for the latest must-have toy. And a literacy specialist extolling the virtue of sharing a bedtime story seems positively antediluvian compared with a shiny new way of teaching the alphabet with computer graphics.

What's more, the marketers and media men behind the ads are specialists in ensuring a message hits home, while academics are not usually famed for their snappy one-liners. Some experts like the psychologist Dr Tanya Byron have tried to use the power of multimedia to put serious research findings across. She worked for several years with the BBC on series like *Little Angels* and *The House of Tiny Tearaways*, explaining and illustrating techniques for managing children's behaviour. Eventually she came to the conclusion that rather than empowering parents, her programmes and others like them might actually undermine their confidence. In 2007 she wrote a book recommending that parents should trust to their own instincts rather than feel there's some sort of 'correct' solution to every problem – a solution that needs a media star to mediate it.

Dr Byron's dilemma illustrates the problems of spreading personal human E-type messages in a high-tech commercial S-type world. You can't commodify love, talk, song and play. As soon as you try to turn something natural into a product, it ceases to be natural. You can't give a foolproof formula for behaviour management, because every child, every family and every situation is different, and it takes personal, hands-on knowledge to decide on the right balance of warmth and firmness on the day.

This means that packaged 'solutions' to child-rearing problems can never be an adequate substitute for parental love and attention, just as 'educational' toys and materials can't be as effective as warm-but-firm support for a child's natural drive to learn. Parents have to take personal responsibility for raising their sons. All experts can do is remind them about age-old wisdom and point out the 21st century pitfalls.

The tyranny of choice

The message of this chapter is that many of these pitfalls relate to our increasingly complex relationship with the concept of choice. It's always been an attractive concept for human beings, since making a choice is a way of exercising control over our destiny. The wealthy half of our planet now lives in a world of plenty, with endless opportunities for choice in all sorts of areas – what we eat and wear, where we live, how we spend our leisure time, and so on. Indeed, to keep our consumption-driven world turning on its axis, the producers of consumer goods have to keep us keen on making choices. Earning enough to fund all the choice increasingly leads into difficulties with work–life balance.

Parents who value freedom of choice often offer it to their children as a way of showing their love. However, the obesity crisis has already alerted us to the potentially disastrous consequences of allowing small children choice over what they eat. Their Stone Age brains and bodies are still designed for survival, so they naturally choose the high-fat, high-carbohydrate foods that would have kept them alive longest in Cro-Magnon times. The market provides lots of products with the sweet and salty tastes that make these foods attractive, and once children – particularly boys – are hooked on these products, it's difficult to change their minds.

Real love means giving children real food that nourishes rather than poisons them. Once they've established healthy eating habits, the odd 'treat' is unlikely to do them any harm (although parental love is necessary throughout childhood to balance marketing messages and keep boys on the straight and narrow). In the same way, real love means giving children real-life experience of the world and loving human attention, as described in Chapter 2 rather than palming them off with second-hand, screen-based entertainment. Boys are drawn to TV and computer games in the same way they're drawn to junk food, so parents have to help them set up a healthy default mechanism during the first few years and ensure that, as they grow older, screens don't take over from other important activities. Two of these are the real play described in Chapters 4 and 6, and real education, as discussed in Chapters 5 and 7.

So, until boys are old enough to make informed choices for themselves, parental love involves making choices for them, which in the first thousand days means most of the choices that crop up. It's always been slightly more of a problem for the parents of boys, who have fewer natural social instincts than girls. They aren't, for instance, usually as easy to convince of the importance of personal necessities like learning to dress themselves, hygienic niceties like toilet training or teeth-cleaning, or social skills such as saying please and thank you. Deciding when and how to introduce a little boy to such habits is another exercise in balancing warmth (respecting his personal wishes and level of maturity) and firmness (knowing what's good for him in the long run). But letting him choose whether or not to bother isn't an option in civilised society: in the long term his self-respect and the respect of others depends on his having them.

So the job of 21st century parents is to make sensible choices for their sons. To some extent this is a question – as Tanya Byron pointed out – of tuning into one's own child and trusting to instinct about what seems right for him. But in a culture so far removed from the world in which our instincts developed, it also depends on knowing about children's developmental needs and how a 21st century lifestyle might be at odds with these. And now that cultural change happens at electronic speed, most parents need occasional advice from experts on specific issues.

Here's the expert advice on laying down sensible habits in the first thousand days that, despite the blandishments of the market, I'd be inclined to follow if I were bringing up a 21st century boy:

- Feed him regular meals based as far as possible on fresh ingredients (remembering to wash fruit and vegetables first), and no snacking between meals.
- Develop a pleasurable bedtime routine, including a gentle wind-down to sleep, and no electronic equipment in the bedroom.
- No television or other screen-based entertainment before the age of two, and no more than a couple of hours a day thereafter.
- Give plenty of opportunity to explore, indoors and out, and encourage imaginative creative play with whatever safe (preferably natural) materials come to hand.
- Provide some toys, especially the tried and tested variety, but don't waste money on expensive stuff, avoid technology for the time being and don't give in to pester power.

- Base the development of personal habits and social behaviour on a balance of warmth and firmness.

And finally, keep away from smart-arses and listen to those whose main motivation seems to be kindness.

During the first thousand days of a boy's life, his parents' decisions and behaviour will influence his future a great deal, for good or ill. The report on a famous neuroscientific conference on early childhood held at the White House at the end of the last century concluded: *'What happens during the first months and years of life matters a lot, not because this period of development provides an indelible blueprint for adult well-being, but because it sets either a sturdy or fragile stage for what follows.'*

In the long term, if we want a healthy society, big business has to recognise that selling junk to little children and undermining their parents' authority isn't just smart-arsed behaviour, it's against everyone's long-term interests. Sadly this epiphany seems a long way off, so in the meantime it's up to parents to guard their sons against over-indulgence peddled by marketers. In the first thousand days, it is perfectly possible to exercise control over what happens in one's own home and, since babies are born without preconceptions, to influence a boy's habits of behaviour in positive ways.

Parents' aim in exercising such control, however, must be to help their son develop increasing *self*-control, because as the thousand days draw to a close, the 'mollycoddling' has to stop. As they reach the age of three, children need to spread their wings beyond the closed world of the home. Boys have to learn to be boys.

Chapter summary

Chapter 3 looked at how marketing and screen-based culture can thwart parents' efforts to instil good habits – such as healthy eating, good sleep routines and free play – from an early age. Instead, there is considerable pressure on children and parents to set up unhealthy habits of behaviour which may be very difficult to break as boys grow older.

Marketers also encourage parents to place increasing emphasis on early learning and pre-reading products. The chapter concludes that these can never replace age-old learning techniques involving time and attention on the part of the parent: love, talk, song and play.

Building good habits, avoiding bad influences

What can parents do?

- Since habits of behaviour are formed through imitation, make sure boys have male as well as female role models from their earliest years. This provides an added challenge for single mothers. I met one recently who said her choice of childminder was greatly influenced by her childminder's husband – he was happy to involve himself in her little boy's life, thus providing a surrogate father figure.
- Let your 'dance of communication' help you tune into your son's sleep needs and guide him gently towards healthy sleep habits. The expert advice collected in my book *Toxic Childhood* amounts, very briefly, to the following:
  - infants between 3 and 11 months need 14–15 hours sleep over 24 hours; toddlers up to 3 years need 12–14, and daytime naps are important throughout this period (children's napping requirements change over time, so stay well attuned and responsive to your son's needs)

- ensure a quiet, calm end to the day, and a darkened bedroom; put your son down to sleep when he's drowsy, leave him to fall asleep by himself and if he wakes give him a few minutes to 'self-soothe' before picking him up. The same gentle lullaby or soft music on CD every night can help condition him to feel sleepy as he grows older
- develop a calming bedtime routine and stick to it (e.g. a milky drink; bathtime and teeth-cleaning, etc; a bedtime story and/or songs; a security object such as a blanket or soft toy; a particular form of words for goodnight, with your goodnight kiss)
- make sure the bedroom is cool, if not cold (if its snug in bed and chilly out of it, there's much less chance that he'll want to get out and wander)
- if he doesn't settle, don't reward him with attention – just kindly but firmly return him to bed
- keep TVs and other electronic equipment out of the bedroom.

See also www.sleepnet.com/children2000 and www.sleepfoundation.org

- Maintain total control over your son's diet in the first few years, and lay down healthy eating habits. The advice of experts I consulted for *Toxic Childhood* can be briefly summarised thus:
  - for at least the first six months, 'breast is best' (see www.breastfeeding.nhs.uk)
  - don't encourage a sweet tooth by giving him sugary drinks instead of milk or water (when you introduce fruit juice later, dilute it)
  - when you introduce cow's milk, make sure it's whole milk (skimmed milk is not suitable for the under-threes)
  - when you introduce solids, preparing real food yourself not only gives you control over the content but also over

consistency – mash it less finely over time so your son learns to enjoy a variety of tastes and textures (many young children these days are addicted to gloop)

- check with dietary guidelines to ensure you provide a balance of nutrition (see www.eatwell.gov.uk/agesandstages)
- introduce your son to plenty of tastes at an early age – once he reaches two or so, he's likely to enter a 'fussy' stage so it's worth trying to widen his taste range early
- encourage social eating from as early as possible; model civilised table manners, and gradually expect your son to pick them up as he develops greater control over his behaviour (since status-driven boys are anxious to be 'grown up', there's great motivation for him to copy adults, especially males).

- Suggestions for encouraging healthy indoor and outdoor play habits are given in the box at the end of Chapter 1 – play develops out of children's natural urge to explore – and developed in Chapter 3. In addition:
  - avoid technological toys at this stage, and don't worry that your son will be 'left behind' (computer technology is designed to be intuitive, so he'll pick it up quickly enough once it comes into his life – in the early stages first-hand exploration of the real world is much more important)
  - avoid exposure to the sorts of manipulative marketing described on pages 86–91, which are designed to hijack 'real play' and turn it into 'toy consumption'.

- To prepare your son for reading when he starts school, talk and sing to him. The website www.talktoyourbaby.org.uk was actually set up by the National Literacy Trust. To ensure he's interested in books, choose a small number of picture books you enjoy yourself and read them repeatedly from the moment he's born, or even before. The story of Max, who was born very prematurely and spent several weeks in a special baby unit, is testament to the power of early reading. While he was poorly in the incubator, his parents took turns to read him a small selection of books: when he came home, they carried on reading the same stories. By four months, Max would concentrate intently on whole stories (watching his parent's face, listening fervently, and laughing in delight); at two and a half he joined in with all his old favourites and was well on the way to being a committed reader.

- As your son gains increasing control over his body, help him become increasingly independent. While it's much easier to dress a young child yourself than wait while he struggles into his T-shirt, the more independent he is on starting school or nursery, the more he'll thrive. Encourage his desire to be a 'big boy' by giving him time and support to acquire these personal skills, and praising every small improvement. Responsive help in making your son independent is one of the best ways to develop a warm but firm relationship – if you tune into his aspiration, you can gently help him overcome frustration and achieve his goal.

- The other area in which to develop a responsive balance of warmth and firmness is in teaching manners. Start by modelling table manners, 'please' and 'thank you', family rules and respectful behaviour (especially to other adults in the community, who you want on your side as he grows older), for instance:
  - addressing all older people as Mr – or Mrs – , unless they suggest another name, and being especially careful with 'pleases' and 'thank yous'
  - letting adults go first, giving up a seat if they don't have one (and perhaps sitting on mum's lap instead), and so on
  - not disturbing adults with noisy play or behaviour
  - teaching acceptable behaviour takes a long time, and requires patience and warm-but-firm consistency. Once you've decided he's ready to cope with a rule or boundary, stick with

it – repeat the instruction every time it crops up, and expect him to comply. If he doesn't, try to work out why and help overcome the problem – that's the warm bit. But keep insisting, gently and firmly. See the suggestions on www.bbc.co.uk/parenting/your_kids/toddlers_discipline.

- It's clear from the above that establishing good habits of behaviour takes time, energy and self-control. It's not something that can be done in your spare time, or when you're exhausted at the end of a working day. But when a little boy is carefully reared by loving adults, he not only develops the beginnings of self-discipline – *he also learns empathy by imitation.* So if you can't care for him yourself, move heaven and earth to find someone else whom you trust to do it.

- Everyone involved in bringing up a boy – especially women – should read Steve Biddulph's classic and highly readable book *Raising Boys* (HarperCollins).

- To ensure your hard work isn't undermined by marketers peddling a different lifestyle, try to keep your son screen-free for the first thousand days. Not only will this protect him from manipulative marketing messages, but research also suggests it's much better for healthy brain development. To keep up to date on marketing strategies and campaigns aimed at children, see www.commercialfreechildhood.org.

- Make sure others who look after your boy (e.g. grandparents, childminder) know your feelings about this, and your reasons. It won't, of course, do him any harm to see the odd bit of television now and again, but at least you can arrange your home-life so it doesn't come within his radar.

- Alongside the LOVE and LANGUAGE highlighted in chapters 1 and 2, the key message in this chapter is the importance in the modern world of introducing DISCIPLINE at an early age, by being warm but firm both with your son and yourself.

What can the rest of us do?

- Since research suggests that authoritative parenting is only possible within authoritative communities, it's in all responsible adults' interests to support parents in developing good habits in their infant sons. Community opinion-formers could use their influence to:
  - ensure all parents know how much sleep children need at different ages
  - advise parents to keep TVs and other screen-based entertainment out of children's bedrooms
  - make healthy food and drink available for children in community buildings and at family events, and discouraging the sale of junk food
  - provide facilities for breast-feeding mothers
  - model good manners and considerate behaviour whenever children are present.
- At the same time, adults have a right to expect reasonable behaviour from parents and children when they're out and about in the community. Since babies and toddlers aren't fully in control of their behaviour, other adults can help parents by refraining from judgemental glares. When parents exercise consideration (e.g. by removing a screaming baby or toddler from a public place), recognise their efforts with smiles and nods; if they don't, perhaps they'd benefit from some friendly help in working out the best way forward?
- Through community recognition of 'well-brought-up youngsters' and concerted adult efforts to set a good example, the message could begin to spread that teaching good habits of behaviour in early life sets boys up for a more successful future.
- It would, of course, help enormously if this message were also

spread by opinion-formers in the wider world of the global village. The rest of us could persuade these public figures to lend the world a hand by complaining to broadcasting authorities whenever unhealthy messages or bad examples of behaviour occur onscreen in the hours before the watershed (see page 253). If enough responsible adults make their voices heard about junk broadcasting the message will eventually get through. But if not, communities can scarcely blame parents when their sons copy the onscreen behaviour.

- In the light of the revelations about marketing in Chapter 3, we could all help parents by letting national politicians know that these changes are damaging community life: a childhood directed by marketers is increasingly 'toxic'.

What can politicians do?

- Support local authorities in child-friendly policies, including:
  - restriction of traffic in residential areas, introducing more traffic calming measures and many more 20 mph zones
  - 'greening' urban areas and providing more spaces for outdoor play
  - welcoming children into public areas, including pub gardens
  - phasing out junk-filled 'children's menus'.
- Support children's centres, schools and other agencies in issuing information to parents about children's developmental needs, e.g. sleep, diet, exercise, talk, song, stories.
- Introduce immediate regulation to make big business and the marketing industry clean up their act, e.g.
  - by providing more positive, realistic images of family life and children's outdoor play (as, for instance, in Persil's *Dirt is good* campaign)
  - by abandoning the portrayal of idealised family life in which

consumer products are associated with parental love and
children's happiness
- by removing the claim (or even the suggestions) that products are 'educational' for young children, unless they have
been subjected to rigorous independent testing
- by stopping all marketing – in every form – to children under
the age of eight.

Chapter 4

ONE OF THE BOYS

Why little boys need to play,
run about and fight ...
and why adults must let them
get on with it

Mothers can teach their infant sons a great deal, but they can't teach them how to be men. For this, boys need fathers or, if that's impossible, other loving male role models. The research showing the significance of paternal involvement in boys' social development and educational success is now incontrovertible. From the age of three or four, boys are aware of their gender and influenced by the behaviour of the men they see around them – not just in real life, but on screen and online. But arguably the most important male influence in any boy's childhood is the other boys he meets in the playground.

Play is another vital ingredient of childhood that has been taken for granted throughout history. In an S-type man-made world, the activities of small children have even less status than women's work. Even E-type mothers haven't particularly valued children's private, independent play, because until recently it happened out of view, without any input from them. Play has always been kids' stuff, practically invisible in the grown-up world, adults' own memories of it buried under all the 'serious' things that happen later. But it's during their free play with other children that boys learn some of the most essential lessons of their lives.

Child's play

Play is a universal feature of childhood, not just in humans but in all higher animals. Apart from anything else, it provides opportunities for learning essential life skills. Lion cubs, for instance, learn how to be lions through play hunting, play stalking and play fighting. Their play is like a natural rehearsal for adulthood, but also a joyous, personal response to the wonder of being alive and being a lion.

Human children's free play, if uncontaminated by adult interference, can be just as joyous, uninhibited and exhilarating. It grows out of the natural learning instincts described in Chapters 2 and 3, and – like all their other learning – is exploratory, imitative, repetitive and vital for development. Children play because their brains and bodies scream out to play, and if the need is thwarted, there are likely to be long-term repercussions. There are clear gender differences in the way boys and girls play, which appear to relate to evolutionary differences in gender roles, and these too we ignore at our peril.

Through independent play, a boy begins to take increasing responsibility for his own physical and mental growth, an important development in terms of self-respect. Self-chosen play also helps his self-control (physical and mental), bodily co-ordination and powers of concentration. This is how he learns to focus his attention on the activity in hand, as he'll one day be required to focus it in the classroom or at work. And as will be shown throughout this chapter and in Chapter 6, all the key qualities associated with secure attachment are further developed through free play: emotional resilience, social competence and the potential for academic success. Indeed, it's likely that play can develop these qualities even in a child who hasn't been securely attached. On the other hand, lack of free play could mean that the seeds sown by secure attachment are unable to grow.

Since play is 'kids' stuff', however, this litany of significance for our species' progress has counted for nothing in a man-made world. For evidence of its low status, just look at the lack of vocabulary for talking about it. That one word, 'play' covers a vast range of activities – from a baby blowing bubbles in the bath or playing with language sounds to a teenager's serious experimentation with a chemistry set or grown-up wordplay; from making mud pies or dens to constructing working models or a full-blown treehouse; from solitary Solitaire to communal cops and robbers; from macho playground wrestling bouts to playing mummies and daddies or the wild abandonment of kiss-chase. In the words of evolutionary biologist Mark Berkoff, *'it's a behavioural kaleidoscope'*, but when everything's lumped together as 'play', it's difficult to notice the variety or to consider what each activity adds to the sum of a boy's development.

Once adults do start noticing it, the lack of vocabulary can lead to other problems. Some play activities clearly underpin future learning – play with sounds, words, numbers and materials like sand, water, clay and paint. Educational experts have popularised the significance of these as a link between tiny children's instinctive drive to learn and the primary school curriculum. So parents who want their sons to do well at school are keen to direct them towards this more civilised, obviously productive type of play – and, as mentioned in the last chapter, marketers have been quick to capitalise on their concern. Indeed, we now have toy shops that call themselves 'Early Learning Centres'. When we home in on 'structured play', it's easy to forget the significance of the other less obviously educational stuff.

The idea of 'structured play' also fits with our increasingly risk-averse attitude: letting children out of adult sight, or allowing them to engage in raucous, uncontrolled activity could be very dangerous ... And, as more small children do more and more of their playing in organised preschool environments which can't afford the threat of litigation for negligence, opportunities for unstructured, loosely supervised, child-chosen play have – for many three- to six-year-olds – practically withered away.

Everything to play for …

Despite their ready dismissal of child's play, however, adults
throughout the ages have gained enormous satisfaction from
grown-up ways of 'playing'. There's a shortage of vocabulary
here too – the same two words 'play' and 'game' crop up in all
sorts of contexts involving first-hand, personal enjoyment, relaxation and exhilaration. For instance, some adults let off
steam on the sports field when they *play* cricket, football, tennis
or some other adult *game*. Another hugely important form of
emotional release is music – and anyone who can *play* the piano,
guitar or another instrument can encourage others to let go of
grown-up inhibitions through the age-old human activities of
singing and dancing. Risk-taking adults enjoy *playing* cards,
chess, the National Lottery or other *games* of chance; creative
adults relish *playing* with words to make poems, stories or jokes,
or *playing* around with colour, shape or materials to make pictures and artefacts. And in that most universal of human recre-
ational activities – sex – we're extremely *playful*: *playing* the field
to find a mate, *playing* flirtatiously with their emotions, then
completely letting our hair down and getting very personal indeed with *foreplay* and sex *games*.

As human culture developed, however, our species has also
learned to enjoy play at second hand. We enjoy watching expert
players play games on the sports field, music in the concert hall
or parts in theatrical *plays*. All art, entertainment and sport is,
to a great extent, creative play – and the creative playfulness of
great artists, entertainers and sportsmen is highly valued – in
an S-type world they gain enviable status and success through
their specialised high-quality play. Our enjoyment of this is often
less personal and spontaneous than the first-hand type though
– there are systemised conventions for response (from football
chants to polite applause) that register our engagement but keep
us firmly in our place as spectators.

The arrival of the electronic media has given grown-up play

yet another dimension. We can now bring expert players into the privacy of our homes. Over the 20th century record *players* and TV familiarised us with the pleasure of such convenient, personal entertainment, and recent developments mean we can now *play* our own choice of DVDs whenever we like, watch endless *replays* of sporting events or download the latest music to *play* on our iPods. Then over the last 30 years, computer technology moved us from merely watching or listening to virtual 'participation' in this second-hand entertainment. Adults can now be '*players*' in an ever-expanding range of highly systemised virtual *games*. As a result the limited language of play is now strongly associated with the electronic media (*PlayStation*, computer *gaming*), and we increasingly equate adult recreation with electronic entertainment.

All this has led adults into a strange relationship with play. We value entertainment highly, and many people are prepared to pay a fortune to join the audience for a great sporting or artistic event, while most of us feel that the electronic gadgetry of home entertainment is a 21st century necessity. But we engage less and less in first-hand grown-up play involving real, personal interaction and lack of inhibition. Apart from anything else, people have to work so hard these days that it's difficult to fit real-life sport, music or other time-consuming hobbies into our lives: the personal satisfaction of participation is eroded by the effort of getting round to it. And anyway, with so many wonderful electronic alternatives available at the touch of a button, why bother?

On the other hand, most parents dream of their sons becoming famous sportsmen, entertainers, artists, musicians or other expert 'players', able to make a fabulous living by doing whatever it is they love best. Hence the interest in educational games to give them a good start on the ladder to success, and the increasing trend for 'hot-housing' tiny children.

But ask any successful sportsman, entertainer, artist or musician and it's not the hot-housing or coaching that made him a star – it's a deep inner love of playing for its own sake. This is what provides the motivation to learn and perspire, and sets free the spark of genius. Success springs from a mixture of natural talent and opportunities to release it – opportunities that first arise through the messy, first-hand, unsystemised joy of child's play. While endless practice is indeed necessary to refine skills, the feeling of 'flow' described by star players in all areas of life is a continuation of the timeless joy of young children's 'free-flow' play.

If, through our increasing sophistication, risk aversion or embarrassment about natural (as opposed to controlled) behaviour, we close down children's opportunities to play freely, we cut off their potential for genius. But if instead we can open up opportunities for *all* children to play, independently and without unnecessary adult interference, not only will the odd genius continue to make it through and stun us with his (or her) skills, but there'll be more happy, successful learners in our schools and adults in our workplaces.

When the mollycoddling has to stop

The encouragement of natural play, arising from a boy's own instincts and interests rather than adult influences, and taking place away from adult eyes, is clearly at odds with the 'mollycoddling' recommended in Chapter 1 and the eagle-eyed exercise of parental authority suggested in Chapters 2 and 3. But if in his first thousand days parents are able to build up their son's resilience, help him develop a mind of his own, and encourage a healthy behavioural default mechanism, they'll find, by the time he's into his third year, that coddling and protection from the outside world are no longer what he wants and needs.

By this time, their son will already be a 'player'. His enjoyment of play grows out of their influence during the first year, when they join in with games he initiates (those tediously repetitive activities such as 'Drop the rattle out of the cot and wait for someone to pick it up') or interest him in the baby games adults instinctively play ('*Peekaboo!*'). As he grows, they influence the general direction of his play by the sorts of experiences and toys they provide. In fact, if they can manage to avoid the blandishments of the marketers, they usually find that manufactured toys aren't necessary. The most genuine, active play grows from children's imaginative use of whatever items are to hand, especially items from the natural world. The more a boy is encouraged to pursue his inborn lust to learn, the more sustained and self-controlled his play is likely to become. But inevitably, as self-control develops, earlier levels of adult involvement become a barrier to future learning, personally, emotionally and socially.

To develop social skills, for instance, he now needs to play with other children. Up to the age of about three, most boys don't play socially – they play alongside other children (so-called 'parallel play') but not with them. And when they first begin interacting, the skills for social play seldom come easily. Not being natural empathisers, boys don't tend to take other children's feelings into account – if they want the toy someone else is holding they grab it; if the play seems to require bashing a 'playmate', they bash him. The natural tendency of parents on such occasions is to leap in and protect their own son's interests, but intervention in social play isn't always helpful.

Just as spoon-feeding prevents a boy from learning to feed himself, and keeping him strapped in a pushchair inhibits his physical development, parental interference in his relationships with other children can prevent him from making progress. On the whole, social skills are caught, not taught. Parents can't *teach* their son how to make and maintain friendships – he has to find out through experience, and sometimes that experience is painful.

It's not just that being bashed by a playmate is an excellent way to find out that bashing hurts. Psychologists also believe that 'rough and tumble' play helps boys to learn the ropes of social encounters. They're opportunities to learn to read facial expressions and body language, and to work out their position and status in their peer group – in this respect, they're an important male addition to the lessons learned in the 'dance of communication' (see Chapters 1 and 2). Adults can provide house rules and models of more civilised methods of getting along; they can be there to tend bruised limbs and egos, to listen to problems and give general advice and loving comfort, but the more they take over the social organisation of little boys' play, the less the little boys will learn.*

In previous generations, it's been taken for granted that after the first thousand days or so, children would be socialised largely by their peer group. Before the availability of contraception, mothers seldom had longer than this to tend to one offspring's needs before another one arrived to supplant him. Most toddlers, once weaned, were handed over to the care of older siblings or other children from the extended family or neighbourhood, where they took up their place at the bottom of the childhood pecking order. According to social psychologists, well-attached older children have a natural urge to protect their younger charges, initiating them gradually into playground culture, so close adult supervision is perhaps less essential than modern parents suspect.

As well as social development, play is where a boy develops self-confidence and independence through opportunities to make his own (sometimes wrong) decisions. Adults should of course ensure that the play area is safe – without making it so safe as to be boring – but if they're always hovering at his elbow to protect him from physical harm, he won't learn how to take 'safe risks' and may become unrealistically over-confident or excessively timid. Again, he's likely to encounter pain when allowed the freedom to make his own decisions about what's safe and what isn't, but the odd bump, bruise or skinned knee is a small price to pay for long-term emotional resilience and physical confidence.

* However, children from violent or neglectful homes may by nursery age operate within a different paradigm from others, and need specialised support (see Note and References)

Some researchers link ADHD to deprivation of play, especially between the ages of three and seven when, in the words of Jan Panksepp, one of the world's top experts on the subject, '*the urge to play is particularly insistent*'. Others suggest that timid children whose parents shield them from rough-and-tumble play in the preschool years may grow up socially withdrawn and fearful. The eminent developmental psychologist Professor Jerome Kagan says that '*mothers who protect their [timid] infants from frustration and anxiety in the hope of effecting a benevolent outcome seem to exacerbate the infant's uncertainty and produce the opposite effect*'.

Fathers are often more willing than mothers to let their sons fend for themselves in early play, since a male parent has experienced being a boy himself and is instinctively less risk averse than a female one. For a loving mother, this is the point in rearing a son when she has to rally all her E-type skills, and tune in empathetically to his growing need for independence. He needs to feel that she has confidence in his ability to manage new experiences ... while still being close at hand when needed with the cuddles and comfort that help keep a newly independent boy on track.

So this is when the mollycoddling has to stop. Warm-but-firm parenting at home is still vital for emotional and social development (see Chapter 6), but as soon as they're ready to stretch their wings – which is usually around the end of those first thousand days – boys need time and space to grow on their own terms.

Boys' toys and adult obsessions

Once boys start to engage in independent and social play, it's clear that their interests are very different from girls'. Boys are far more physically active and inclined to 'naughty' or risky behaviour, they're more likely to enjoy high-contact 'rough and tumble' activities and much of their early imaginative play tends to focus on weapons and superheroes. They also gravitate to certain sorts of 'boys' toys'.

These differences can all be explained by the arguments from evolutionary biology outlined in the Introduction, but there's also no doubt that social forces operating from the moment of birth drive boys towards life on Mars and girls to Venus. This self-evident fact leads to endless chicken and egg dilemmas. Is adults' traditional treatment of boys from the moment of birth – tickling and bouncing them about, and making sound effects like 'Brmmm, brmmm' and 'Wheeee' rather than quietly sitting and chatting as they do with girls – a stimulus or response to so-called 'boyishness'? Do the toys parents tend to provide for their sons – building blocks, mechanical gizmos, bats and balls, trucks, cars and so on – appeal to natural instincts or do adults just think they do? Are sexual stereotypes the result of nature or nurture?

There really is no answer. Clearly babies and toddlers won't respond positively to the way they're treated unless it rewards them in some way, just as they won't play with a particular toy unless it appeals to them. But just as clearly, in their earliest years they're at the mercy of adults in terms of the treatment, toys and, to a great extent, the rewards available. And while children under three aren't aware of gender and gender stereotypes (so could scarcely make decisions on the basis of them), adults certainly are. Throughout the latter half of the 20th century, therefore, well-meaning adults attempted to free themselves and their children from the negative effects of this stereotyping.

They were guided in this humanitarian endeavour by an avalanche of academic research into sexism that poured out of universities. However, with hindsight, much of that research was itself influenced by preconceptions and bias. One psychologist whose work affected the actions of generations of parents and teachers was Dr John Money. In the 1970s he reported the successful 'gender realignment' of an unfortunate baby boy called Bruce Reimer, who had lost his penis in a botched circumcision. Dr Money persuaded Bruce's distraught parents to have their son's testes removed too, to change his name to Brenda and to bring him up as a girl. Since 'Brenda' had an undamaged twin brother, she was the perfect subject for a comparative experiment in sexual stereotyping.

Dr Money's reports on the boy's apparent transition to a happy female existence ('*the child's behaviour is clearly that of an active little girl, and so different from the boyish ways of her twin brother*') convinced many in the educational, medical and political establishments that gender was indeed a social construct. However, in the later 1990s, it was revealed that Dr Money had been at best a victim of his own unconscious desires and at worst engaging in academic deception. 'Brenda' was in fact never at ease in a girl's body. Her mother later told a documentary team, '*I could see that Brenda wasn't happy as a girl. No matter what I tried to do for her, no matter how I tried to instruct her, she was very rebellious, she was very masculine and I couldn't persuade her to do anything feminine.*'

Indeed, at the age of 13 Brenda threatened to commit suicide rather than see Dr Money again. When, at 15, s/he discovered the truth, s/he was devastated, had surgery to restore as many masculine features as possible, and took the new name of David. But, perhaps as a result of the deception, Bruce/Brenda/David and his twin brother both suffered long-term mental instability. The twin became schizophrenic and died of drink and drugs in 2002 and two years later Bruce/Brenda/David shot himself with a sawn-off shotgun.

The moral of this story seems to be that adults, no matter how well meaning, need to be tuned into children's needs, not just their own obsessions. These obsessions are powerful ones: academics and politicians are keen to exercise control over children from as early as possible, generally in the hope of changing human nature for the social good; big business and marketers want control so that they can hijack human nature in their own commercial interests. Both groups want to enlist parents and others who care for children to help fulfil their aims. But the more zealously adults try to control every aspect of a boy's behaviour without taking account of his natural biological drives, the more long-term damage we're likely to do.

'We don't play with guns here'

At the end of 2007, the British government published guidance
that nursery workers should value boys' self-chosen play, even
when it centred on 'characters with special powers and
weapons'. The resultant media flurry about whether little boys
should play with toy guns summed up this knotty problem of
control.

The traditional liberal (and feminist) line of argument is that,
if adults want children to grow up eschewing violence, we
shouldn't condone it in their play. This means a zero tolerance
approach to violence and an emphasis on helping boys to empathise and collaborate. As nursery worker Gina explained to
some small miscreants: *'We don't play with guns here. Guns hurt
people. We're all friends at nursery, and we don't want to hurt each other,
do we?'* It seems a reasonable argument.

But what if it doesn't work? Little children aren't famed for
their susceptibility to reasoned argument, and parents and nursery workers who try to stop violent play soon realise that they
merely drive it underground. Their young male charges then
learn from first-hand experience that, by working as a group,
they can find a way around grown-up rules – a practical lesson
that's not helpful in the long run for authoritative parenting or
teaching. The ban also pushes them into a 'naughty boys' role
which is often self-perpetuating.

Across cultures, little boys of around three or four have always begun playing violent games centred on goodies versus
baddies – this violent play reaches a peak at around seven years
of age, then gradually declines. Perhaps, as some theorists
maintain, boys are struggling through play to come to terms
with fundamental questions of good and evil, or perhaps the
younger they are the closer they are to their Stone Age heritage,
and they need a way of getting aggressive instincts out of their
system. Their play is, of course, affected by the cultural context
of their lives and times – our tribe versus another tribe; Tommies

versus Huns; cops versus robbers; cowboys versus Indians – and their pretend weapons reflect the weapons they see being used by grown-ups. Today's boys usually identify with magical super-heroes battling various monsters and villains. Since they see guns used regularly on TV and films, it would be strange if guns didn't come into their games.

However, in preschools that allow superhero play, nursery workers find the pretend violence soon dies down and boys start devising rules of engagement – their own ways of ensuring 'fair play'. Often (especially with the odd subtle nudge from grown-ups here and there) the play can then develop into something much more positive and social. The male urge to fight seems closely allied to the urge to build, make and protect. In one case study, a particularly aggressive little boy was transmogrified through his own play into Dr Darren, his 'gun' changing miracu-lously into surgical instruments.

Critical to this transformation was that the 'gun', fashioned by Darren himself, was his own imaginative construction and could thus become whatever he wanted. A shop-bought toy gun doesn't have that same transformational power. In the words of the major British researcher in this field, Penny Holland, when a child is given a manufactured replica toy, 'the toy determines the play, not the child'. So the problem is not little boys running about shouting 'Bang bang you're dead' but a society that commer-cialises every aspect of children's lives.

Children's lust to imitate adult behaviour means they crave grown-up-looking replica toys and costumes, but the greater the verisimilitude (including those ubiquitous Spiderman out-fits), the less their imagination is unleashed, and the more boys are trapped in a manufactured adult fantasy. As Holland points out, children now live in a media-saturated world awash with 'real and fantasy violence and aggression generated by adults'. In these circumstances, adult attempts to impose liberal values on three- and four-year-old boys is an act of 'ostrich-like hypocrisy'.

Boys versus girls

Studies of other primates show that young males deprived of the opportunity to fight grow up more violent, not less. It's highly possible that rough and tumble, pseudo-violent play is not only a rehearsal of fighting skills, but also a way of learning to defuse aggression. It's now well established that when fathers 'wrestle' with their sons, they demonstrate how to restrain behaviour so that no one is hurt. There's evidence that boys (like lion cubs) pass on this lesson among themselves: certainly nursery staff who reversed their zero tolerance approach noted that *'children are far more effective at managing play-fighting themselves, both to avoid injury and to sustain the play, than they had previously thought possible'*. It seems very likely that the close physical contact of play-fighting is a way for boys to 'get in touch' with each other's feelings and develop empathetic engagement with their peers.

As mentioned above, if there is a natural urge in little boys to fight, banning it is rather like trying to crush something deep in their soul. Not a good introduction to the institutionalised world they're going to inhabit for at least the next 15 years. But it's not just fighting that can get boys sent to the naughty table. They are also born to run ... and to jump, climb, slide, scramble, stalk, chase and all the other physical activities required of an apprentice hunter. Unfortunately, most British nurseries and preschools don't have much room indoors for large-scale exuberant activities, and many have little or no outdoor space. On the other hand, they do have rafts of government regulations to observe, and the prospect of parental wrath – and possibly litigation – if an accident should happen. There are inevitably difficulties in containing little boys' behaviour and their opportunities for natural learning through active play are limited.

Little girls, on the other hand, usually take to the nursery environment like ducks to water. Naturally inclined to chat and socialise, to excel at small-scale tasks and to get along in a domestic setting, their behaviour is in marked contrast to that of the boys. Kindergarten teacher Vivian Gussin Paley, a seasoned child-watcher, describes her struggle to let boys be boys in her book *Boys and Girls: Superheroes in the Dolls' Corner*. Touchingly, one little boy explains to her why girls aren't naughty: *'It's because they like to colour so much. That's one thing I know. But boys have to practise running.'*

Colouring fits very well into what most adults think of as 'structured play', and most girls are naturally interested in and good at it. The pictures they draw at preschool age tend to be neat, brightly coloured representations of people, houses, trees, flowers, and so on, all likely to appeal to a nursery teacher's tastes. Boys' pictures tend to be messy, less colourful attempts to represent action and movement (*'This is a rocket crashing into the earth!'*). In the same way, girls' role play is more 'structured' – based on familiar domestic scenarios and stories – and usually involves talk, including the sort of 'narrative' talk (a running commentary on what they're doing) that prepares them for reading and writing.

As mentioned above, when boys are allowed to be boys, playing their own self-chosen active games, they too move from shouts, jeers and sound effects to using language in increasingly constructive ways. As well as making up rules and negotiating roles and boundaries, they may eventually begin, like the girls, to provide narrative commentaries. Given plenty of opportunities for large-scale physical activity, boys also gain in bodily control and balance, so are more able to sit still and take part in small-scale activities like the girls.

In her review of superhero play, Penny Holland wonders – along with other recent commentators – whether the restrictions in many nurseries and preschools are due to their being overwhelmingly run and staffed by women, who are not naturally sympathetic to boys' natural urges. Maybe, in an unequal world *'perceived sexist patterns in children's play'* are *'an area in which women could take some control'*. However, my own conversations with nursery workers suggest most feel instinctively that boys need more freedom to play in 'boyish' ways, and would like to find some way to give it to them. The empathetic child-caring skills that have helped women provide for little boys' needs through the millennia are still around. Unfortunately, nursery workers are usually young women with few educational qualifications, little self-confidence and the natural reticence of low-status employees, so they don't question the rulings of risk-averse employers, parents and government inspectors.

Band of brothers

There's one type of 'structured play' in which little boys tend to excel: construction. Most make a beeline at nursery for Lego, Duplo, Mobilo and other construction toys, and their noisy domination of these activities often deters girls from having a go. Even more popular and attractive for boys' construction purposes are natural or real building materials in the great outdoors, and access to simple tools allows them to refine the small-scale motor skills they'll need when teachers later ask them to pick up a pencil and write.

Given the opportunity to build their own den, boat, fort, spaceship or Batmobile, even three- and four-year-old boys can become deeply involved in complex collaborative effort. This again involves them in all sorts of talk – instructing, explaining, describing. Social worker Sandy Campbell (whose project Working Rites has helped many disaffected lads back on to the straight and narrow by 'apprenticing' them to self-employed craftsmen) believes it is easier for males to strike up conversation if sitting side by side, engaged in work together, than in the face-to-face situation preferred by females.

Boys' talk is less obviously social than girls', and the products of their labour are seldom neat and tidy. But it's through immersing themselves in the physical world, collaborating to make and build, to chase and ambush, and to create their own rule-based play, that boys have learned how to learn through the millennia. They need adults to ensure their safety, to support and – sometimes – help them extend the play in more creative directions (and children who haven't played much in their earliest years may need more adult help), but until the age of six or so, their interests should drive the activities.

In most European countries, this is understood and provision for boys' (and girls') free play, indoors and outdoors, is considered essential. Indeed, even in Japan, where there is very limited space for play, the need for freedom is acknowledged. I met some English teachers in Tokyo who were horrified when they visited a Japanese indoor nursery where children were issued with just two rules – 'Don't do anything unkind and don't do anything dangerous' – then left to get on with it. But after a while the English observers noticed, like the nursery workers who abandoned zero tolerance, that the children were able to regulate their own behaviour: on the whole, they didn't do anything unkind or dangerous.

The urge for institutionalised control of little children's behaviour seems greatest in Anglo-Saxon countries. Some boys are able to adjust to a more contained, indoor existence at preschool (especially if there's a garden or somewhere for them to let off steam at home), but there's usually a hard core (perhaps a quarter) for whom a too-structured approach is anathema. Often these include powerful personalities, who by fair means or foul draw other boys to join them, and peer pressure can then work against adult influences.

Boys are particularly susceptible to what Gary Wilson, an authority on boys' education, calls the 'peer police'. Given the choice of pleasing an adult or a group of their own sex, they are more inclined to play to the crowd, so conflict with authority may begin very early. From around the age of three, children are highly aware of gender and without positive opportunities to express their masculine identity, the band of brothers may begin to rally around the flag of '*not being girls*'. Hence sexism too can get off to a very early start – despite (perhaps even because of) adults' resolute attempts to prevent stereotyping.

Yet researchers find repeatedly that, given the chance to express their male identity through free play, boys become more laid-back about gender, feel accepted in the preschool environment, and are more likely to join in play with girls. When boys and girls are brought closer together in this way, the combination of male and female interests allows them to go beyond gender stereotypes and explore through play the great themes that affect all human lives – attachment and separation, life and death, sickness and health.

Screenplay for the future

For several decades now, liberal parents and teachers have made a concerted effort to ignore, or at least downplay, gender stereotypes. This is partly to avoid social expectations that may promote sexual inequalities, and partly to protect the interests of those children who don't conform to established gender roles. If 'inclusivity' is a 21st century aspiration, it should surely begin as early as possible.

All their efforts are, however, in vain when marketers home in on gender stereotypes from the moment of birth. The pink/blue division of baby paraphernalia leads straight into the pink/steely grey division of major toyshops. From the moment they become conscious of toys, boys are steered towards construction materials, mechanical devices and, increasingly, screens. There are now computer games for infants as young as nine months, worked with a joystick rather than a mouse. From then on, screenplay increasingly dominates the toy marketplace, especially the metallic, male sections of the superstores.

Just like real food, real play (active, creative, social, outdoor) nourishes the natural development of body and brain. So far, the contribution of 'processed play' to the physical and mental health problems that beset 21st century children has not been fully acknowledged, probably because of play's low status in the adult world. But there have certainly been profound changes in play habits: Scottish researchers into children's activity levels recently found that two-year-olds were as sedentary as office workers.

Second-hand screen-based play appeals to many of boys' primal needs: there's plenty of movement and action to watch, opportunities for pattern recognition and spatial skills, the chance to compete without fear of failure. A child tuned early to screens through TV often moves effortlessly to simple computer games, and – if this becomes his major focus of activity – increasingly misses out on the essential physical, emotional, social and conceptual lessons gained through real first-hand play.

The targeting of electronic entertainment at very young children has happened very suddenly, and its potential effects are only just beginning to dawn on the scientific community. In the last couple of years, there have been urgent calls from neuroscientific experts in both the USA and the UK for more research, but what little has been done is not cheering, particularly in terms of the damage to children's concentration spans. One American study found that, for every hour per day of TV watched under the age of three, there's a 9% increase in attention deficit by seven. Even just having the TV constantly on in the background may damage children's capacity to concentrate: behavioural psychologist Daniel Anderson, who devised *Blues Clues* (one of the few 'educational' TV programmes rated by educators) for Nickelodeon, has found that when a small child is playing in a room where the TV is on – even if it's an adult programme he's not watching – he tends to look up in response to sounds and movements onscreen. Thus children are constantly interrupted in their own free-flow play, probably interfering with the development of focused attention.

As Anderson puts it, *'we are engaged in a vast and uncontrolled experiment with our infants and toddlers, plunging them into home environments that are saturated with electronic media'*. In the UK

Baroness Susan Greenfield, Director of the Royal Institution and one of the country's foremost neuroscientists, has set up an all-party committee in the House of Lords to investigate the effects of modern life on children's brain development. She points out that screen-based entertainment provides '*a gratifying, easy-sensation "yuk and wow" environment, which doesn't require a young mind to work ... We cannot park our children in front of the TV and expect them to develop a long attention span.*' Meanwhile, a primary head teacher recently told me that many children – especially boys – now arrive on their first day at school completely unable to learn: '*They just have this jumble in their heads – a chaos of images and odd words, with no connections, no structures, no schema.*'

Low-status 'play' is one of those embarrassing four-letter words that underpins human development, much to the irritation of S-type thinkers. It's spontaneous, arises from deep emotional needs and gives children intense personal satisfaction. It's also vital to their physical, social, emotional and cognitive development, but the lessons concerned are caught rather than taught. It can't be quantified or marked, systemised or controlled.

No wonder such tricky stuff doesn't appeal to control-freak politicians. No wonder it frightens parents who've been brainwashed into thinking that only education can educate. And no surprise at all that media and marketers are desperate to own it as early as possible, defusing boys' own imaginations with plastic man-made toys, off-the-peg costumes and sedentary screen-based entertainment, in order to sell them the second-hand, virtual thrills that nowadays satisfy the majority of the adult population.

But if lion cubs stopped playing, what would happen to lions? Would they be able to keep up in the chase, work as a pack, make the fine judgements of space and distance needed to feed themselves and their offspring? In the words of naturalist David Attenborough: '*Play is a very serious business.*'

Chapter summary

This chapter looked at the importance of independent play for a boy's physical, social, emotional and cognitive development and discusses how 'play' in our society has become increasingly less hands-on and ever more associated with technological gadgetry. It suggested that it is vital for a boy from his third year to follow his instinct for play, and considered whether attempting to eliminate 'violent' play may be counter-productive.

It also explored some of the differences between the play of boys and girls, and current gender-stereotyping in the marketing aimed at children. One result of this is the growth in screen-based entertainment aimed at boys which may interfere with the development of focused attention and lead to a more sedentary lifestyle.

Keeping little boys on track

What can parents do?

- In the first thousand days, as your son develops increasing control of his actions, watch how his exploratory instincts develop into 'play'. His two scientific quests will drive him to play with almost any object that crosses his radar and to enjoy social play with adults. Rough and tumble play with his father (or father substitute) is likely to give particular delight.
- As well as outdoor and indoor activities suggested in previous chapters, as he grows older let him experiment with:
  - cardboard boxes, which can become cars, boats, spaceships, and other household junk
  - cloths, sheets, ribbon, discarded clothing for dressing up and making things

- making dens (outdoors using branches and so on, indoors using a sheet over the table)
- pots, pans and containers (filling and emptying them, banging to make music, piling them up and knocking them down, etc.)
- mixing and messing with water, paint, bubbles, playdough, cooking ingredients, etc., indoors – and sand, grass cuttings, leaves, mud or snow outdoors
- when he's sensible enough, things he can take apart (old pieces of machinery, clocks, etc. – but still watch out if there are small parts).

● Don't feel you've always got to join in. When he's focused on his own self-chosen play, try not to interrupt his concentration, and make sure that he's not distracted by the TV or computer flashing in the background.

● Make sure he has opportunities to mix with other children from as early as possible, as it helps build immunity to childhood illnesses and prepares the way for social development. However, don't expect him to play *with* other children till he's about three. From then on he'll need plenty of opportunities for social play, so (in a 21st century world where he's unlikely to have many siblings) he'll benefit from being enrolled in a nursery for several hours a day.

● Look for a nursery with:
- plenty of space for active physical play
- an outdoor area – the bigger and more interesting the better (with grass to run on, slopes to roll down, trees to climb – or manufactured alternatives if real ones aren't available)
- plenty of opportunities for making and building, including making dens, forts and so on
- a very strong 'play ethos', rather than an early concentration on formal schoolwork
- well-qualified, empathetic nursery staff.

● Accept that, if your son engages in the active physical play boys need, he'll come home with the occasional bump, scrape or bruise (and pray that it's never anything worse). The point about 'real play' is that it must involve an element of risk, and as long as the nursery takes reasonable safety precautions, they're doing as much as any caring parent can do. Excessive risk aversion is in the long term more damaging than the small short-term risk of minor injury. Indeed, bumps, scrapes, bruises, etc., are all themselves useful learning experiences.

- Accept also that boys naturally engage in physical rough and tumble play. Your son needs to learn the social ropes of boyhood, so it's not in his interests to have too much adult intervention. At this age, 'bullying' is rare among well-cared-for children, so expect nursery workers only to intervene if a child is 'unnaturally' violent and unable to control behaviour. Most boys' injuries in play-fights and so on are forgotten almost as soon as they've happened.

- Once children start to play out – even when they're loosely supervised – problems like 'stranger danger' begin to rear their head. Don't let these fears get out of proportion (see Chapter 6). The best way to put your mind at rest – and to keep your son safe – is to teach him sensible safety precautions. There's a useful free leaflet on www.kidscape.org.uk – use it as background knowledge to inform your informal chats with your son. Remember that you want to help him keep safe, not terrified of the outside world.

- One way to make sure your son has enough space to grow is to share outdoor experiences with him. There's a wonderful book called *Nature's Playground* by Fiona Danks and Jo Schofield (Frances Lincoln) that could lure even the most citified parents to share the great outdoors with their sons. See also their website: www.goingwild.net.

- In terms of creative work, don't compare boys' efforts with those of girls of his age. When your son makes pictures and

artefacts at nursery or at home, they're unlikely to be neat and
tidy. Value them for their verve, and talk about what it is he's
depicted.

- Keep up the stories, song (encourage him to join in) and talk
  around all your activities, as described in the last chapter. Give
  lots of opportunities for him to initiate talk, and tune into
  what he has to say. Always respond to both verbal and non-
  verbal communication. If you listen, he's likely to talk more.

- Once your son is at nursery, it's increasingly difficult to shield
  him from the influence of media and marketing. He'll now
  learn about consumer 'must-haves' from the other children,
  so you don't want him to feel excluded and will need to
  change strategies. Here are some suggestions gleaned from
  parents and experts I've met:

  - don't have junk food in the house, but don't completely ban
    it (the occasional burger or fizzy drink when out and about is
    unlikely to do much harm)

  - however, don't make it into a treat – show you're unimpressed
    by the stuff, and stress that it's not healthy ('The marketers
    don't care about whether it's good for you: they just want our
    money')

  - never give in to pester power

  - introduce TV and other electrical equipment into the house
    when *you* want to and on your terms: keep them in family
    space where you can monitor and mediate their use

  - limit time spent on electronic entertainment and be firm
    about it: 'junk play' shouldn't take over from real play any
    more than junk food takes over from real food

  - stick to your bedtime routine – between three and seven
    years, children should have 11–13 hours sleep a night and if
    your son's engaging in plenty of active physical play during
    the day, he'll need it!

- Previous chapters have fo cused on LOVE, LANGUAGE and DISCIPLINE. No surprise, then, that this one is concerned mainly with importance of PLAY in developing the physical, emotional, social, creative and cognitive foundations for life and learning. If you want to read more about the significance of play in young children's lives, the most readable and long-established authority is the delightful Vivian Gussin Paley. Try *A Child's Work* (Chicago University Press).

What can the rest of us do?

- Small boys' play is not always convenient in a crowded adult world – it's usually noisy, and they often make a mess. When preoccupied by his game and showing off to friends, even the best brought-up boy may forget his manners. Older citizens who live near a nursery, park or busy family garden are often irritated by these infringements of their peace. So are some customers in pub gardens on sunny afternoons (one of the few places these days where city children get to enjoy outdoor play). If you fit either of these groups,
  - remember that you were small yourself once (perhaps you also have children or grandchildren who were/are small boys)
  - in a few years' time these same small boys will be rather larger, and it's in all older residents' interests to forge good relationships now
  - indulgence towards genuine children's play is a great sign of kindness.
- If you live near families with young children, show an interest in their play and stop for a chat (make sure you're known to the parents first). In doing so, you'll provide another model of responsible adult behaviour, and help break down the

generalised 'fear of strangers'. The more friendly community contacts children make outside their immediate circle – and across the generations – the more social skills they'll develop.

- If you're one of the people entrusted with the care of young boys, move heaven and earth to give them plenty of unstructured, loosely supervised, outdoor play. If there's no outdoor area handy, find somewhere in walking distance and negotiate its use (maybe the park? a pub garden during closing hours? maybe the primary school would let you use its grounds during lesson times?). And go out in all weather: boys should not be cooped up.

- If you're a community leader, put children's play at the heart of public policy. You can find advice (including information on how to employ playworkers) at http://www.skillsactive.com. By emphasising the needs of the youngest members of society, you'll immediately raise the profile of kindness within your community and start to break down the insanity of the current health-and-safety culture (see Chapter 6).

What can politicians do?

Preschool provision for three- to five-year-olds has developed haphazardly over the last few decades, usually on the cheap. Much of it (especially in the private sector) is far from satisfactory, and current regulation tends to be concerned with:

- health and safety considerations
- long-term educational goals, emphasising cognitive development over the social and emotional development that really matters at this age.

In terms of raising healthy boys, serious political attention to childcare between the ages of three and seven is second only in importance to support for one-on-one care in the first three years.

- Review the commitment to play in current legislation and regulation, from planning to education. If you can find any, revise it to ensure *real* commitment, not just lip-service.
- Provide a proper 'kindergarten stage' between the ages of three and seven, modelled on the Nordic system – see next chapter.
- Make it a regulation that all nursery and preschools have access to outdoor areas for children to play.
- Apologise for the shameful sale of so many school playing fields, and look for ways of greening brownfield sites to provide more open space for play in communities.
- Support local councils, charities and community groups in putting children's play at the heart of their communities. This has implications for town planning, traffic regulation, community facilities and many other aspects of social welfare.

DYLAN'S STORY: BIFF! BAM! KAPOW!

Remember little Dylan, the five-year-old boy who can't sit still? It's possible that he has a genetic predisposition to ADHD – there's no way of telling. But if so, this natural tendency may certainly be nurtured by a 21st century lifestyle.

Dylan's staff nurse mum Mandy found adjusting to motherhood difficult but was ashamed to admit it, even to herself. As a competent health professional, she was shocked to find herself struggling to fulfil the demands of one little boy. But there was no one to talk to about it: her husband Craig was really stressed about his workload and needed her support; she didn't really know anyone on the estate where they lived; her own mother was hundreds of miles away; and when friends from the hospital visited she had to keep up appearances – they were all so impressed by her lovely home, handsome husband and gorgeous little boy. So she struggled on, covering her feelings of isolation and depression with careful make-up and a bright smile for Craig when he arrived home, exhausted, from work.

It wasn't too bad when Dylan was tiny. Mandy would sit for hours, feeding and rocking him – she became quite addicted to daytime TV. *The Contented Little Baby* book helped him sleep through the night, and as he got older she kept on top of the housework while he watched *Baby Einstein* from his baby seat (the DVD was for slightly older children, but Mandy thought you could never start too soon). But Dylan never seemed a contented baby, or an Einstein. When she held him, he was always hitting out and grasping. She wasn't entirely convinced that he loved her.

Once Dylan was mobile, the trouble really started. He was into *everything* and Mandy had to be on constant watch. There were so many sharp corners, electrical items, expensive pieces of furniture, and rugs she and Craig had spent a fortune to own. Reluctantly, she stashed most of the soft furnishings away and installed every safety device she could find. But it still seemed the only word she ever uttered was 'No!' and every time she uttered it was like hammering another nail in the emotional barrier between herself and her son. She tried fencing him into a corner with his toys, but he just screamed. She tried taking him outside, but he got splinters from the decking. There seemed only two ways to keep him and their home safe: take him out in the buggy, or plug him into CBeebies.

Her salvation was Elmo. When Dylan was nine months, she found a video of *Sesame Street* she'd loved as a kid. When he liked it too, she bought him an Elmo doll. Until then he hadn't shown much interest in toys – just threw them about – but Elmo went everywhere. It became a point of emotional contact between them, and they made up their own Elmo games. Dylan was late to talk, but when he did, his first word was 'Mo!'.

Mandy and Craig put their old TV in Dylan's bedroom when he was 18 months old. That was when she went back to work part-time and Dylan started going to nursery three days a week – suddenly he was really difficult to settle at night, and his *Best of Elmo* DVD calmed him down. He'd lie there in his Elmo jim-jams, under his Elmo duvet, with his beloved Mo toy in his arms and drift off to sleep to the sound of Elmo's song.

He looked so sweet when he was asleep – Mandy's heart used to swell with love. But by sunrise, he was back on the go, and the older he got, the more of a handful. By the time he was two, he was fascinated by anything mechanical, so you always had to be on his case because he'd put his fingers into everything, including the bread-maker. In the car, you had to stop him from pressing all the buttons and wiggling the gear lever. Mandy strapped him in the back with Elmo, and closed her ears to his screams.

It was wonderful to leave him with the professionals. Despite her prickles of guilt, she was sure it was the right thing to do – it widened his horizons and helped his social development. Also the healthy eating policy improved his diet. Knowing he ate healthily there meant Mandy didn't feel so bad about the occasional chicken nuggets the rest of the time, and once back at work full-time she was grateful for fast food. Not that there was any fear of Dylan being overweight – he was always on the go, as the nursery staff ruefully confirmed. Unfortunately, they were short of space so his rumbustiousness often got him into trouble. Frankly, Mandy didn't know how they coped.

She nearly didn't cope herself when it came to potty training. Dylan hated it and – perhaps as a protest against the Elmo potty and training pants – transferred his allegiance to Spiderman. So as well as trying to convince their son not to wee on the carpet, Mandy and Craig had to adapt to life with a superhero. To start with, they were amused as Dylan tore round the house, humming the theme tune in a high-pitched voice and striking dramatic poses, but the novelty soon wore off. On one occasion he tried to climb the dining room curtains and pulled the whole lot down, curtain pole and all. He now insisted on wearing his Spiderman costume when Craig took him to the park, their traditional 'boys' afternoon out' on Sundays. Dylan loved going out with his dad, who was much more laid-back than Mandy about antics on the play equipment.

Eventually, he got the hang of the potty, seemed to settle into nursery, and started to talk a lot more. From being slightly worried about language development, Mandy and Craig were suddenly bombarded with questions, but sadly Dylan had such a butterfly brain he never seemed to listen to their answers. Still, he was doing projects at nursery, and occasionally surprised them with chatter about dinosaurs (*'saurs*) or volcanoes (*'canoes*).

He had several friends now, all of whom seemed possessed by superheroes, and the family's diary began to revolve around Dylan's 'playdates'. The friend he cherished most had a large garden, where three of them charged around, shrieking, doing Ninja kicks and ambushing each other. But Dylan always seemed slightly calmer after an afternoon at Brett's.

And then, suddenly, he was old enough for school – only a few months after his fourth birthday! As she dressed her little boy in school uniform for his first day, Mandy's heart nearly overflowed with love. He seemed so small and vulnerable, despite all the bravado and Shrek impressions. She'd heard the teacher was quite a stickler, and wished she'd persevered in teaching him to use a knife and fork, dressing himself and everything. And she was worried about the nursery head's final report: '*Dylan is a cheerful and active little boy, but still very immature. He can sometimes be aggressive. He enjoys outdoor activities and the construction area, but has so far shown little interest in small-scale motor tasks, literacy or numeracy.*'

Mandy found herself gulping back tears. Somehow she didn't think that dressing Dylan in a smart new uniform would make him show more interest in small-scale motor tasks. All he wanted to do was run …

Chapter 5

UNWILLINGLY TO SCHOOL

Why literacy is vital to boys' all-round
development ... but starting
too early does more harm than good

A few years ago the journal *Nature* published a report about chimpanzees passing on cultural knowledge to their young. It described how adult chimps show the younger generation how to harvest termites, a useful source of protein if there's nothing better to eat. They select a strong reed, insert it into the termite mound, wiggle it around, then carefully withdraw it – and lo! a termite lollipop.

The little girl chimps sit around watching this procedure with rapt concentration, and are soon selecting reeds for themselves, trying to copy the routine. The little boy chimps watch for a while, then lose interest and run off to play-fight, play-hunt, and scramble about in the trees. All is as one would expect according to their biologically ordained gender roles.

However, adults go termite-harvesting many times over the days and weeks, and the boy chimps therefore have plenty of opportunities to come back and watch over again. Eventually, they too start selecting reeds and learning to make termite lollies. It takes boy chimps roughly twice as long as girls to learn the skill, and they interrupt what they're doing four times as often. Interestingly, in an experiment carried out for a TV programme at the end of the 1990s, two groups of six-year-old human children (one of boys, one of girls) were given a task to complete with plasticine. It took the boys twice as long as the girls, and they interrupted what they were doing four times as often.

Passing on the culture

Like chimps, humans are born programmed to learn essential survival skills naturally, partly through play and partly through watching their adult carers. In the earliest stages, the skills children need to learn tend to be personal and domestic ones related to feeding, dressing and hygiene, and boys – with their yearning for the wide open spaces – usually take longer to learn them than girls, and therefore attract more maternal indulgence. But as time goes on the skills to be learned become more 'work-related'. Most children, in most times and places, have been needed as soon as possible to help their families or communities survive, contributing in whatever ways they could: fetching and carrying, labouring in the fields, tending the beasts and so on. Just like the chimps, adults would demonstrate how to perform the task and gradually the children would learn it. But, boys being boys, their drive to explore and play didn't go away, and parents have always struggled to keep them on task.

In his book *Naughty Boys*, psychologist Sami Timimi describes boys' transition from indulged infants to lowly work-horses across a range of cultures. The general worldwide wisdom seems to be that 'the mother's years', during which boys' boyishness has been generally indulged, covers the period up to about six or seven years of age, and 'the father's years' cover the next six or seven. Interestingly, scientists investigating human consciousness suggest that six or seven is the age at which children become able consciously to control their thoughts. Before this, they're ruled largely by emotion, so would need the input of an E-type thinking specialist. It's only once the capacity for reasoned thought is developed that they're ready for more formal instruction.

In cultures with a written language, some boys have always

escaped an early introduction to hard physical labour. Their society needed them to learn reading, writing and other lessons their parents couldn't teach, so they went to school instead. And as humanity acquired ever more cultural capital to be passed through the generations, more and more children needed at least a basic level of education. Again, the transition from playful child to obedient student was seen as happening around the age of seven. Moslem friends have told me that the prophet Mohammed summed up the change in these words: '*The first seven years are for play; the second seven are for discipline and education*'. (See also page 284.)

It is now generally accepted across the developed world that universal education (not only for boys, but for girls) is an essential element of civilised society. The fact that UK authorities provide 12 years of state education (soon to rise to 14) indicates how complex our technological culture has become. Nevertheless, the foundation stone on which most learning is still built is literacy – and in most countries, formal literacy teaching begins, as work used to do, around the age of six or seven.

Why literacy matters

Even in a multimedia world, day-to-day survival depends upon basic reading and writing skills, and for a boy to make any progress in the educational system (and to take up almost any career) he'll need a high level of fluency in both reading and writing. The visual media can be a powerful educative force, but so far it has proved far less effective than the written word, especially for conveying complex abstract ideas. This is probably because human beings have spent countless millennia honing their capacity to pass on knowledge through language. So, while multimedia educational techniques will undoubtedly rival literacy as the centuries go by, the spoken and written word are likely to stay the main way of passing on human culture for the foreseeable future.

There are, however, other reasons why literacy matters, which may be of particular significance for boys. The first is that the process of learning to read and write – the 'getting of literacy' – helps human beings become better thinkers. Reading is an enormously complex process, involving simultaneous activity in a vast number of different regions of the brain. Interconnectivity between regions enhances brain power, and learning to read increases interconnectivity so much that neuroscientists talk about it 'changing the architecture of the brain' (see also Chapter 8).

There are particular changes in the prefrontal cortex – the area behind the forehead that controls higher intellectual functions. The net effect of all this architectural change is to make human beings more rational, and thus more civilised. It is probably no coincidence that a written language is one of the hallmarks of a civilisation and that the spread of democracy has always been preceded by the spread of literacy.

Rational thought may compensate, to some extent, for boys' initial lack of interest in E-type thinking. Even though they don't naturally 'see' other people's point of view they may be helped to understand it intellectually through reasoned explanation. In the Victorian children's book *The Water Babies*, Mrs Doasyouwouldbedoneby convinces the hero, Tom, of the importance of treating other people as he'd like to be treated himself. Through reasoned argument, even an extreme S-type thinker can be helped to recognise the social advantages of taking other people's views into account.

However, reading may offer boys a way to develop 'people skills' too. There seems to be a deep human need for stories which is extremely strong in children (see 'The foundations of literacy', overleaf), and which reading can feed. Reading a story is very different from watching one on TV, because the reader becomes actively involved in decoding the author's words and mentally recreating his meaning. So while viewers are passive recipients of the story unfolding before them, readers are active participants, helping to make the story happen inside their own heads. In this way, readers lock minds with an author or characters in a story, engaging personally with their motivations and feelings. A boy who becomes a committed reader can thus learn to connect with other minds.

Last but by no means least for boys, learning to read and write has a huge knock-on effect on language skills, which research shows come less easily to males than females. Books introduce them to new, more sophisticated vocabulary, and also to more complex sentence structures. Before learning to read many boys have little idea of how to construct a 'literate' sentence. The spoken language they pick up naturally tends to be rather vague and disjointed – speakers bat odd words and phrases back and forth to make sense between them, and since they're usually in the same place they don't need to be particularly explicit.

Written language, on the other hand, is produced for an unknown, unseen audience, so it has to be clear and carefully crafted. The boy who learns to read, and then reads widely, gradually absorbs written language patterns and can start to use them himself. This too increases his powers of reason and understanding: the wider his access to language, the better he'll be able to explore and express his own ideas and communicate socially with others.

The foundations of literacy

Unfortunately, however, learning to read doesn't come naturally. Like termite-harvesting for chimps, the skills involved have to be passed on to each new generation. These skills are built on other human abilities that *do* come naturally to most children – as long as they're sufficiently well nurtured. So the ease with which a boy learns to read and write depends both on his innate talents and his early experiences.

For instance, he has to be able to talk. You can't make sense of written language until you have a reasonable command of spoken language. This is a natural human talent but, as we saw in Chapter 3, it has to be nurtured by interactive engagements with adults. As described in Chapter 4, it can be further developed through creative, social play with other children. Research in English preschools has found that one of the best ways to prepare children for a successful school career is 'sustained shared thinking', when children and/or adults talk together about a shared experience.

Literacy skills also depend on a boy's ability to listen. This doesn't just mean attending to what other people say, although that's very important in a classroom. It means being able to listen discriminatively, so as to hear the individual sounds that make up a word. You can't read and write the word 'dog' unless you can hear the three speech sounds /d/, /o/ and /g/ and link them to alphabet letters on a page.

As described in Chapter 2 ('Dance to the music of time'), discriminative listening starts in the cradle, and is nurtured through songs, nursery rhymes and baby talk. As children grow, their own playground language (rhymes, songs, chants, jeers and jingles) also tends to emphasise speech sounds through rhythm and rhyme. If these early experiences are lacking, school lessons in phonics may be less than effective.

Reading and writing also involves control of physical behaviour. To read a boy has to keep his head and body still while tracking along a line of print with his eyes. Writing requires finely judged control of the wrist and fingers, and good hand–eye co-ordination. As prototype hunters, programmed for an active outdoor life, boys are not naturally fitted to such small-scale activities. Most of them need plenty of opportunities for large-scale active play, preferably outdoors, to hone bodily control before settling down to fiddly desk work.

Even just sitting still can be a problem. According to experts in physical development, keeping still is one of the most difficult physical skills. It depends on a mature sense of balance and awareness of the position of one's body in space. A movement specialist at a conference I attended pointed out that teachers often ask children to 'find a space on the floor and sit in it'. While little girls usually do this with ease, little boys tend instead to sprawl full-length on the ground, to lean up against a wall or piece of furniture or, very frequently, to sit on each other. Teachers assume they're being naughty but if physical control is not fully developed, the boys may actually feel more secure when their body's in contact with another surface. Without contact, they feel unbalanced and unsupported in space.

When the surface a boy chooses to make contact with is another boy, he's probably also working on his social skills – as seen in Chapter 4, boys bond with each other through physical rough-housing and play. To help them adopt the more civilised social behaviour needed in a classroom, most need careful training. This can be provided through structured play, simple games or other activities that have been used since time immemorial to socialise young children: moving to music, singing and listening to stories.

Tuning the mind

Human brains are hardwired to respond to music, just as they're programmed to respond to language – indeed, the two instincts are probably related. Scientists are only just beginning to investigate the 'music instinct', but it may have much to offer in terms of preparing children for formal learning. For instance, moving together to music, in predetermined ways, can help boys develop bodily control while working alongside and together with others. Men have used music in this way through the ages, from sea-shanties and other working songs that helped labourers co-ordinate their movement, to war dances, marching tunes and the rhythmic chants soldiers use to keep in step.

When dancing was an important part of community life, children soon learned how to move to music at an early age by copying the adults. They practised it too through play: many traditional children's games involved songs and simple dance steps, such as 'Here we go round the mulberry bush' or 'The good ship sails through the alley-alley-o'. The musical accompaniment for these games was provided by the instrument most readily available: the human voice. But in the modern world, we no longer have to make our own music. Professional renditions are readily available in most homes, via CDs, iPods, TV and radio.

So just as we've become sporting spectators rather than active players, we've stopped singing and dancing for ourselves, and instead merely listen to expert singers or watch expert dancers. With few real adult models, children no longer sing as naturally as they once did, and though they love to move to music they tend to dance alone, improvising their own steps rather than moving as a group steered by convention.

But even though modern adults now delegate musical activities to experts, music continues to be a powerful vehicle for human emotion. On the few occasions where people still do sing and move together (such as swaying to a football anthem, singing a protest song as they march, or happy-clapping a gospel hymn) the activity draws them together socially and emotionally. When I helped run an early years pre-reading project, we found in classes that opened with a 15-minute singsong (including action songs), children settled much more readily into the rest of the day's routine.

Song is also helpful for training another important skill: memory. To read, children must hold sequences of sounds and words in their heads – indeed, 'auditory memory' underpins almost all learning. The melody and rhythm of songs help words stick in the mind. This is why the church has always placed great store by psalms and hymns, and why generations of teachers have taught their classes to sing the times tables. The more boys sing familiar songs and exercise auditory memory, the stronger this 'mental muscle' is likely to become. I once asked a Finnish kindergarten teacher why she threaded so many musical activities throughout her class's day – action songs, little dances, musical accompaniments to activities and so on. 'Music,' she replied, '*trains the mind to pattern and the ear to sound*.'

Yet in UK preschools in recent years, there's often little time for music and song. Particularly in England, where nursery staff must chase innumerable learning objectives, it's often seen as a distraction from the important business of preparing children for literacy and numeracy. In fact, I suspect that singing, dancing and moving to music may be the very best preparation we could provide.

Worlds of words

Another technique for training children's minds and ears, popular through the ages but no longer common in a multimedia world, is storytelling. It's long been accepted that the ancient fairy tales were used to pass on practical and moral lessons to the young, including knowledge about the workings of the world and the human mind. But while many parents now accept it's important to read to their children from an early age, the art of telling a story has almost disappeared. Sharing storybooks with children is indeed an excellent introduction to the pleasures of reading and the conventions of literacy, but by going straight to the printed word today's parents and teachers miss natural opportunities to teach language, listening and attention skills.

A storyteller (like a mother engaged in the dance of communication) keeps the audience's attention through eye contact, facial expression and body language – and even eye-resistant little boys can be persuaded to attend to these features by the lure of a story. They also have to listen carefully to follow the plot (no pictures to focus on as in a TV programme or book), thus learning unconsciously to attend to the spoken word. And the repetitive patterned language of oral storytelling, a blend of simple speech and rhythmic song-like cadences, can be almost as memorable as music.

A storytelling project run by literacy specialist Pie Corbett in many UK schools has shown how even preschool children can, with frequent repetition and support from pictures and action cues, learn to recite many stories by heart. The aim is to build up children's store of literate vocabulary and language structures orally, well before they are taught to write. Before beginning the project, Corbett asks teachers to send him one high-achieving, one average and one below-average pupil from the class, whom he invites to tell a story into a tape recorder. Almost inevitably, the above-average child retells a simple fairy story, while the others look blank. 'I've come to the conclusion,' says Corbett, 'that the reason they're above average is that someone's been telling them stories, over and over again.'

The memorable, patterned language of story, which is also used in good children's picture books, may help boys develop their own powers of narrative. An important stage in language development is the 'running commentary' children often give while concentrating on their play ('The car's going up the road, and over the hill, and down here and round here... and now the monster's chasing it... and it goes up here and round there... '). Girls tend to be better at this than boys, as they usually engage in more small-scale play and like talking to their toys. The Russian psychologist Vygotsky suggested that these playtime monologues are a way of thinking out loud. As children grow older, the monologues gradually become internalised as thought processes (as he points out, adults, when faced with a challenging task, often find themselves regressing and 'talking it through'). So the more skilful a child is at spoken narrative, the better his adult thought processes are likely to be.

The better also will be his deep inner confidence to control and access words. Although language is a human instinct, boys need an enormous amount of early input from adults and frequent opportunities for practice before they achieve a reasonable degree of fluency. And since the artificial skills of reading and writing are built on their natural competence in speaking and listening, singing and storytelling are important precursors of literacy.

Since all these foundations of literacy and learning have always been laid in early childhood, they've been taken entirely for granted. It's only when they no longer happen naturally through children's daily interaction with adults and other children – through lullabies, nursery rhymes, playground songs and bedtime stories – that their loss is felt. Some lucky boys, endowed by nature and nurture with good memory, language and listening skills, still sail through the early stages of learning to read. But in an increasingly impersonal, institutionalised, screen-based world, more and more British children are embarking on the most important educational lessons of their lives without a sound foundation.

Too much too soon

In fact, learning to read seems to be particularly difficult in the UK and USA, as politicians have discovered when they've poured millions of pounds into the enterprise, to little noticeable effect. Their supporters claim this is because English is a complex language with a fiendish spelling system. But most specialists in early education and a growing number of specialists in literacy now believe it's because we expect children to read and write far too early. For boys especially – who've been lagging behind girls developmentally since their time in the womb and by this time can be as much as a year behind in general maturity – this can mean starting their educational career at a serious disadvantage. A 2007 government report noted a fairly stable 10% gap in achievement between boys and girls, starting in the preschool years and continuing throughout their school careers.

In most European countries, formal schooling begins at six or seven, the age when most boys seem ready to settle down and cope with formal work. Until then all children follow a play-based 'kindergarten curriculum', usually from the age of three. This is based on a mixture of children's own self-chosen play and teacher-led activities to develop the listening, language, attention and social skills described in previous sections. There's great emphasis on playing outdoors, and on learning activities that come naturally to small children – stories and drama, music and song, painting and modelling – and no child is forced to pick up a book or pencil unless they want to.

In the UK, however, children have historically started school at five. There's no sound educational reason for this early starting age – Victorian politicians anxious to get poor children off the streets and into the new state elementary schools just plucked the figure out of the air. There's an apocryphal story that in the late 1860s Prussia settled on six as a starting age, and with true British competitive spirit we decided to round up our children a year earlier and get a head start.

In the last 15 or so years, the 'head start' theory has pushed the formal approach down to four- and even three-year-olds. In the middle 1990s, playgroups, set up by parents so that their little children could play together, were told by Ofsted (the Office for Standards in Education) that they should introduce maths and literacy activities – within a few years, they'd changed their name to 'preschools'. Meanwhile, a 'bums on seats' funding policy in primary schools meant head teachers began luring children into their reception classes as young as possible. 'Early learning goals' published in 2000 aimed to have these tiny children reading simple texts and writing in sentences (using punctuation!) by the end of the year, so preschools, nurseries and even childminders have since felt obliged to crack on with these formal skills as early as possible.

Both Wales and Northern Ireland have recognised the madness of this 'too much too soon' approach and have reformed their systems to be more in line with the rest of Europe. The Scottish government too increasingly bases advice to early years classes on successful European models. But the English government refused to relax its early emphasis on literacy skills and in 2008 enshrined these 'early learning goals' in law. An outcry by experts and parents forced them to 'review' the two most ridiculous goals (including the one about punctuation) but even so many English children still start formal reading tuition two years before everyone else. When you're only four, that's the equivalent of half your life span.

The drive for too much too soon seems to be peculiarly Anglo-Saxon, since the USA, where formal education used to begin at six, has in recent years also pushed it down into the kindergarten. This is the result of legislation designed to ensure 'No Child Left Behind', but which, according to teachers, is leaving behind the very children it aimed to help. In fact, research consistently indicates that an early start confers no long-term advantage, and may be damaging. One study in Philadelphia found that children who'd spent their early years in a rigidly academic nursery were no further ahead by age seven or eight than children from play-based ones – they were, however, more anxious and less creative. Even more worryingly, a long-term study from the 1960s found that children from poorer homes taught in formal kindergartens grew up to have more problems with personal relationships and more trouble holding down a job than those who'd been allowed to play. They were also more likely to have been in trouble with the law.

Nor does an early start seem to raise a country's educational standards. In international comparisons of school achievement, European countries with play-based kindergarten provision consistently out-perform the UK and USA. Both Finland, which tends to top the league in literacy, and Hungary, which is particularly strong in numeracy, delay formal teaching till children are seven. This doesn't mean they hold them back – books and writing materials are available, any child who shows an interest in reading or writing is encouraged and supported, and from the age of six there are daily oral language and maths lessons. But the main emphasis in these early years is on physical, emotional, linguistic and social development through the tried and tested methods of music, story, drama, art and creative play.

When Ofsted visited Finland and Denmark in 2004, it commented on the difference between six-year-olds there and in England. The Nordic children's attention spans were longer, their boredom threshold higher and their teachers were not constantly distracted from their work by behaviour management. On the other hand, in the last few years, the behaviour of four- and five-year-olds in England has become an ever greater problem, to the extent that in 2006 60 were actually expelled from school. All of them were boys.

Too clever too soon?

There's no doubt that many children – far more girls than boys – do learn to read well before the age of six. However, this usually says much more about their home background than their schools' teaching policy. They tend to come from educated homes where parents are keen that their offspring should want to read and therefore usually share books from an early age, along with plenty of chat about the stories and characters. This means these children arrive at school with good language and attention skills, enjoy stories and relate well to the adults in their lives. If they're also gifted S-type thinkers – naturally skilled at what reading specialist Dame Marie Clay called 'the patterning of complex behaviour' – they often just 'see' how print works and start reading fairly effortlessly.

Children are, on the whole, getting 'cleverer'. Ever since IQ tests were first devised early in the 20th century, average scores have increased steadily at around three IQ points per decade – this means most of us are about as third as 'bright' again as our counterparts in the years after the First World War. The skills IQ measures are problem-solving, abstract reasoning, pattern recognition and spatial skills – in short, S-type thinking – and analysts reckon the improvement, known as the Flynn Effect, is because the type of mental activity encouraged by a fast-moving, urban, increasingly screen-dominated existence develops these skills.

So a good S-type thinker who's had plenty of exposure to language and books may well start reading earlier. The politicians who now run education are all examples of such 'lucky children' – high-functioning S-brainers who did very well in the education system – and therefore value S-type gifts. But in an S-driven world, they seem unable to 'see' how E-type nurture is necessary to release these gifts. Hence their conviction for many years that putting very young children into cheap institutionalised childcare can somehow substitute for the experience of being brought up in a loving, educated family.

Politicians' attachment to S-type skills and values has now locked the English education system into a competitive 'winners and losers' culture predicated on tests, targets and an early start. Not unnaturally, the parents of those lucky children who pick up reading skills early want schools to build on this head start, rather than holding them back waiting for the rest of the class to catch up. And since successful educated parents are also politically influential, their opinions fuel the system. Thus the widening gap between rich and poor is now fed by education – the very force that should be narrowing it. Too early a start damages the chances of success for children who aren't ready for formal work. So early failure at school locks them into poverty not only in economic terms, but in richness of aspiration, confidence and social expectations (see Chapter 10).

This is the very reason that the other European countries mentioned earlier don't emphasise literacy skills until they reckon most children can learn them with relative ease. They see the overall good of society as more important than accelerating the academic achievement of a select few. Developing all children's self-belief, confidence and social skills during the kindergarten stage is the best way to ensure society's long-term health.

Not only would better foundations for every child's literacy level the academic playing field, but it would give precocious readers the chance to play for a little longer, with all the benefits that brings for physical, emotional and social education. Their home background may ensure they get on well with adults, but for well-rounded social and emotional development they also need time to play and socialise with other children. In the long run, the most successful learners are those who are not only bright but balanced. So concentrating on *all* children's *all-round* development (emotional resilience, social competence, physical fitness and intellectual curiosity) is the best way for our society to recalibrate an S/E-type balance currently running out of control (see also Chapter 10).

Can't read, won't read?

If children are inadequately prepared to learn and get along together, they're prime candidates for educational and behavioural problems. Ironically, high-functioning S-type thinkers can suffer as much as their less 'gifted' classmates.

For instance, if a boy's social, emotional or physical development hasn't kept pace with his systemising capacity, he may have difficulty relating to other children or attending to the teacher. When he can't do as he's told, he becomes frustrated and starts applying his analytical skills in ways that hinder rather than help make progress. And when their son starts playing up or failing to learn, articulate and aspirational parents want to know why. Over the last 50 years or so, the educational establishment has found labels for their children's failure.

The first widely recognised developmental condition was dyslexia. When I was teaching in the early 1980s, it was dismissed by most educationists as an excuse for poor teaching or parental paranoia, but it's now widely accepted that most UK children diagnosed with dyslexia have problems discriminating language sounds. These problems may be the result of nature (some sort of neurological malfunction), nurture (not enough language and song in their first few years – see page 63) or a mixture of both. A bright child who makes no sense of phonic decoding often covers his problems with inspired guessing in the early stages of reading, and once he's committed to a guessing strategy, it can be very difficult to help him slow down his brain and learn, painstakingly, to decode.

After mountains of research on dyslexia, experts are still divided on the best ways to help children overcome it. It's also clear that many of its 'symptoms' overlap with those of other developmental conditions, and usually boil down to problems with concentration (discussed in more detail in Chapter 8). One educational psychologist I interviewed, whose job it is to discover the reasons behind Special Educational Needs said: *'Boys? Well, at the moment we're driving the poor little devils towards either ADHD or Asperger Syndrome, depending on their home background and psychological makeup.'*

She wasn't denying that these two developmental conditions (like reading difficulties, with which both are often associated) have a neurological basis, that some boys are predisposed to them, or that in some cases this predisposition is so great that little can be done to help. Her point was that modern lifestyles, including our early-start policy at school, may well be making many boys' problems much worse. And that maybe in some cases, the 'symptoms' of a developmental disorder are entirely the result of environment and experiences. In the five years since she uttered those words, I've repeated them to hundreds of teachers, psychologists and others working in the field of special needs. The responses – ranging from wry smiles to solemn faces and nodding heads – are not cheering.

It is undoubtedly a step forward that schools and society try to understand children's educational problems rather than merely labelling them 'backward' and writing them off. But it's also possible that our new scientific labels can help make things worse for some children. ADHD, dyslexia, dyspraxia and Asperger Syndrome are labels for the way children behave when a neurological predisposition is triggered – or not triggered – by their experiences. But once a boy finds himself failing socially or educationally, emotional problems are added to the mix, and whatever label we attach to his Special Educational Need, these can make it progressively harder to address the underlying causes.

The very fact that he *has* a label can propel a boy in a particular direction. Many of the boys I taught in the days before 'Special Educational Needs' existed might qualify for one of these developmental conditions today. But in a less toxic, technological age, they were just 'boys' – naughty boys, perhaps, or wayward, reserved, awkward, shy or clumsy boys. 'He's a little professor type,' I remember saying about one lad who'd definitely be up for Asperger Syndrome today. They often had their problems, both in class and in the playground, and I know my Asperger candidate struggled socially – but we nevertheless thought of them, as they thought of themselves, within the range of 'normal'... and this helped them to *be* normal for much of the time. They may not have thrived in class, but at weekends, playtime and around the edges of the school day they had opportunities to deal with their differences through loosely supervised outdoor play with other children – and with luck to find a niche in the band of brothers. We called it 'knocking the corners off', and it wasn't always easy for them – but then, it isn't easy for Special Needs children today.

In the modern world, boys diagnosed with ADHD are often kept under constant adult supervision. Like zoo animals prowling in their cages or primates denied the chance to play-fight, they may become steadily less socially adept and even more inclined to antisocial behaviour. Similarly, an Asperger boy protected from a very early age from all social engagement with his own peer group doesn't get the chance to learn any social ropes through experience. Adults shielding him from slight pain in the infant years – by, for instance, letting him cultivate an isolated 'academic' image from a very early age rather than being sent out to play with the other boys – could well be sentencing him to far greater pain in the future.

This is surely a case where attempting prevention is better than attempting (and so far failing to find) a cure. Delaying the start of formal education to six, or preferably seven, and substituting an excellent kindergarten curriculum of the type found in successful European countries, would not only lead to greater social cohesion but could save many boys from a lifetime of Special Educational Needs.

Since time immemorial, human beings have let children socialise each other through play during the first six years or so of their lives. They've also sung songs and told stories to pass on their culture, the tunes of their language, and the words youngsters needed to construct thoughtful narratives and to explore and express their ideas. They've used music and movement to draw children into their community, to attune their minds to the patterns of social interaction and their ears to sound. These were the foundations upon which written language was eventually constructed, so that culture could henceforth be transmitted across time and space. They're also the foundations upon which every human child builds literacy skills – particularly important for boys who need more help with social patterning, auditory tuning and language learning than girls.

However, just as adults through the centuries have failed to value free-flow play, sophisticated 21st century adults have lost sight of the importance of music, movement, stories and song in children's learning. Instead, we try to rush them straight into reading and writing, and to fast-forward them into our technological culture. But without the essential nurture that triggers neurological connections, children's brains don't develop naturally. When we try to skip or accelerate stages in development, we risk causing long-term damage to development.

Until they're old enough to control their own thought processes, little boys need time to mature, respect for their natural play, and help to acquire the social and linguistic capital of our culture. It's a gradual process, and teachers around the world have found that most boys aren't ready to settle to formal learning till they're six or seven. So patience is of the essence. We could learn a lot from chimpanzees.

Chapter summary

This chapter describes how successful learning of literacy is built on other skills – discriminative listening, spoken language and the conscious control of physical behaviour. All of these are naturally developed through social play, storytelling, music, dance, song and – especially for boys – outdoor activity. It looks at the failure, particularly for boys, of current early start policies in the UK and USA, and compares them with the education systems of other European countries that do not start formal education until six or seven. It suggests that early start policies are the result of politicians' attachment to S-type skills and values, and that education is widening, not reducing, the gap between rich and poor. It also proposes that current policies may be increasing (perhaps in some cases creating) Special Educational Needs.

Helping boys go willingly to school

What can parents do?

- Don't be impatient for your son to start formal education. Long experience in many countries has shown that six or seven is quite soon enough to worry about the 3Rs.
  - If he shows an interest in reading, writing and/or doing sums before that, encourage him but don't push – a leisurely start

at his own pace is most likely to pay dividends.

- If he doesn't show an interest, don't worry – it's perfectly normal for boys to take longer getting to grips with formal work, and pushing him before he's ready can do more harm than good.

● Look for a school that concentrates on laying secure foundations for learning up to the age of six or seven – that means plenty of outdoor activity, play-based learning, music, song, stories, art and drama. Phonics and basic number skills can be adequately covered through fun activities, games, songs and rhymes. Although state schools are required to follow national curricular guidelines (and in England in recent years these have been 'aspirational'), the best – like Montessori and Steiner schools in the independent sector – find ways to avoid formal teaching in the early years. See the *Too Much Too Soon* video on YouTube:
http://www.youtube.com/watch?v=nmheYOoZ72o

● Remember that boys develop more slowly than girls, especially in terms of the skills needed for formal school-based learning. For successful long-term development, the most important lessons for your son in the first few years are in:
  - how to get along with the other children
  - how to fit into institutional life
  - how to get on with teachers and enjoy school.

● He's designed by nature to enjoy playing and learning through play for his first seven years, and robbing him of these childhood experiences isn't good for his developing brain.

● He's also born to run! All the advice in the previous chapter still holds good. Look for a school that encourages outdoor activities and has plenty of room for unstructured, creative play.

● Around the edges of the school day your son will still need plenty of LOVE, LANGUAGE, DISCIPLINE and PLAY. If you can't be around to deliver these yourself, make sure there's someone else who knows and cares about him to take your place. A good childminder is ideal, and if it's the same one who's looked after him previously, even better.

- To achieve the final must-have of LITERACY, you or your surrogate can help the school by doing the following:
  - Carry on singing songs and rhymes. By now he'll probably enjoy playground rhymes and so on. A favourite with boys I know is this version of Postman Pat:

    Postman Pat, Postman Pat
    Postman Pat ran over his cat.
    Postman Pat was crying
    All the guts were flying –
    Never seen a cat as flat as that

  - Keep on reading favourite picture books, even if by now you feel vaguely ill with all the repetition. Encourage him to join in with repeated lines, to finish off sentences, and – once he knows the story really well – to join in and recite it with you.
  - Don't worry about phonics – he'll get plenty of that at school, and doing extra at home isn't going to make him warm to reading.
  - If you're determined to do more to help at home, read *Flying Start to Literacy* by Ros Bayley and Lynn Broadbent (Network Continuum).

- Continue to limit screen-based activity (see Chapter 8: Thought control and Digital natives, digital learners?) and to monitor and mediate its use. If your son complains that other children in his class have a TV in their bedroom, explain that you love him too much to give him one:
  - there's scientific evidence that it's very bad for him
  - anyway, you enjoy his company and don't want him going off to his room when he can watch with you.

- If your son is unlucky enough to be diagnosed with a 'learning difficulty', consider whether it might be related to
  - diet (see www.fabresearch.org)
  - sleep (see www.behavior-consultant.com/discuss-sleephygiene)
  - lack of outdoor exercise and play (see Chapters 3 and 5)
  - language problems (see www.talkingpoint.org.uk).

What can the rest of us do?

- A community can't hand over total responsibility for its children to schools any more than it can expect parents to bring them up without support. Schools need neighbours who are tolerant about children's play and other noisy activities. And most schools are deeply grateful for community involvement, such as volunteers for hearing reading and supervising break-times.
- Community opinion-formers can also help change the 'too much too soon' culture (see the YouTube film listed on page 158) by accepting that small children need to play before they settle down to learn. By promoting – and demonstrating – a generally more relaxed attitude to childhood, headteachers, religious leaders, health workers and other professionals can spread the message that adult anxieties should not be visited on little children.
- While schools are expected to follow national curricular guidelines, it's possible to cover literacy targets without requiring children to engage in inappropriate formal work. Creative nursery practitioners and teachers can find ways of ticking government boxes without pushing little boys to achieve beyond their physical, emotional and cognitive

potential (see *The Foundations of Literacy* by Sue Palmer and Ros Bayley [Network Continuum] and *The Bumper Book of Storytelling into Writing at Key Stage* 1 by Pie Corbett [Clown Publishing]).

What can politicians do?

- Urgently review policy for the early years of schooling. There have been welcome moves around the UK – less so in England than elsewhere – in recent years towards a genuinely more play-based curriculum, but we still concentrate far too much on literacy and numeracy skills without paying sufficient attention to the natural foundations on which they are built.

- Successful European systems take account of the realities and subtleties of child development, provide an appropriate kindergarten stage, and then work upwards, building their curriculum on secure foundations. But English education has traditionally taken a top-down approach: planning the curriculum on the basis of where we want children to be by the end of primary school and 'topping down'. The 'Foundation Stage' was put in at the end as an afterthought.

- Don't assume – as most politicians seem to – that parents would be opposed to reform, and somehow terrified that their children would be 'left behind'. Welsh teachers tell me that, throughout their country's abandonment of a tests and targets primary agenda and the institution of a Nordic-style foundation phase, parents have been highly supportive. Certainly, all the parents I meet are far more concerned by the effects of increasing pressure on their children than they are about the PISA league tables.

- If the UK genuinely wants to create a level playing field for its children, early years education is the obvious starting place (see Chapter 10).

Chapter 6

BATTERY-REARED BOYS

How boys' freedom is increasingly constrained ... and why a 'cotton-wool culture' damages us all

'What do you like about being a 21st century boy?' I asked. 'Oh, it's great,' came the reply. 'I can sit in my room and watch TV or play computer games and if I'm hungry I text my mum and she brings me up a pizza!'

You'll probably be relieved to know that some of the other ten-year-old boys in the group looked as horrified as I at that response. But, talking to boys around the country, I found a remarkable number who spend most of their leisure time cooped up indoors or being ferried between organised clubs and activities. Official researchers, such as those advising the Cambridge Report into *Children, their World, their Education* and the Good Childhood Inquiry, both published in 2008, have found the same: children's leisure time today is increasingly under tight adult control.

It's all a long way from the world of *Huckleberry Finn* and *Just William*. Within a generation, the traditional freedom to roam, explore and learn from first-hand experience of their world has for many boys all but disappeared. Instead, they're closeted away in their bedrooms, exploring the virtual world of screen-based entertainment.

Out to play

In his book *The Invention of Childhood*, social historian Hugh Cunningham describes children's lives from the Middle Ages to the present day, and concludes that '*there has probably been no generation of parents that has been quite so constantly concerned for their children ... as our own*'. This concern is perhaps most startlingly evident in adults' attitudes to children playing outdoors – and out of sight of the adults. For boys, this has traditionally involved roaming the local area, 'messing about' with one's mates and engaging now and then in what most adults would consider risky behaviour. Even though their activities often proved irritating to the adult world (and occasionally had serious, or even tragic consequences), the usual parental tactic was crossed fingers and a blind eye. As Kyle once put it in *South Park*: '*You can go anywhere and do anything so long as Mom doesn't know where you are and what you're doing.*'

Only half a century ago, this freedom of movement began very early. My own memories, and those of contemporaries who grew up in the 1950s, are that even in the inner city children were allowed to play out well before school age. Older sisters or other local girls looked after little lads until they were old enough to join in the boys' games. Once a boy joined the male tribe, at perhaps four or five, there was a strong hierarchical structure based on age, so all little boys had experience of being menial members of the tribe, and all older boys (whether alpha males or not) experienced the joys of being looked up to, and shared the onus of responsibility. By the time they reached double figures, most had achieved a degree of independence unimaginable to boys today.

In the early 1970s, perhaps as a result of increases in traffic, small children were more likely to be kept under close adult supervision, but even then researchers recorded that 80% of seven- and eight-year-old children still made their way to school unsupervised. They seem to have had similar freedom to play out and about – the average nine-year-old was free to wander around 900 yards, a ten-minute walk from home. The journalist Andrew Collins' childhood experiences, recounted in his book *Where Did It All Go Right?* about growing up in the 1970s, were very much in this Huck Finn/William Brown tradition – 'up trees, in water, or just "down the field", snatching whatever bit of earthy nature I could among the suburban seepage of Northampton'. Twenty years later, however, nine-year-olds' freedom to roam had been reduced to about 300 yards. And by 2007, most parents put the boundary just outside the front gate – interpreted by the press as a 'no minute walk'. When the Good Childhood enquiry asked parents what age they felt children should be allowed out alone, a significant proportion settled on 14.

This remarkable change in children's freedom over the course of 30 years is usually put down to parental worries about safety, particularly road safety and 'stranger danger'. Their fears seem also to have been passed on to the children themselves, since Hugh Cunningham reports a survey of ten-year-olds who believed the most important aspect of their upbringing was 'staying safe'. As he points out, 'It is difficult to imagine that this would have been the highest priority for any previous generation of children.' It's also difficult to understand how this level of fear has taken such sudden and remarkable hold.

From a rational perspective, it makes much more sense for parents to confront 21st century fears and tackle them, rather than hiding their offspring away. Teaching one's child to survive environmental hazards – from wolves and marauding invaders to bombs and flying bullets – has always been an important element of parental responsibility. In today's urban landscape, the major source of danger is probably traffic, so the responsible course of action is to help children grow up city-streetwise, by demonstrating and teaching road safety procedures from a very early age.

At the same time, government could help by ensuring residential areas are safe for children to play out. Many parts of

Europe have 'home zones', where a combination of careful town planning and traffic-calming measures are an accepted part of public policy. However, the fears that keep children indoors do not appear to be entirely rational, as the 'stranger danger' phenomenon illustrates. Compared with other risks, the possibility of a child of under 14 being attacked or abducted by a stranger is extremely small, and until around 25 years ago warnings and advice were generally considered enough protection. According to official statistics there has been no increase in 'stranger danger' crimes over those 25 years, but parents' *perceptions* of the danger have greatly increased. They now believe the chances of their children being abducted are so high that the only way to protect them is to keep them hidden away.

This may in itself be partly due to our screen-based lifestyle. Whenever a tragic event of this kind occurs, blanket media coverage ensures that vivid and emotionally disturbing images are blasted into our homes 24 hours a day. Neuroscientists have shown that constant emotional arousal of this kind can make people feel personally threatened – television viewers who repeatedly watched video images of the Twin Towers disaster began to show post-traumatic stress symptoms as if they had actually been there themselves. In over-protecting their children, parents are reacting as though the dangers they see on-screen are just outside their front door.

Cotton-wool kids

Excessive concern for children's safety is now widespread, and has merged seamlessly with a 'health and safety' culture to affect all aspects of childhood. Even supervised play is now circumscribed in ways that would have been inconceivable only a generation ago. Some schools, for instance, have banned traditional children's games, such as conkers, kiss-chase and tag, on safety grounds and in 2006 half of all primary schools in one county of Ireland actually forbade children to run about in the playground. Stringent safety regulations have also been applied to play equipment in public parks, resulting in the removal of many popular items. After a campaign in the 1990s by the television programme *That's Life*, many local authorities felt obliged to install expensive safety surfacing in playgrounds in case children fell from the equipment.

Again there's little rational basis for these measures. Schools usually blame playground bans on fears of litigation, but as long as reasonable safety procedures are observed there is no legal cause for concern. The same applies to public playgrounds, where the whole point of play equipment is to allow children to develop their physical skills and to learn how to take 'safe risks'. As for safety surfacing, there's debate among experts about how far it's reduced accidents (children may simply become more reckless when they expect to bounce), but there's no doubt at all that its cost has reduced the extent of play space available in built-up areas.

In trying to eliminate all possibility of a 'worst-case scenario' in children's play, we seem as a society to have lost sight of the point of the exercise. As childhood campaigner Tim Gill explains, '*if we were always to look at the world through the eyes of the most unlucky, we would always choose the zero option*'. And the zero option in terms of playgrounds is so anodyne that it can scarcely be described as play at all.

When parents expect all playgrounds to be super-safe and supervised, there's little chance of their children engaging in real, fulfilling play, which by its very nature involves risk and excitement. And in an increasingly risk-averse society the 'unofficial' playgrounds in which urban and suburban boys traditionally rejoiced – wasteland, building sites, subways, canal banks and abandoned buildings – have now become absolute no-go areas.

There are bound to be long-term ill-effects of denying children the chance to stretch their wings. A 13-year-old boy expressed the problem pretty well on a BBC website:

To be honest, adults can be very stupid at times. They ban every-thing for health and safety reasons. If they're going to ban very simple stuff like [tag] they might as well lock all kids in empty rooms to keep them safe. Kids should be allowed to experiment and try things. Otherwise, when they grow up, they'll make very stupid mistakes from not getting enough experience in childhood.

Studies around the world show that boys are more likely than girls to engage in risky activities – it's in their genes to enjoy sailing close to the wind, savouring the adrenaline rush that goes with danger. A parental blind eye allowed them to get these risk-taking instincts out of their system, while learning how to work collaboratively, solve problems and rise to challenges. There have always been dangers, of course, and every time a 'worst-case scenario' occurs we are inevitably horrified, but the occasional tragedy has to be weighed against the dangers of over-protection. In trying to eliminate the statistically minuscule chance of a child dying while out to play, we risk damaging the physical, social and emotional development of an entire generation of youngsters, with long-term consequences for society.

Concern about the loss of children's freedom to roam is now growing widespread, not only among childhood campaigners. Sir Digby Jones, former director of the CBI, was the first industrialist to express concern that the 'cotton-wool culture' would lead to a lack of entrepreneurial spirit. Since then many businessmen and entrepreneurs have made the same point that boys who don't learn skills of risk assessment and risk management through first-hand experience in childhood are unlikely to make good business decisions as adults. Indeed, Sir Richard Branson tells in his autobiography how, when he was four years old, his mother used to drive him a mile or so from home and leave him to find his own way back over the fields. She wanted him to develop independence and initiative.

Researchers also believe that the cotton-wool culture is dumbing children down educationally. First-hand experiences of the world bring scientific concepts to life, and without them teaching in school may fall on stony ground. Throughout history, damming streams has introduced boys to the properties of materials, building dens and forts has taught them basic principles of engineering, and they've learned a lot about trees by climbing in them and about gravity by falling out. In 2007, researchers at London University published evidence that 21st century 11-year-olds are two to three years behind their counterparts in 1990 in terms of their commonsense, conceptual understanding of the world. They put it down to lack of play.

Nevertheless, despite the growing academic backlash against risk aversion, it's very difficult for parents surrounded by media scares to stop looking at the world through the eyes of the most unlucky. It takes a positive act of will to subscribe to the slogan of the 2008 *Spirit of Adventure* playworkers conference: '*Better a broken bone than a broken spirit*'.

Fear of boys

That act of will is even more difficult in the face of modern social expectations about 'parenting'. It's not just parents who have to get over their fret about letting boys be boys in 21st century Britain, but the neighbourhoods they live in. As the world has grown increasingly risk averse, it's become the mark of a good parent to keep one's child under careful scrutiny at all times. And as 'responsible' parents increasingly locked their children away, the attitude of the general public to unsupervised youngsters has changed. Within the space of a decade or so, communities in all areas of the country have become far less tolerant of boys' outdoor play, even when it's not particularly rambunctious.

A teacher in North London told me recently of a small group of boys who were playing out behind her house during the school holidays, making go-karts from bits of junk. She was stunned when a letter was posted through her door by a neighbour, urging her to help move the children on. 'They may be making go-karts today,' the letter explained, 'but they could be vandalising our cars tomorrow.' My informant didn't join the witch-hunt, but enough neighbours did; the boys' families were contacted and the lads moved on – presumably back into their homes to be propped in front of the TV or communing with a Gameboy for the rest of the holiday.

In his book *No Fear: Growing up in a Risk-Averse Society*, Tim Gill catalogues press coverage of boys in trouble with authority for behaviour that would have been considered completely normal a couple of decades ago. In 2006, for instance, three boys in the West Midlands (none of whom had ever been in trouble before) were arrested and DNA tested after they'd been caught trying to build a treehouse in a cherry tree on public land. In the same year, a mother in Manchester received a letter registering complaints from local residents about her son's antisocial behaviour – Ben, aged three, had been playing football outside his home.

In the past, adults in the local community used to deal with small examples of boys' unruly behaviour themselves – ticking off lads they saw misbehaving, and offering a word of advice or warning if they thought their play might be dangerous. There was what I called in *Toxic Childhood* an 'adult alliance', whereby all adults in a community took responsibility for children's safety and parents accepted their judgement in return for their help. Nowadays, however, people tend to avoid getting involved on a personal level, and often refer even the slightest problems on to a higher authority.

There are probably many reasons for this abnegation of social responsibility. Communities are far less cohesive than in the past, owing to a more mobile population, increased ethnic variation and the movement of women (who forged much of the old social capital) away from home and into employment. Adults – particularly men – are reluctant to engage with children because of widespread fears of paedophilia. Many people – especially older ones – are frightened by stories of ill-mannered children who might give them 'a mouthful of abuse', make their life a misery with petty vandalism or possibly even resort to violence. They also fear reprisals from their parents.

There's a terrible circularity about these changes. The more boys are locked away and denied the opportunity to play, the more they're likely to lack social skills and emotional resilience, leading to more immature and irresponsible behaviour when they do break out of captivity. And the less interaction between adult members of a community, the less easy it is to see each other's point of view, leading to intolerance and aggression fed by defensiveness on both sides.

So it's not just fear of traffic or stranger danger that stops parents from letting their sons out to play. As Tim Gill puts it, '*Activities and experiences that previous generations of children enjoyed without a second thought have been relabelled troubling or dangerous, while the adults who permit them are branded as irresponsible.*' And in the words of sociologist Frank Furedi, '*Parents are almost forced to fall into line... When your kid is the only one allowed to go shopping, to go to the swimming pool by himself, it looks very strange.*'

Virtual freedom

Meanwhile, many boys – like my pizza-eating interviewee – seem to have adapted to life in captivity. The researcher Roger Louv recalls an eight-year-old who told him: '*I like to play indoors better, 'cause that's where all the electrical outlets are*' and another nine-year-old I met enthusiastically described his 'virtual world': a bedroom stocked with so many electronic items that I lost count. He is not alone: in a 2008 survey of children's leisure activities by Childwise, 80% of British five- to sixteen-year-olds were found to have a TV set in their bedroom and over a third (including a quarter of five- to six-year-olds) had a computer or laptop of their own. When their screen-based activities were totted up, the average time children spent on them per day was five hours twenty minutes – about the same amount of time as they spend in school.

I asked my interviewees where their parents were while they wandered alone around the electronic global village. Some were at work or doing household chores, but many adults appeared to be themselves engaged in virtual activity – watching TV downstairs, on the computer, doing the email, chatting on the phone. Just as communities seem have splintered off into individual households, no longer interacting with each other, the members of those households – including children – have splintered off into individual virtual domains, tailored to their personal interests. It's a huge irony that, as humanity devises ever more ways to communicate, we communicate less and less with each other. In his book *Social Intelligence*, the science journalist Daniel Goleman calls this phenomenon 'technocreep', and describes it as *'nominal communication in actual isolation ... so insidious that no one has yet calculated its social and emotional costs'*.

And out of technocreep is born another irony: parents who live in terror of their children meeting a stranger in the great outdoors seem happy to leave them in the company of strangers on-screen and online for more than five hours a day. The blind eyes and crossed fingers have been transferred to children's escapades in the virtual world.

It's possible that this virtual stranger danger poses no greater threat than the real-life sort. As historian Hugh Cunningham points out, all new developments in popular culture, from 'Penny Dreadfuls' to video, have inspired initial panic in terms of their effects on children: *'The alarmists imagine the child's mind as a sponge, children absorbing every message and every nuance from what they see on the screen.'* On the other hand, *'the sceptics see children taking from what they see what they want, ignoring the rest and also having critical judgement rather greater than is imputed to them'*. This subject is discussed briefly in 'Battery-reared bullies' below and at length in Chapter 7. But whatever children take from the screen, there's no doubt that sitting transfixed in front of it is a very different sort of boyhood from that experienced by previous generations.

The psychologist Professor Robin Moore explains that, in contrast with real world activity the electronic media provides *'secondary, vicarious, often distorted ... vision and sound only, one-way experiences'*. Watching TV is an entirely passive experience, and while computer games may involve decision-making, problem-solving and rapid response, the player's judgements don't involve real space, people or risks, and the experience isn't in any real sense interactive. If it all gets too scary or too boring, you can just switch off and text down for a pizza.

In terms of social development, some computer games are designed to be played by pairs or groups, while texting, instant messaging and social networking involve virtual interaction. But none of these are a genuine substitute for the real-life first-hand experiences shared with real-life playmates by which children have always learned to make friends, get along together and resolve disputes. Since virtual communication is a 21st century skill, 21st century boys need opportunities to acquire it, but not at the expense of the 'old-fashioned' social skills on which it's based.

Children in the Childwise survey also appeared to miss out on 'old-fashioned' family activities. More than half of them ate their main meal of the day in front of a screen, so there was no chance of family time and social chit-chat over the dining table. Nearly two-thirds went to sleep with the TV for company, which fits with other research findings cataloguing the death of the bedtime story. The developmental significance of these family activities was outlined in Chapter 3, and their importance doesn't decline as children grow older.

Family values

This is another factor in the lifestyle of the battery-reared generation. It's in the family that boys have always learned – through the usual routes of imitation and repetition – the skills, values and attitudes that underpin their behaviour in the wider world beyond the home. Deep-seated attitudes to life, learning and social responsibility are caught, not taught. And in order for their sons to catch them, parents have to spend time in their company, not merely during holidays or so-called 'quality time', but in day-to-day incidental contact. Unfortunately, in an S-type world where personal relationships are accorded little value, spending time with one's children often seems less important than providing consumer must-haves like the latest technological gadgetry, or expensive extracurricular activities such as sports clubs and music tuition.

It's also in daily, personal contact with their children that adults themselves acquire the essential balance of warmth and firmness needed for authoritative parenting. Parents can't be truly warm with their sons unless they spend time tuning into their needs and interests, listening to their point of view, sharing experiences and ideas. Nor can they set and maintain firm boundaries for behaviour unless they're actively engaged in their son's daily life – monitoring his manners and making sure he sticks to agreed routines, such as mealtimes and bedtime rituals. If a boy's locked away in a virtual world, such authoritative parenting is impossible.

So from a boy's earliest days, it's important to involve him in family life, rather than leaving him with an electronic babysitter. Since a small boy's 'help' is inevitably much more of a hindrance, this involves a great deal of parental patience. So it's tempting to park a toddler in front of a screen in order to get chores finished quickly and efficiently. But when parents show their son that they value his company and contribution, they not only help him build confidence and competence but also a sense of self-respect. Outdoor domestic duties (trips to the local shops, bank, post office and so on) take longer with a small child tottering alongside, but it's a chance to demonstrate road safety procedures, to notice possible hazards in the local area and to chat about how to deal with them, so that parent and son both feel increasingly secure that *he* knows the health and safety ropes. It's also a chance to encourage respectful behaviour towards neighbours and shopkeepers, which prepares him and them for future meetings once he's outdoors on his own.

By the time they're six or seven, boys in most times and cultures have been expected to contribute to their family's welfare and fortune. Taking responsibility for chores at this age (possibly linked to pocket money) can be a 21st century boy's first step towards independence. But as well as such regular duties, he also has to learn a vast assortment of practical skills that he'll need in adulthood – how to wire a plug, change a fuse, cook a meal, sew on a button, clean a car, sort the recycling and so on. If parents make a point of sharing family time with their sons, they can teach such things as they arise, through example. And every life-skill lesson is also a vehicle for incidental chat and companionship, building up and sharing memories, swapping the family stories and jokes that are an essential part of everyone's identity. Meanwhile the boy, as a valued apprentice, gradually learns the trade secrets of being a grown-up that will stand him in good stead throughout his life.

This is what growing up is all about. Boys raised in fully functioning families grow in confidence and competence as they're initiated into the adult world, and learn through experience and example how to balance their own needs with the needs of others. Parents who watch their sons develop in this way learn to trust and respect them, so they're more inclined to encourage independence in other aspects of life. On the other hand, if a boy just lounges for five or so hours a day in front of a screen, or spends his time being ferried from class to club, he retains the status of a dependent child (or perhaps a sort of pet) rather than a fully paid-up member of the human race.

Nobody realised, back in the 1990s when children's TV channels and computer games first took off, that they would gradually take over so many of the younger generation's waking hours. As it is, they have changed family life profoundly, and the changes display the same depressing chicken-and-egg circularity as those that stop boys playing outside:

- Parents frantically juggling work and domestic responsibilities come home exhausted, wanting to get chores done
  quickly and grab an hour or so's relaxation.
- They start relying on TV, computer games, social networking sites, etc. to keep their offspring safe indoors, while
  also out from under their feet.
- Boys who spend hours engrossed in electronic entertainment don't develop competence and manners and thus become increasingly less pleasant to be with, especially when
  exposure to marketing messages translates into 'pester
  power' (see Chapter 7).
- Parents need to earn ever more guilt money to keep their
  progeny up to date with electronic gadgetry, thus working
  ever longer hours, becoming more exhausted and frazzled
  ... And the cycle continues.

Thus relationships within the family are steadily eroded until,
by the time boys reach their teenage years, communication has
dwindled to nothing.

The problem is exacerbated if the pressures of modern living
also take a toll on adult relationships. One in three marriages
now ends in divorce, so as well as juggling work–life balance,
many parents are often coping with personal emotional dramas,
or – as time moves on – with raising children single-handedly,
or dealing with the problems of step-parenting. For boys, a
father's input is at least as significant as a mother's, which
makes it particularly worrying that, for the one child in four now
raised in a one-parent family, there's an 83% chance that the
one parent is his mum.

While single mothers often make Herculean efforts to do the
best by their sons, the one thing they can never personally provide is a male role model. Children imitate the behaviour of the
adults they see, so a boy needs to see plenty of acceptable examples of male behaviour, and the role models he meets through
the electronic media usually fall well short of the mark (see

Chapter 9). Experts advise that lone mums enlist the aid of male family members or close friends in rearing their sons – but it's never going to be the same as living in the same house as a loving father. For a 21st century boy to grow up with a real understanding of gender equality, he needs to watch male and female role models comfortably sharing domestic responsibilities.

Battery-reared bullies

The profound changes in family structures and values in the last 30 years have made 'authoritative parenting' extremely difficult. It's difficult for parents to be warm but firm in a world where marketers translate warmth into over-indulgence and society confuses firmness with over-protection. But when boys are reared like battery chickens, penned in front of screens, parents – like schools – help push them in the directions described in the previous chapter. As a society, we're 'driving the poor little devils towards either ADHD or Asperger Syndrome, depending on their psychological makeup'.

Research shows that when boys with ADHD are encouraged to play outdoors (especially in 'green places') and given structured routines and rules for behaviour at home there's usually a significant reduction in their symptoms; on the other hand, long hours of screen-gazing appear to increase attention deficit. As for Asperger Syndrome, human beings learn the ropes of social interaction through first-hand experience – which means interacting with family inside the home and playing with other children outside it – not from TV or computer games.

This brings us back to outdoor, loosely supervised play. The significance of children's interaction with each other in determining their emotional resilience and social competence cannot be under-estimated. American social researcher Judith Rich Harris argues powerfully that children left to play together discover their strengths and work out ways of compensating for personal weaknesses – and that this has to happen within the peer group, without interference by parents or teachers. Canadian studies in 2007 found a connection between play and the development of the prefrontal cortex of the brain – the area associated with attention, self-control and empathy – leading them to suggest that lack of play might lead to children being 'less able to make adjustments to the social world'. If a screen-based lifestyle prevents some boys from learning to control their behaviour and others from fitting in socially, we shouldn't be surprised on those occasions when they do rub shoulders that they find themselves involved in bullying incidents.

Reports of bullying have mushroomed in recent years, leading to much adult angst and preoccupation with 'anti-bullying policies'. But maybe policies can sometimes make the situation worse? Adults must, of course, step in to prevent serious harm in playground altercations, but if they're *always* there to swoop in and sort things out, children never learn to cope for themselves with frustration, disagreement or rejection. As psychologist Valerie Besag points out, *'There is a place for some degree of teasing, challenging and critical comment in the normal interactions of childhood.'* The earlier children learn to cope with these challenges, the more resilient they'll become and the less vulnerable they'll be to bullying later on. The eminent US play scholar Brian Sutton Smith is even more explicit and robust, maintaining that in real-life human play *'children learn all those necessary arts of trickery, deception, harassment, divination and foul play that their teachers won't teach them but are most important in successful human relationships in marriage, business and war'.*

Like a skinned knee, a bruised ego can be a valuable learning experience, and when adults attempt to protect children from all harm, they remove the opportunity to learn. Hugh Cunningham suggests that we are now *'so fixated… on giving our children a long and happy childhood that we downplay their abilities and their resilience'.* And when resilience is downplayed, it doesn't develop. As children grow older, teasing and criticism become more unpleasant and difficult to ignore, so a boy who hasn't learned essential social skills by the age of seven or eight is increasingly likely to become a victim or – in retaliation – a bully himself.

It's also worth considering whether the bullying explosion is fed by what boys actually watch during those long hours in front of screens. The debate about the effects of screen violence on young minds has waged for many decades, and a recent review by Dr Tanya Byron for the UK government displayed the usual official ambivalence. It did find, however, that young boys frequently gain access to X-rated computer games involving high levels of violence and antisocial behaviour, and there was a strong recommendation that action be taken to restrict this access. Since there is a mountain of psychological research on the significance of imitation and repetition in children's learning, it is amazing that such a recommendation needs to be made.

But violence is not the only form of bullying. Many reality TV programmes popular with children involve taunting or humiliation of participants, soap opera storylines frequently home in on victimisation and intimidation, and 'confessional TV' hosts like Jeremy Kyle are expert browbeaters. The media culture to which boys are exposed provides plenty of examples of the sort of behaviour the real-life adults in their lives frantically try to discourage.

It takes a village ...

The jury may still be out on the direct effects of electronic entertainment on children's minds, but evidence is mounting that wrapping the next generation in cotton wool, keeping them locked up 'safe' in virtual worlds, and compensating for parental presence with electronic presents is doing them much more harm than good. When boys are eventually released from captivity, those who lack emotional resilience and social competence are likely to pose problems not only for themselves and their peers, but also for society at large (see Chapters 9 and 10).

If their parents have indulged and protected them rather than teaching them how to observe boundaries and behave responsibly, they're very likely to come into conflict with other citizens, and the prophecies of those frightened neighbours on page 289 will be fulfilled.

But the community's behaviour towards boys is just as important as boys' behaviour towards the community. The contrast between the British attitude to children in general and that of other European nations is becoming quite stark. For instance, in the Scandinavian countries where parents, politicians and the general public are generally aware of the younger generation's developmental need to play, even very young children still play out in the area around their home. They're also expected to spend a significant proportion of their school day playing outside. With time and space to develop physical, emotional and social skills, they acquire greater levels of self-control and empathy. As time goes by, they can therefore be expected to behave with greater consideration to their more venerable neighbours. Meanwhile, those neighbours, having smiled indulgently at little lads when they saw them playing out as toddlers, are less likely to feel threatened by them as they grow up. In the UK, however, unsupervised children are today seldom seen or heard – at least in 'respectable' neighbourhoods.

There's something extraordinarily joyless about a community devoid of children. I recently visited Amersham in Buckinghamshire – a lovely place, with plenty of parkland and open space, including water meadows and woodland that looked like paradise for growing boys. But during two hours in late afternoon on a beautiful summer's day, I didn't see a single child playing out. It was as though the Pied Piper had spirited them all away – and perhaps he has (see Chapter 7, 'Life on Jupiter').

The parks, natural amenities and public spaces in towns like Amersham are beautifully maintained and manicured, which is probably a source of deep satisfaction to the older residents (who tend to be the ones with time to attend to civic duties, and thus establish the community's priorities). It's easy to imagine what would happen if children were playing all over them: they'd make dens and mess, the cultivated parkland would start looking the worse for wear, riverbanks would become muddy, lawns would lose their sheen. Just as an exploratory baby ruins the order and appearance of an ideal home, a crowd of playful youngsters can soon give their local area a lived-in look, unlikely to go down well with the people who write letters to local newspapers. But just as a mother obsessed with interior design risks thwarting her son's mental growth, a community preoccupied with keeping up appearances at the expense of children's freedom may damage the development of a whole generation. And thus, as time goes on, the community as a whole.

There is probably less contact now between the generations in the UK than at any time in human history. As the extended family broke down over the 20th century, children became less likely to live in close proximity to uncles, aunts and grandparents, so older citizens have been increasingly cut off from day-to-day contact with children. Fed by the media with stories of feral youngsters, and ever less likely to bump into well-raised boys out and about in the neighbourhood, the older generation is becoming ever less tolerant. But if we're to raise a generation of boys fit to meet the challenges of the 21st century, every adult living in a neighbourhood has to support parents in bringing them up – and that means allowing them growing independence. Authoritative warm-but-firm parenting is only possible in authoritative, warm-but-firm, child-friendly communities.

In a complex social world, freedom depends on being able to balance one's own rights as an individual with the rights of everyone else. Children learn to do this through example (by watching how their parents and other adults act towards them) and experience (by playing and learning how to get along with other children). This can only happen if parents make the effort to spend time bringing up their offspring rather than relying on electronic babysitters, and communities make the effort to tolerate children's loosely supervised outdoor play, while keeping a general eye on their welfare. It depends on adults acting responsibly, so that the next generation can grow up to be responsible too. A 2007 report for the Economic and Social Research Council found that *'the more parents were involved in the lives of their neighbours, the more free-dom they gave their children. At the same time, the more social networks children have in a neighbourhood, the greater parents' confidence in the safety of that area.'*

Back to my interviews. Another 21st century boy – an eight-year-old – was rhapsodising about his Nintendo Wii machine: *'You can, like, be it. I can, like, be the superhero and save people and all that!'*

'But you can do that in real life,' I said. 'You can *play* at saving people!'

He stared at me, first with incomprehension, then, as my words sank in, with something that looked very like pity. This boy, like many I've spoken to over the last two years, thinks real play is 'babyish'. He's so accustomed to a battery-reared exis-tence that he's handed over his imagination to the games manu-facturers. The home-grown, spontaneous, free play in which children have indulged their creative impulses for millennia is no longer 'cool'.

And by losing out on creative play, and the unsupervised, so-cial messing about that's been boys' birthright across all times and cultures until this one, this little boy has also lost out on op-portunities to develop:

- his independence, self-control and ability to assess and take risks – all important elements of *emotional resilience*
- the ability to get along with other children, make new friends, deal with disagreements, collaborate on joint proj-ects and find his niche in a group – essential skills for *social competence*
- his physical co-ordination, bodily control, stamina and general *physical fitness*

- his first-hand knowledge about the real world and real people, acquired in real time and space – the *conceptual understanding* that underpins learning
- a general '*mental suppleness*', making for a more creative, flexible approach to life and, later, work.

Meanwhile, the community loses out on the chance to get to know him, and to help his parents socialise and civilise him as he take his first steps on the long road to responsible citizenship, balancing individual rights with social responsibilities.

These are highly significant losses, and anyone who cares about the long-term fate of our society should be concerned to reverse the trend. In a world paralysed by 'technocreep', re-inventing community spirit isn't going to be easy, but I've met many adults who've overcome their 21st century diffidence and made the leap. Parents worried about the loss of play are already banding together with other local parents to get their children playing outside, drawing neighbours into an adult alliance that's transformed the local area into a safe 'home zone'. By refusing to take the zero option on play, they're starting to rebuild the trust and hope for the future upon which human communities depend.

Chapter summary

This chapter looks at how children's freedom has been increasingly constrained over the last 30 or so years due to excessive concern over their safety. This leads to a stunting of the development of initiative, independence and resilience, as well as to a more sedentary lifestyle. It also considers society's increasing intolerance and fear of boys' outdoor play, and the impact upon community cohesion when children are no longer allowed the freedom to roam.

But while boys are increasingly less free to explore their real-life environment, they are now allowed more 'virtual freedom', resulting in reduced contact between the generations, and a lack of development of personal responsibility and manners. The recorded increase in reports of bullying is also explored, as possibly resulting from lack of social skills and empathy once developed through free play (perhaps exacerbated by exposure to bullying on-screen).

Getting boys (and girls) out to play

What can parents do?

- Start by remembering the anonymous, very wise advice that parents' job is to give children 'roots to grow and wings to fly'. There's no right age for letting boys out and about by themselves, but if you want your son to develop emotional resilience, social competence, physical fitness, intellectual curiosity and a creative spirit, one day you have to let him go.
- You'll feel better about doing this if you've developed his skills and self-confidence. If you've followed the suggestions in earlier chapters, he should by now be quite independent and know the ropes of good manners. Increase his confidence and self-esteem by:
  - getting out and about with him yourself, demonstrating and discussing safety procedures and getting to know your local area so you know where he might go and what he might get up to (see the Kidscape leaflet on child safety available from www.kidscape.org.uk)
  - spending plenty of family time with him: preparing, eating and clearing up after meals; sharing everyday chores; going shopping and on other errands together; continuing with the

bedtime routine (even big boys need a goodnight kiss) – all these are opportunities to chat, share jokes, listen to his news and views, and pass on adult wisdom

- making sure you teach the life skills he'll need for the future, like sewing on a button or mending a fuse (there's a list in my book *Toxic Childhood*, along with lots of other suggestions for shared activities and things to chat about)
- sharing your hobbies and interests with him (this is especially important for fathers and father-substitutes)
- watching TV and playing computer games together, and talking around them
- discussing the marketing messages you see on TV, the internet and in daily life, and helping him realise why you refuse to be influenced by pester power (and, of course, resolutely NOT being influenced by it).

- The sort of everyday activities listed above will, in the long run, be far more advantageous to your son than endless extra-curricular clubs and classes. A few organised activities each week, such as sports or music tuition, are useful for developing skills, interests and time-management. But they should not become a substitute for family time and free time for 'messing about'.

- Be firm about restricting and monitoring your son's use of TV and other screen-based entertainment. As well as occupying time that could be better used for family activities (above) or the outdoor play that's good for his mental and physical health,
    - it exposes him to the marketing influences described in more detail in Chapter 7
    - there are many other potential dangers in excessive screen activity – see *Remotely Controlled* by Aric Sigman (Vermilion).

- If you're reluctant to let your son play out because of fears about traffic and other dangers in your local area, try one or all of these:

- get together with other local parents and discuss how to make your area as safe as possible – if necessary, contact your local council for traffic calming measures. Agree with other parents on sensible boundaries for children's play, and collaborate to ensure there's always someone 'on duty' to keep an eye on the streets when children are out.
- investigate the local area to find the best places for your son to play out with other children, work out the safest routes to and from home, then find other parents who'd like to join you in starting a 'Playing Out Club'
- ask to discuss the issue with your son's headteacher or 'extended schools co-ordinator'. Convince them they need – with you – to work on a strategy for getting all the local children 'Out To Play'.

● If it's concern about being thought an irresponsible parent, look at the suggestions for reforming the 'adult alliance' in Chapter 7. The local community needs you to give parental insights into this problem.

● And if it's because your son is himself frightened, you really do need to talk – what's he worried about? And how – between you – can you work out plans and strategies to allay his fears? By discussing the sorts of things that might go wrong, and working out solutions, you (and he) take control of the situation.

● As political concern about the changes in children's play habits grows, you'll doubtless hear more about this subject. There's now a regular National Playday (usually in August: see www.playday.org), and each of the UK countries has its own play organisation: www.playengland.org.uk, www.playwales.org.uk, www.playscotland.org and www.playboard in Northern Ireland. But really, encouraging play is about letting your son out and leaving him to it.

What can the rest of us do?

- It's once boys reach the age of around eight or nine that the relationship between them and adult neighbours often becomes strained. Boys are not, on the whole, well-behaved social beings – no one would enjoy having William Brown or Huckleberry Finn living next door. And the less contact adults have with their local community, the more intolerant they seem to become of natural boyish high spirits. But to reforge communities for the benefit of all – young and old – everyone has to make an effort. And it behoves adults to remember their own childhood and show tolerance to the next generation.

- We also need to recognise how much society now demonises children, especially boys (there's disturbing evidence of this on YouTube: 'Barnado's children in trouble campaign – hunting'). These attitudes must be challenged. Just as children's right to play must be balanced by the responsibility to behave decently towards adults in their community, the rights of those adults must be balanced by their responsibility to help rear the next generation. It should be a sign of responsible citizenship to encourage children and young people's freedom to roam, and also to help keep them on the social straight and narrow.

- Boys who've grown up since babyhood in a child-friendly community are likely to be much more biddable in terms of social responsibility than those who haven't. So if everyone exercises their civic duty to talk to babies and so on, as suggested in previous chapters, the next generation of lads should be relatively easy to civilise. In the meantime, communities need to reforge the 'adult alliance', which in the past helped keep growing boys under control – see Chapter 7.

- When parents get together to arrange for their children to go out to play, this can be a starting point for more generalised neighbourly collaboration. Other responsible adults could offer their help, e.g.

- in providing 'eyes on the street' to keep children safe from harm in campaigning for safer streets
- by influencing neighbours to challenge the 'no ball games' culture.

- On a more 'official' level, local councils could employ play-workers or play rangers to supplement the loose parental supervision of outdoor play (see www.skillsactive.com). Like old-fashioned park keepers, these professionals supervise children's activities within a particular area – but they also help organise activities and support children in carrying through their own ideas. Male playworkers can also provide another positive role model for boys.

- Local councils could also work towards more child-friendly policies in public areas. Instead of concentrating merely on the appearance of public space, they could emphasise its productive use. One useful target for judging success might be to increase the number of children playing out on a regular basis in residential neighbourhoods and parks.

- All this would, of course, require prioritising the needs of pedestrians (especially children) over cars (see www.home-zones.org). This would also, of course, also make communities more environmentally friendly.

What can politicians do?

- In recent years there has been a growth of political interest in outdoor play, but it has tended to revolve around the creation of more purpose-built playgrounds in inner cities. While more playgrounds – especially well-designed ones – are welcome, they are only part of the answer.

- many children don't live within easy walking distance of a playground, and true creative play doesn't happen in specially created child ghettos. The 'everyday adventures' through which boys develop emotionally, socially and cognitively involve wandering further afield.
- reforging community isn't about corralling children in special areas away from adults, but reintroducing them into the social realm.

- Reintroducing children into the great outdoors has implications for national policies in terms of town planning, transport and community work. And putting children's need for wide-ranging outdoor play at the heart of policy-making makes sound political sense in many ways:
  - it can help create community cohesion, by encouraging inter-generational contacts
  - it gives an extra, human reason for the introduction of environmentally friendly policies, including the 'greening' of inner-city areas
  - it should, in the long run, reduce teenage disaffection and crime figures.

- So it's not just a question of creating children's services run by professionals (which tends to bolster the 'ghettoisation' of children and families) but of turning the UK into a child-friendly society. While this isn't something that can be achieved by legislation, politicians can facilitate it by:
  - drawing attention to the issue in speeches and policy statements
  - putting it at the heart of public policy in every area
  - providing support – including financial support – for local and national initiatives.

- Finally it's essential that government begins to unpick some of the most damaging 'health and safety' legislation, and defuse the many health and safety myths that have arisen from it. A recent political edict that local authorities should assess the 'risk benefits' of any play provision is a good start. But, in our excessively risk-averse culture, it needs concerted action to help everyone – parents, public servants, the general populace – recognise the huge significance of risk *benefits*.

OZZY'S STORY: LITTLE PROFESSOR OR LITTLE EMPEROR

Time to catch up with Ozzy, the eight-year-old fossil enthusiast we met on pages 1 and 48. He looks like a prime candidate for Asperger Syndrome, but might he just be ... 'spoilt'?

During his early childhood, Sarah and Josh were thrilled with Ozzy's progress. He was a bright-eyed baby, fascinated by the world around him. They used to watch him in his cot, gurgling at his electronic mobile and the lights and shadows it threw on the wall. As he grew older they were proud of his interest in educational toys and the speed with which he sussed them out. Ozzy was late to talk, but Sarah didn't panic. She suspected their policy of avoiding silly 'coochy-coo' language meant he might skip a stage or two, and she'd read that many brilliant people didn't utter a word till they were two or so, then started talking in complete sentences. And, indeed, when he did start to speak at around 18 months, he made rapid progress, and by two-and-a-half could conduct quite a grown-up conversation. He could soon count too, and say the alphabet. But his interests were wide-ranging, and he was always asking Josh to sit with him to watch DVDs of David Attenborough's *Life on Earth*. People commented on what a solemn little thing Ozzy was, and how self-contained. When the family went visiting, he would watch with interest as other children played, but made no attempt to join in. He much preferred adult company, and Sarah and Josh giggled about the 'little professor act' with which he used to charm their visitors. But underneath it all he was just a little boy at heart, who loved to sit sucking his thumb and listening to Thomas the Tank Engine stories read over and over again. Fortunately, his big sister Sabby liked reading them to him, because Sarah found the repetition rather wearing. In fact, in the end, she cracked and got a CD: Ozzy enjoyed following the story in his book and she reckoned the constant repetition would eventually teach him to read.

All Ozzy's excellent progress was, however, no thanks to the various nannies who came and went over the first couple of years. The Portuguese girl lasted only six months because she and Sarah didn't get on (Josh suspected jealousy because he knew how hard it was for Sarah to leave Ozzy with someone else, but Sarah just felt that the nanny and Ozzy never really bonded). Then there was an Australian who missed her boyfriend and was gone within weeks. Anna from Romania lasted 19 months until they discovered she was letting him watch CBeebies for several hours a day – she claimed it was the only way she could keep him out of mischief. Since he didn't get into mischief at all during the four days a week Sarah and Josh looked after him, it seemed the problem lay with her.

After that they decided he might be better off in a nursery. Apart from anything else, at nearly three he needed more stimulation than could be provided at home. And it was about time he learned to get along with other children – as Josh said, he'd been living a 'little emperor' existence, with hired help and an adoring mother and sister waiting on his every command. They found a small pre-prep nursery with a lovely garden and an excellent pupil–teacher ratio. It cost even more than the prep school but then, the early years are the most important, and

Ozzy certainly seemed to flourish there. By the time he went up
into pre-prep one he could read quite well, and do little sums.
He still preferred to play alone rather than with the other children, but the teachers said that lots of children – particularly the
bright boys – were often like that.

He still seemed very happy at home. The Thomas fetish
meant they bought him a train set for his fourth birthday, and he
and Josh spent days organising layouts and routes and timetables. But he also played with it on his own, chatting away to
himself as he arranged and rearranged engines, carriages and
track. When Josh found a superb railway website, he was desperate to share it with Ozzy, but Sarah disagreed – she didn't
want the pair of them turning into virtual train-spotters … This
was when they decided they all needed to get out more.

They were staying with Sarah's parents in Devon when fossils entered their lives. A chance finding on the beach electrified
the five-year-old Ozzy – once he'd had the principle explained to
him he practically dragged his parents to the local library to find
out more. From then on, the Thomas books and train set were
history, and Ozzy settled down to become the world's greatest
expert on fossils. Sarah began to wonder whether it might be
nice to have a slightly less intellectual son.

It wasn't till he was nearly six that the trouble started. The
school rang her at work to collect him because he was behaving
uncontrollably. Apparently there'd been trouble in the playground and when Ozzy was urged to 'make friends and shake
hands' he refused point blank, then got violent. Sarah could
scarcely believe it, but his tearstained distraught face and shaking body convinced her. According to the school, Ozzy had just
flown into a rage (apparently a relatively common occurrence);
according to Ozzy he'd been systematically bullied.

From then on, their lives changed. There were increasingly
frequent calls from school about 'misbehaviour', not only in the

playground but in the classroom. Ozzy grew withdrawn and reluctant to go to school. There was also a constant stream of experts – educational psychologists, psychotherapists, Special Needs advisers – and debate. Did he have Asperger Syndrome, or was he just a very bright little boy who found social interaction difficult? Was he bully or bullied? At home, he was still the same old Ozzy – a sadder, less easily managed Ozzy – but still their 'little professor' who could be lost for hours in his fossil collection.

Josh decided to hunker down and concentrate on getting his son through the next ten years unscathed – after that, he'd be free of the system and would probably have a glittering academic career. But Sarah wasn't so sure. What about friends? What about all the other delights of life, apart from fossils … ? What about – in a few years time – adolescence and girlfriends? Would Ozzy ever know what it's like to fall in love and have a family? She lay awake at night wondering whether the glittering prizes Josh dreamed of were worth Ozzy's strange dissociation from the rest of the human race.

Chapter 7

SCHOOL VERSUS COOL

How education and marketers are battling
for control of boys' minds ...
and why schools and parents must
redraw the battlelines

So far this book has concentrated on where boys are coming from – their natural inclinations, how these affect behaviour, and how their nature can best be nurtured to ensure they grow up bright and balanced. Nature and nurture, however, can only get them so far. There comes a point when society joins in to impose its expectations ... and for 21st century boys this means school.

Play – whether outdoor active play in the William Brown tradition or indoor sedentary, screen-based play – won't earn them a living. School is where boys learn how to knuckle down to work, so that one day they can become self-sufficient, responsible citizens. It's about learning to follow the teacher's lead rather than their natural inclinations, working towards distant rewards rather than the pleasures of immediate gratification, and suppressing individual whims to rub along with other children in a rule-governed institutional environment.

Throughout history boys have not, on the whole, taken well to school. Shakespeare's schoolboy crept there unwillingly, like a snail, and Shelley complained that '*shades of the prison house begin to close upon the growing boy*'. The reason behind their distaste is probably summed up in one word: 'discipline'. Revealingly, the Latin word *discipulus* (meaning 'schoolboy') is closely related to *disciplina* (meaning 'scourge or whip'). Schoolmasters throughout history have usually needed to impose discipline – often harsh physical discipline – to keep boys in line. And while scourges and whips can be effective in quelling insubordination, they don't win many hearts and minds.

A question of discipline

Yet even a Stone Age hunter needs discipline. Skills must be honed, knowledge acquired and, if you're working in a team, conventions followed, so boys have always had to submit to instruction and learn the ropes of their culture. A successful apprentice hunter took the discipline offered by his elders and internalised it, to guide his behaviour for life. To succeed in today's world, boys must submit to the discipline of school, but as long as they *want* to learn, there's no reason for discipline to be painful. Indeed, successful schoolmasters throughout the ages have never relied on scourges or whips, but on motivation.

As described in earlier chapters, children want to learn from the moment they're born. As they grow, they learn essential lessons through play (especially outdoor play), stories and song. Problems tend to arise when 'play' turns into 'work'. If the gulf between the two is very great, adults may have to apply harsh discipline to enforce a boy's co-operation. But if the distinction between work and play can be minimised (particularly in the early stages), so the boy learns that work can be just as rewarding as play, the discipline problem scarcely arises. Just as a Stone Age boy was hardwired to progress from play-hunting to real-life hunting, a 21st century boy who never loses the will to learn should easily develop the self-discipline needed to flourish at school.

This is the philosophy behind the play-based curriculum recommended in Chapter 4 for the three- to seven-year age range. In European kindergartens where teachers build on children's natural inclinations to develop language, listening, social and attention skills, boys usually arrive at primary school bright-eyed, bushy-tailed and motivated to learn more. If we want

British boys to have the same positive introduction to school, we should follow their example. Indeed, in a society where the use of scourges or whips to ensure co-operation is no longer tolerated, if we don't follow the European example we're likely to have ever greater problems with boys' education.

Once formal schooling begins, the primary teacher's job is to instil the basic skills of reading, writing and reckoning as quickly and efficiently as possible, to equip her class for further learning while still maintaining their interest and enthusiasm. She (there's an 85% chance it'll be a she) also has to ensure that every child settles well into classroom life, so their behaviour doesn't interfere with other children's learning. All children learn best when they're enjoying themselves, and there are many playful methods of introducing the 3Rs. But all children soon work out that – playful or not – schoolwork is serious, and their performance is being carefully monitored by the grown-ups. This realisation matters particularly to boys, whose male drive for status means success is profoundly important for their self-esteem. Every little boy *needs* to be a winner.

So the boy who settles straight into the social life of school *and* picks up basic skills effortlessly has drawn a winning ticket in the lottery of life: he'll reap rewards by the barrel-load and need little help from teachers to acquire self-discipline. On the other hand, the boy who doesn't fit in or can't get the hang of the 3Rs is a 21st century loser – and it doesn't take him long to find out. His status-driven nature means failure hurts bitterly, and at this young age he has no way of brushing it off. As explained in Chapter 5, the British early-start policy means many boys fall unnecessarily at this first fence. Huge amounts of money, time and effort are then poured into catch-up programmes to get them up and running again, but so far no one's found a magic formula. Since failure breeds failure, their motivation to learn steadily fades.

Most boys, however, are neither natural winners nor natural losers in the education stakes. They're constitutionally capable of learning the 3Rs and fitting into school life, but they still need time to develop the necessary powers of focused concentration, self-control and working memory. If a good teacher can keep them motivated – helping to blur the work–play boundaries as often as possible and keeping them buoyed up with positive feedback – self-discipline and long-term success are perfectly attainable. But if their teacher isn't particularly inspired, or if the behaviour of 'born losers' in their class mean she's distracted from good, sensitive teaching by the demands of crowd control, they're likely to drift off course.

Keeping the boys on board

Over the last 15 years or so, as it became increasingly apparent that boys were falling behind the girls in the educational stakes, the need to find ways of 'raising boys' achievement' has become more pressing. So far research into the subject hasn't yielded any startling surprises – in fact, the majority of studies merely reaffirm strategies used by generations of teachers throughout the ages.

For instance, males – at both primary and secondary level – tend to learn best when there's plenty of structure: classroom rules and routines, timetables and deadlines, clear instructions and marking systems help them stay on task and focus concentration. They also need opportunities for physical activity to help them control body and mind: the less intrinsic appeal a topic has, the more boys benefit from active learning, rather than being stuck at a desk. If it's necessary to be deskbound, they need to stop work at regular intervals and run off steam through organised sport and PE, outdoor activities and 'playtime' breaks.

Not unnaturally, they also learn better if teaching builds on male interests, such as competitive classroom games or finding out (preferably by experimentation) how things work. They appreciate humour and a light touch: light-hearted or quirky lessons go down well, and when factual information has to be dinned in, short punchy lessons work better than long tedious ones. Modern boys cleave to technology and will often stay on task on computer for longer than on paper. And as language doesn't always come naturally to males, they need time for reflection before answering questions – but they also benefit from building up their language strength through plenty of directed opportunities to speak and listen, such as role play, drama, discussion, debates, quizzes and prepared performances and talks.

If boys are to become truly literate (as opposed to merely ticking the boxes on a test paper) they have to be helped not only to acquire basic skills but to build up 'literacy stamina', so that – over the course of a decade or so – reading and writing come as easily to them as watching TV or playing on the computer. Not all boys are, of course, academically inclined, but given that there's nothing seriously wrong neurologically, enthusiastic teachers can generally keep them switched on to reading, whether it's newspapers, manuals, blogs or serious literature (although these days, boys also need reassurance that reading is an acceptable male occupation).

No matter how wonderfully a teacher applies all the research, however, most boys will still occasionally wander from the straight and narrow. The need to take risks and push boundaries is deep within their souls, so teachers, like parents, must always be in authoritative control. While rifling through books and attending conferences on raising and educating boys, I've come across the same story from three experts on this subject – from the USA, Australia and the UK. It's about an old Scoutmaster who took on the job of disciplining a wild bunch of youths and, when he'd successfully tamed them, explained that boys all need to know three things: *Who's in charge? What are the rules? Will those rules be fairly enforced?*

The international acclaim for these words of wisdom suggests that, in this respect, a tribal hunter's instinct works in education's favour – young males respect their pack leader. If a teacher is clearly in charge, lays down clear rules for classroom behaviour and enforces them firmly but fairly, most boys are happy to accept adult discipline.

So the underlying message of both ancient wisdom and contemporary educational research is that to help boys thrive at school, teachers must be authoritative – 'warm but firm', just like a parent. On the one hand, they have to take boys' interests, strengths and weaknesses into account to ensure they stay motivated; on the other, they have to be absolutely clear about goals and boundaries and insist that everyone sticks to the rules. Teaching is personal. As with parenting, an authoritative stance depends on a genuine relationship between teachers and pupils. It also requires that the teacher feels in complete control of what happens in the classroom.

There's one further important element involved in keeping the boys on board. The education on offer has to be appropriate to their needs, and as boys enter their teens these needs become increasingly varied. Over the last 50 years, there's been a general assumption in academic circles that pencil-and-paper achievement somehow has more intrinsic worth than other types of attainment (probably because pencil-and-paper achievement is what academics are good at). Our education system has therefore focused excessively on 'book learning' and written exams, even though for many boys of about 14 and over these activities hold no intrinsic motivation whatever. If the point of schooling is to instil the sort of self-discipline that helps a boy become a responsible citizen, we have to recognise that a one-size-fits-all, exam-based system isn't going to suit these boys' needs.

The trouble with systems

Sadly, as society's love affair with computers and data has burgeoned over recent decades, the individual needs of the human beings who people the education system have been forgotten. The focus of educational policy today is not pupils and teachers, but the creation and management of data. Increasing bureaucracy and centralised micro-management have replaced teachers' personal control of classroom practice with data-driven systems of tests, targets and accountability procedures. This is particularly the case in England where even day-to-day teaching strategies are now prescribed in minute detail by government agencies, ready-made scripted lessons can be downloaded from the internet, children are tested more frequently than in any other country on earth, and schools have government-imposed targets for every pupil's attainment.

This is a long way from the authoritative, personalised teaching described above, or the sorts of exciting, personally tailored lessons that lead boys to self-disciplined learning and behaviour. When teachers merely follow centralised instructions in how to 'deliver' a centrally prescribed curriculum, teaching becomes bland and learning boring. And when politicians measure schools' success only in terms of test scores and the capacity to hit prescribed targets, teachers start drilling pupils in pencil-and-paper exam techniques – 'teaching to the test' rather than developing pupils' real-life useful skills or stimulating their intellectual curiosity. In these circumstances, some boys switch off completely. Others adjust to a narrow, utilitarian approach, but their brains shut down (one teacher told me that these days if he wanders from the syllabus his sixth-form lads narrow their eyes and ask: '*Is this in the exam, sir?*'). And others – especially the non-academic ones – rebel. When this happens, schools can become a social battleground, where teachers' main job is to uphold order rather than encourage learning.

Exams are undoubtedly essential. They're needed to check up on how school pupils are progressing, to help determine their educational career path, and – especially in the case of boys – to help keep noses to the grindstone on the inevitable occasions when intrinsic motivation fails. But when they drive the whole process of schooling, something has gone seriously wrong. Education in a civilised nation must have wider purpose than the mere accumulation of assessment data. In his 2007 book *Education by Numbers*, journalist Warwick Mansell describes the full extent of England's *reductio ad absurdum*. His survey includes details of widespread cramming (on textbooks purpose-written by examiners to get more pupils through), loosely disguised cheating and slow but steady grade inflation.

The steady dumbing down of the public examination system has become a national scandal. Academically inclined pupils now habitually gain fistfuls of A and A-star grades, making it difficult for universities to select entrants without examining them all over again, while a third of businesses have to send staff (many of them graduates) on remedial courses in literacy and numeracy. Meanwhile, less academic pupils are consistently failed by the system: in 2007, fewer than half of the nation's 16-year-olds gained the five A–C grades, including English and Maths, that the government regards as an acceptable baseline performance. In the absence of any other way of proving their worth, 11% of 16- to 19-year-olds are now classified as NEETs (not in employment, education or training) – this is double the proportion of school failures in other European countries.

So it's not just observers like Mansell who now speak up against this data-driven system. In the last couple of years, a massive independent review of primary education led by Professor Robin Alexander of Cambridge University has criticised almost every aspect of current policy, and the Oxford-based Nuffield Review of education 14 to 19 has pointed to the risk of '*damaging the values that define an educated and humane society*'. In fact, practically every educational organisation, from the General Teaching Council to the government's own quangos, has lined up to denounce aspects of the current educational culture. The National Audit Office has reported that there is '*no quantified evidence*' that league tables or similar schemes help improve performance and the head of QCA (the organisation in charge of the English examination system) has complained that 'the assessment load is huge. It is far greater than in other countries, and is not necessary for the purpose.' The 2008 fiasco with the marking of SATs rammed home this message.

If ever a system were in need of root and branch reform, this is it. A recent international review by the consultancy firm McKinsey points the way. This found that in the most successful country (Finland) 'the national curriculum specifies only general outcome goals, rather than the path by which to attain them' meaning that 'teachers and schools have to work together to develop the curriculum and instructional strategies tailored to the needs of their school'. In the end, it is good teaching rather than relentless assessment that produces educated school pupils. A report from the IPPR think tank backs up this conclusion: they found that, once children's backgrounds are taken into account, the quality of their teacher is the most important factor determining school performance.

Good teaching involves attention to both systems and relationships – balancing the needs of the curriculum with those of the pupils in the class. This varies from individual to individual, day to day, school to school, and requires two essential qualities in the teacher: humanity and professionalism. For those two qualities to be put to best use, another essential human quality is required from parents, politicians and the general public: trust.

As major figures in the lives of children and young people, it goes without saying that teachers should be highly trained for their positions and subject to rigorous professional standards. But once in charge of a classroom they must be allowed to maintain authoritative control. This means of course that teaching is subject to human frailty: like parents, teachers can only hope to be 'good enough', and some will inevitably be better than others. But as in other professions, day-to-day management by promoted staff within their own organisation, combined with supervision by an authoritative professional body, is the most effective way to monitor their performance.

At time of writing, one region of the UK – Wales – has taken the route of trusting the profession. In recent years, they've introduced a European-style kindergarten stage for children under seven and dropped SATs, leaving teachers to assess pupil progress before the age of 16. As a regular visitor to Wales I've noticed a distinct improvement in teachers' morale, and a much more can-do creative attitude among the profession. It will be many years before the results of the Welsh Assembly's brave decision become clear, but it'll be interesting to see if they have a noticeable effect on the educational performance of boys.

Don't mention the gender wars

England's data-driven, impersonal, systemised approach certainly doesn't seem to suit them much. A 2007 research report found that 27% of them (nearly 90,000 in all) didn't gain a single good (A–C grade) GCSE and only around a fifth gained five good GCSEs, compared with nearly a third of girls. While 44% of girls stayed on to take A levels, the figure for boys was 36%. On the other hand, 72% of fixed-term exclusions were of boys, as were nearly 80% of permanent school expulsions.

Boys, with their risk-taking, status-driven nature, don't take well either to boredom or failure. So if learning becomes bland and tests are the only measure of success, it's increasingly difficult to keep them interested in the whole educational enterprise. Chris Ford, who's worked for many years on projects to enhance boys' achievement, puts it like this: *'In a rich and lively school culture, both boys and girls do well, but in the absence of that, girls cope, but boys quite quickly fall apart, either in a quiet sense of opting out, or with behaviour issues and so on.'* Neither is it just the low-achievers who fall apart – bland 'education by numbers' and lack of opportunities for creative thought can make school just as depressing for the academically able. Oxford neuroscientist Professor John Geake summed up their problem: *'Boys are having a tough time... some who can do extremely well aren't being challenged – they either mind their own business or go nuts.'*

On the other hand, girls are making steady progress. They now out-perform boys in almost every subject on the curriculum and 70% go on to further and higher education, as opposed to 50% of boys. So less than a century after women were first granted the vote, there are now more female than male graduates, and women are making serious inroads into professions previously dominated by men, such as medicine and the law. It's a remarkable achievement, but also rather worrying. If girls continue to prosper and boys to decline, it won't be long before the seesaw starts tipping towards female domination. Then society will either go from one gender imbalance to another or – much more likely – the gender wars will break out all over again. And this time things could get very nasty.

One increasingly female-dominated profession is, of course, teaching. In 2002, 85% of primary and 55% of secondary teachers were female, and the proportions have almost certainly increased since then. According to government figures the ratio of women to men among young newly qualified teachers is now almost seven to one. Not surprisingly, commentators have begun to wonder whether the feminisation of school staffrooms could be contributing to boys' educational problems. Sadly, however, these speculations are seldom raised in the staffrooms themselves. Today's teachers (male and female) all lived through the sexism debates of the late 20th century, and education is still in thrall to the feminist orthodoxy that gender is a social construct. Anyone who crosses the line tends to get their fingers rapped. When Celia Lashlie, an education adviser from New Zealand, recently suggested that female teachers should make specific allowances for boys' learning needs, she drew a typically orthodox response in the *Times Educational Supplement* from a (female) union leader: *'It's disappointing that a woman has felt the need to pander to the views of a tiny group of men who present themselves as the oppressed minority.'*

But my research for this book suggests that certain aspects

of modern childhood *are* more oppressive for male children than for females. To ensure all pupils are genuinely offered equal opportunities, the educational establishment must consider whether female domination of schools might now disadvantage boys just as male domination of society disadvantaged women throughout the millennia. For instance, if women are more inclined to talk than to action, might this affect their teaching style in ways that unintentionally favour girls over boys? And if women are more naturally risk averse than men, might highly feminised institutions have gradually grown less tolerant of boisterous 'boyish' behaviour? Indeed, could female concern to quell this boisterousness be helping make school cultures less 'rich and lively' than they could be? Discussing such issues is not a betrayal of deeply held beliefs about sexual equality – it's a rational response to a professional problem.

Once the influence of gender on teaching and learning is accepted, there are also rational ways forward. While co-education is clearly desirable in a sexually equal world, there's no reason that co-ed school pupils shouldn't be taught, for at least part of the day, in single-sex groups, if it helps them to learn more effectively. This would make particular sense once pupils move into their teens and hormonal changes intensify the effect of gender differences (see Chapter 9). It might also improve male recruitment in subjects like science, at present seriously understaffed. There are also calls from many policy advisers outside education for teenagers to take part in community projects, which may become the responsibility of schools. In Chapters 9 and 10 I argue the case for taking boys' specific needs into account, which means seeking out suitable male mentors.

The problem is, of course, that while everyone's politely not mentioning the gender wars in the staffroom, all too often they're raging back in the classroom. In many schools, the effects of what Gary Wilson calls '*the peer police*' help to pull down both standards and morale. Boys who fail to prosper in the system save face by condemning education as 'girly', pouring scorn on the whole educational process, and disparaging any lads who do make an effort to succeed. So while girls continue to make progress, boys become increasingly disengaged. The effects of the gender wars on girls' and boys' achievement are now so obvious that even infant children have a playground aphorism about it: *'Girls go to college to get more knowledge,'* they chant, *'but boys go to Jupiter to get more stupider.'*

Life on Jupiter

In previous generations, boys who chose to follow their natural inclinations rather than accepted social patterns were given short shrift by the adult community. Indeed, in less humane societies than our own, scourges and whips were regularly employed to bring them back on track. But when today's boys decide not to accept the enlightened discipline of education, there are no such sanctions. Instead, there's an increasingly well-defined alternative route to status – the pursuit of 'cool'.

The 21st century culture of cool infiltrates every aspect of children's and young people's lives – toys, food, fashion, music, media. Since it's controlled by the market forces that finance the media and produce the toys, food, fashion, music and so on that children consume, this isn't surprising. And the survival of the word 'cool' as an expression of approval for over 50 years is a testament to its enduring nature – and its influence on the younger generation.

Cool culture has an extremely clear gender bias. Teachers (and liberal parents) may have spent the last 30 years trying to iron out the differences between the sexes, but marketers have been doing exactly the opposite. Indeed, ever since psychologists first alerted big business to young children's acute awareness of gender (see Chapter 4), they've been using it as a major selling tool. The briefest of visits to Toys R Us makes it clear. One side of the building, the female side, is pink; the other is dark, metallic and filled with electronic bleeping.

As if boys didn't have enough problems in 21st century society and education, all their disaffection – including the conviction that learning is a 'girly' pursuit – is now fed by well-established marketing lore. In his 1997 book, *Creating Ever-cool: A Marketer's Guide to a Kid's Heart*, Gene Del Vecchio explains that there are '*timeless truths about children... emotional needs that demand satisfaction*' – which are deeply gender-specific. Successive marketing manuals have refined this list, until it's become widely accepted that the best buttons to press when underpinning sales pitches to boys include:

* power: being the best, gaining applause, admiration and attention
* dominion: vanquishing the foe, putting other people down
* grossness: anything coarse, disgusting or bizarre
* humour, especially crude physical humour, pranks and practical jokes
* 'edge' – the capacity for risk-taking or pushing boundaries
* mastery – winning or overcoming challenge.

This list tallies neatly with evolutionary biologists' list of male traits. Indeed, all the 'needs' are established elements of playground culture through the ages. The first two are found in almost all traditional boys' games from conkers and 'I'm the King of the Castle' to play-fighting and superhero role play. Interest in grossness is obvious in the enormous pleasure boys take in burps, farts and so on, in anything ghoulish, ghastly, weird or wacky. Their humour is famously scatological, while also involving a lot of 'dominion' – ribbing, joshing, hoaxes and tricks. As for the final pair of emotional needs, all boys like to indulge in risky activities – which in a contemporary social context often means pushing the boundaries of acceptable behaviour – and they all delight in mastery of new skills.

Sensible parents and teachers have whenever possible turned a blind eye to playground excesses in terms of this sort of behaviour, letting boys be boys. Indeed, as described in Chapter 6, outdoor play away from adult supervision gives boys a chance to work through their 'emotional needs', making it easier to accept discipline at home and in school. And when imposing discipline, empathetic adults usually exploit boys' instincts and interests to blur the distinction between work and play. They know it helps if they provide educational challenges with a tantalising edge of risk, or link attention and applause to the mastery of specific skills. They often exploit boys' interest in the bizarre or their sense of humour to catch their attention. And wise adults have always tried to direct boys' lust for dominion into the ancient struggle of good against evil – when the instinct to vanquish foes works positively, there's a nobility in boys that can be quite inspiring.

Marketers, on the other hand, are not concerned to draw on boys' noble impulses, enhance their education, or see good triumph over evil – they just want to sell lots of stuff. So the way they exploit 'evercool needs' is to pander to inner demons, baser instincts and brazen self-interest. In this, the culture of cool is in direct opposition to the culture of school.

So battle is joined between the forces of self-discipline and self-indulgence. Teachers try to develop boys' social skills, while the cool-merchants happily encourage antisocial behaviour, regularly demonstrating how to achieve dominion by putting other people down, shocking, mocking or 'grossing them out'. School-based mastery requires boys to focus on what the teacher requires them to do and often takes a fair bit of dull, repetitive effort – a direct contrast from mastery in marketing-land, which can be effortlessly acquired by handing over your money. And while teachers stress the value of self-control, rational thought and civilised behaviour, the ethos of modern consumer culture is narcissism, thoughtless consumption and no sense of responsibility for anyone's welfare except one's own.

Life is short – play more!

Research now indicates that children in the UK spend as much time each day engaged in electronic, screen-based 'play' as they spend in school. We've already seen in Chapter 6 the links between this trend and the loss of 'real play' – with profound consequences in terms of boys' mental and physical health – and in Chapter 9 I explore further implications for their emotional, social and cognitive development. But when the values promoted through screen-based media are in direct opposition to the values taught in school, there are also clearly significant educational implications.

Strangely, the educational, political and liberal establishment has so far failed to acknowledge the potential effects of 'cool culture' on children's behaviour and ability to learn. Indeed, just as this elite assumes that pencil-and-paper tests are a Good Thing (never did them any harm, after all), and that gender differences can be ironed out by refusing to admit they exist (the sexes seem to rattle along well enough in universities and at the BBC), they often cling to the opinion that screen-based media is just the 21st century version of 'play'.

But TV and computer games aren't the old-fashioned child's play of previous generations, in which boys ran off high spirits, exorcised their demons and indulged their baser instincts out of sight of the grown-ups. Such play arose naturally from children's own needs and interactions, and drew on adult culture only so far as children themselves decreed. The invasion of playground culture that's taken place over the last ten to 15 years has been devised by child psychologists, backed up by million-dollar budgets and carefully crafted by experienced marketers and media operators. And in the case of boys, the message all too often is that macho aggression, self-indulgence, gross-out humour and the desire to put other people down are desirable 'cool' features of male behaviour, while status and success are to be gained not by hard work and effort but by ownership of consumer goods.

Just as adverts for junk food clash with parental advice to eat up your greens, the message that every boy is entitled to be the powerful, edgy, wisecracking master of his own universe is at odds with school's role in encouraging social behaviour and self-discipline. The official motto of children's commercial channel Nickelodeon is 'Kids Rule', and one sure-fire way to help kids feel powerful and masterly is to ridicule the adults in their lives. As psychology professor Mark Crispin Miller explains, it's become *'part of the official advertising world view that your parents are creeps, teachers are weirdos and idiots, authority figures are laughable, nobody can really understand kids except the corporate sponsor'*.

'Lighten up!' say the marketers, media men and broadsheet columnists when old schoolmarms like me dare to point out the commercial pressures on children. 'It's only a bit of fun.' And indeed, authentic boys' play and playground culture did turn aggressive masculine instincts into relatively harmless fun, which is why sensible adults left them to it. But this isn't authentic play: it's the cynical manipulation of children's minds by commercial interests for commercial gain. What's more, the culture of cool actively *discourages* real play. It was clearly no longer cool for the eight-year-old boy I described at the end of Chapter 6 to exercise his own imagination – he was dependent on game developers for every aspect of his play. And I was a creepy old weirdo for suggesting he play out with other children and develop his own powers of creativity.

Fun, like play, has been hijacked by commercial forces. According to investigative reporter Eric Clark, author of *The Real Toy Story*, the toy industry is now *'a harsh corporate world, driven by social and demographic changes, concern about stock prices and fierce battles between global brands'* while the entertainment industry and big business are two sides of the same coin: *'It is all about profit. The role of the children is a clear one – they are cash cows to be milked.'*

The pursuit of happiness

This milking of children is constant. Almost every programme now has a product tie-in, including many on public service channels such as CBBC and CBeebies. Clark describes many commercial TV shows as 'programme-length commercials', with children skilfully directed from TV programme to website 'advergame' to the parental pocket. Between the shows are more ads for a wide range of products boys can pester for. And in an 'evercool' consumer-driven world, the more products they can attain, the more status they achieve.

This early grooming for a consumer lifestyle is based on another deep emotional need in every human being, the need to belong. Children have a profound craving, rooted again in their tribal ancestry, for acceptance by their peer group. Nowadays, boys learn from every TV show, ad and website that acceptance into the male tribe depends on cool behaviour, closely related to ownership of cool products. The prime motivator to buy these products, according to Sean Brierly, author of *The Advertising Handbook*, is *'the fear of social failure. You have to have the latest. You don't want to feel like an outcast.'*

'Cool' is not a static phenomenon – marketers expend enormous effort keeping track of its latest manifestations via focus groups and surveys, and successful marketing involves linking this week's cool behaviour with their product in such a way that the product itself imparts cool to the owner. This technique has been so successful that children's self-image and relationships in the playground now often depend on consumer choices: 'I love brands,' said one 12-year-old in a marketing survey. *'Brands not only tell me who I am; they protect me from others in my class.'*

According to a recent survey, boys are even more concerned than girls to have the right label on their possessions. To be part of the in-crowd, a boy now needs the right trainers on his feet, the right sweatshirt on his back, the right crisps in his lunch box. He needs to listen to cool music, watch cool TV shows, and know the latest cool games and websites. So messages linking cool and consumer products now dominate many boys' out-of-school lives. They're ingrained in the ads and content of the commercial TV channels they choose, they pop up on their favourite internet sites and their mobile phones, and they're an integral part of the commercial websites and social networking sites they visit. Since TVs, computers and so on are now usually in children's bedrooms, most parents are unaware of the marketing bombardment, but even marketing executives have started to worry about it. One told the advertising magazine *Campaign*, *'The rate at which mass marketers encourage children to consume frightens me. I find it obscene.'*

They're right to be worried. Pursuing the elusive genie of cool while gobbling up endless consumer goods doesn't make children – or anyone else – happy. There is now a branch of neuroscience concerned with well-being or 'happiness studies', and the findings of research are highly consistent. To some extent, we're genetically programmed for a certain level of happiness – some people are naturally more sanguine than others. But beyond one's 'set point' (probably around the 50% mark of one's happiness quotient), feelings of well-being depend on lifestyle and values.

According to Professor Felicia Huppert, Director of the Well-Being Institute at Cambridge University, after the obvious criteria of physical health, adequate exercise and the fulfilment of basic material needs, the most important feel-good factors in human life are:

- curiosity, interest, being absorbed by first-hand engagement in an activity such as 'real play', work or sport
- feeling supported, loved and respected by the people close to us
- feeling some degree of control over our lives.

Where schooling works successfully, education and the acquisition of self-discipline equip boys to pursue the authentic happiness described by researchers. But if it doesn't, and boys turn instead to media and marketers, they'll learn to seek happiness through consumption, self-indulgence and screen-based entertainment. The culture of cool not only lures boys to indulge their baser instincts; it sells them a lie.

Redrawing the battlelines

Many 21st century boys have been trapped in recent years between an arid, test-and-target-based educational culture at school and a screen-based culture of cool at home. During the school day they learn that education is about ticking boxes and passing tests, with the long-term aim of a job that might earn them money and status (but might, for all they know, just mean more of this tedious box-ticking business). During their leisure hours, they learn that happiness consists of instant gratification, personal self-indulgence, and lowest common denominator screen-based entertainment.

And both school and cool work on a 'winners and losers' ethic – if you've got the grades or the goods you're a winner; if you haven't, you're a loser. Parents now find themselves urging boys on in the educational rat race, or buying off the brattishness arising from pester power. They thus become complicit in a system devoted to turning their sons into mere units of production and consumption, with little concern for their future personal life or well-being.

To make matters worse, the highly competitive nature of both school and cool often drives a wedge between the two groups of people who have youngsters' best interests at heart. As education agony aunt Hilary Wilce puts it, *'Teachers and parents come from different corners, and have different goals. Parents want red carpet treatment for their children; teachers want to keep their classroom show on the road. Parents get frustrated when schools don't take their concerns seriously; schools get hostile and defensive when parents make demands they think unreasonable.'* This conflict of interest often results in parents closing ranks with their sons against the school, with consequent erosion of schools' authority and even further damaging effects on boys' development.

If the adults who love and teach them can't agree on answers to *Who's in charge? What are the rules? And will those rules be fairly enforced?* boys will never acquire the self-discipline they need to be responsible men. Lucinda Neall, author of several excellent books on dealing with boys, points out that '*boys are hard-wired to test boundaries. And the adults' job is to hold boundaries firm. If a boundary's not upheld and the boy goes through it, he finds himself in uncharted territory – that's scary. Boys need, and want, the security of those boundaries; if we don't provide firm boundaries we damage our boys.*'

Every school – primary and secondary – needs all its parents' support in creating a disciplined environment where all pupils can learn. At the same time, all parents need to know their sons will be well taught, so as to reach their full potential. This requires communication, commitment and, above all, trust between parents and teachers. I have come across such schools, and know this sort of collaborative ethos can be achieved. But establishing genuine, mutually respectful relationships between school and home means that parents and teachers have to accept personal responsibility for their part in boys' lives, rather than over-reliance on systems at school or electronic babysitters at home. It also involves parents and teachers working together.

This doesn't mean parents should become involved in the running of schools: education is teachers' responsibility. Similarly, schools have no place interfering in the way parents bring up their sons: child-rearing is up to the family. And I'm not referring to involvement on 'boards of governors' or 'school councils' – organisational committees are necessary, as are a few committee-minded people to run them, but most people simply don't have the time or inclination. What's needed is genuine, human, social contact between the people who have boys' best interests at heart. When teachers and parents get to know each other personally they can provide a united front on discipline, and establish shared values to counter the siren voices of the market.

Successful schools prove that when all the adults in boys' lives are committed to a 'lively educational culture', it's relatively easy to develop a disciplined approach to learning. But if adults are disengaged and distrustful of each other, unable to decide on shared values to underpin an alliance between home and school, it's extremely difficult. Engagement, trust and shared values don't happen by accident: they require that people get together, and talk face to face. For the teachers and parents of boys, there's plenty to talk about – how to re-establish boys' right to roam, for instance, and to balance real and virtual play, or how to nail the marketer's lie ...

As for the ways schools could change to provide that 'lively culture', that requires another book. Fortunately, Professor Guy Claxton, a respected authority on children's learning, has just written it. He's been conducting school-based educational research for many years, and in *What's the Point of School?* (2008) sums up what we now know about how human beings learn, and the best ways to teach them.* Claxton suggests an approach based on developing eight human qualities:

- curiosity
- an explorative and investigative mind
- imagination
- sociability
- courage
- the ability to experiment
- reason and disciplined thought
- the capacity for reflection.

* My only addition to Professor Claxton's suggestions would be to stress the importance of a structured play-based preschool stage, with formal written work in the 3Rs not beginning until seven. When formal work does begin, there should be rapid, structured teaching of the literacy and numeracy skills needed to underpin the 'magnificent eight' qualities listed.

Some of these 'dispositions' draw on natural male strengths; some require more input from teachers and effort from boys. But concentrating on them would fit youngsters to face the challenges of the 21st century far better than a sterile obsession with tests and targets. Changing to Claxton's approach doesn't necessarily require change to the curriculum (although with time it should point the way to a curriculum better suited to the 21st century than the present one) or withdrawal from public exams. It simply changes the culture of a school, putting the focus back on learning and teaching, and relegating tests to their rightful, tangential place. Interestingly, in my experience this usually also leads to improved exam results, for both boys and girls.

In Chapter 6, I argued that authoritative parenting was only possible within authoritative communities. All communities need a hub – somewhere people can meet, chat, form friendships and establish the 'adult alliance' that's essential for socialising and civilising boys. Schools can provide that hub. Social events – talks, discussion groups, book groups, parents' clubs and classes, parties and other excuses for a get-together – can provide opportunities not only for parents, teachers and others concerned with children's welfare to meet, but for adults to discuss ways of 'detoxifying' childhood in their street, their block of flats or their neighbourhood.

At the very least, when parents and teachers forge a personal relationship they can ensure that the key adults in a boy's life sing from the same hymn sheet. But with luck, collaboration between a school and the families that feed it could be a force for regenerating social capital within the whole neighbourhood, and creating an authoritative community to the benefit of all local children. If enough responsible adults work together to establish communities committed to raising responsible young men, we'd soon see a change in public attitudes to discipline.

On the other hand, as long as adults ignore their personal responsibility to the children in their care, boys will be left to endure the dreary discipline of a sterile educational system or to absorb the anti-educational, anti-authority, antisocial ethos of the culture of cool. And their chances of developing the self-discipline needed to pursue authentic happiness and become decent responsible 21st century men will be well and truly scuppered.

Chapter summary

This chapter looks at how the current education system may be antipathetic to boys. Their status-driven nature means they take badly to early failure and their motivation is eroded by an over-emphasis on pencil-and-paper work. Their need for warm-but-firm classroom discipline often cannot be met in a system where teachers do not have genuine authority in the classroom. It surveys the vast range of research suggesting that an over-centralised, data-driven test-and-target curriculum is failing all children, particularly boys, and discusses whether the system may be further skewed against boys by the increasing 'feminisation' of education.

The chapter also looks at the effects on boys' motivation of the screen-based 'culture of cool' which now dominates children's out-of-school hours, encouraging narcissism, 'edgy' behaviour and the substitution of consumption for effort. It looks at what studies have found contributes to human well-being and at how the culture of cool is in direct opposition to this. The author suggests that parents and teachers have to collaborate to help boys resist cool culture and accept the values of school. One way would be to aim for the development of eight human qualities defined by Professor Guy Claxton rather than the current obsession with targets.

Tackling the problems of school and cool

What can parents and teachers do?

Throughout full-time education, parents and teachers share respon-sibility for boys' development. So it's essential that they share the same values and attitudes, especially about the importance of self-discipline and a responsible attitude to work and lifestyle. If they don't, boys will receive mixed messages about acceptable be-havioural boundaries, which isn't in the interests of parents, teach-ers, the community as a whole, or – most importantly – the boys themselves. When parents and teachers don't work together, the field is wide open for other influences to affect boys' behaviour – including the highly pervasive influence of marketing.

- As the responsible adults in boys' lives, parents and teachers need – from the moment children start school – to be in regu-lar contact and to agree on ground rules for behaviour. A good starting point for thinking about this is Human Scale Educa-tion: www.hse.org.uk.
- For schools, partnership with parents means:
  - providing school prospectuses and home-school agreements which lay down institutional ground-rules (and which are genuine guidance and agreements, not merely box-ticking paperwork)
  - maintaining contact through regular written reports, the school website, email, text messages, etc.
- But parents and teachers also need to engage on a personal level, which means face-to-face meetings, e.g.
  - an initial meeting, or series of meetings, when children join the school, or at the beginning of each Key Stage, for gen-uine two-way discussion of children's developmental needs and the part played by school and home (some schools

already offer three-session 'Start Right' meetings when children start school, which all parents are expected to attend)

- a 'Meet the Teacher' (and teaching assistants, and other relevant school staff) evening when children move into a new class
- regular parent-teacher meetings to discuss children's progress and behaviour
- enjoyable social events at which parents and teachers can meet informally
- a coffee shop, library facilities or internet café on school premises, for leisure use by both parents and staff.

- From parents' point of view, partnership with the school involves:
  - being clear about school rules, routines and requirements (it helps to keep a folder for school literature, for ready reference when specific issues crop up)
  - attending both formal and informal meetings, and establishing a personal relationship with school staff
  - keeping in touch with your son's teacher via the accepted channels (parents' evenings, reading records, homework diaries, etc.)
  - keeping the school informed of anything that affects your son's learning, attendance, and so on
  - accepting that, when he's at school, his teacher (and beyond her/him, the headteacher) must have authoritative control
  - supporting their decisions regarding discipline, if your son steps out of line. (Obviously, there may be exceptional circumstances when this advice doesn't apply, but every time parents and schools fall out, it weakens the 'adult alliance' and makes it more difficult to hold the boundaries for boys' behaviour.)

- Parents and teachers also need to talk openly about educational issues. I've lost count of the number of parents who've told me that although they hate tests, targets and league   tables, their son's teachers really care about them; meanwhile those same teachers tell me how they personally detest test-based culture, but sadly their pupils' parents are devoted to it! (At primary level, there are often similar crossed wires with regard to homework.) Unless the politicians who impose the tests-and-targets culture know that both parents and teachers are unhappy with the current regime, they're unlikely to change it. Parents especially could make their feelings known about it to their local MP and through the press.

- Some schools promote home-school contact through a parent-teacher book group. If you try this, and want some educational fodder to discuss, try:

    Education by Numbers Warwick Mansell (Politicos)
    What's the Point of School Guy Claxton (One World)

- Another successful way to encourage home-school contact (and collaboration) is to hold Open Forum evenings, at which parents and staff can discuss and decide policy on issues that affect them both, e.g.

  - disciplinary procedures, dealing with bullying, mobile phone use in schools, school meals, uniform, etc.
  - problems such as car parking, or policies for encouraging children to walk or cycle to school
  - wider issues affecting childhood, such as marketing influences (for instance, showing and discussing the film clip 'Consuming Kids' – see YouTube: http://www.youtube.com/watch?v= maeXjey_FGA)
  - specific issues concerning parents, such as new technological developments and teenage behaviour. If teachers and parents regularly debate such issues, so that everyone understands each other's point of view and decisions are arrived at democratically, the essential partnership between

the responsible adults in children's lives is significantly strengthened.

- Schools could also invite speakers on aspects of child development, child-rearing and education, such as:

    • 'Bringing up Teenagers' (e.g. Rob Parsons, www.careforthefamily.org.uk)

    • 'Outdoor activities for families' (e.g. Fiona Danks and Jo Schofield, www.goingwild.net)

    • 'Keeping kids safe on the internet' (contact local ICT advisory service)

    • 'Bringing the best out in boys' (e.g. Lucinda Neall, see http://www.bringingthebestoutinboys.com)

    • 'Making it better for boys' (e.g. Ali McClure, see www.mifbfb.com)

    • '21st Century Boys' (see www.suepalmer.co.uk)

    As well as national speakers who usually charge a fee, there are often many local people with an area of expertise who are willing to speak in schools for no more than travelling expenses – the local grapevine is the best way to access these.

    Talks provide an excellent platform for bringing parents and school staff together, to share understanding of the problems of raising and educating boys in a 21st century world.

- Over time, genuine shared interaction between parents and teachers can be developed to draw in the wider community (see below).

- For suggestions for boy-friendly education at all stages, see *Breaking Through Barriers to Boys' Achievement* by Gary Wilson and *Bringing the Best out in Boys* by Lucinda Neall (both Network Continuum).

What can the rest of us do?

The local school is a natural meeting place for responsible adults wishing to improve the quality of childhood. If boys are to be lured away from screen-based entertainment and back into the great outdoors around the edges of the school day, we have to re-forge the 'adult alliance' which helped keep them safe in the past. This begins with parents and teachers working together to enforce boundaries for behaviour at school, but it must eventually extend to other members of the community, for instance:

- When schools provide a forum for parents to collaborate in helping their children go out to play (see Chapter 6), it can be extended to more generalised neighbourly collaboration, e.g.
  - in providing 'eyes on the street' to keep children safe from harm
  - in campaigning for safer streets
  - influencing neighbours to challenge the 'no ball games' culture.
- Community leaders and opinion-formers are needed to promote the idea of an 'adult alliance' to support authoritative parenting, e.g. by developing a neighbourhood code such as:
  - Everyone welcomes children playing out in the neighbourhood, as long as they're reasonably behaved
  - In the case of irresponsible behaviour, an adult will have a word with them and expect to be listened to respectfully
  - Parents are also expected to listen respectfully to other adults' complaints
  - Only if problems can't be sorted out in a friendly manner will they be referred to a higher authority – perhaps a 'parent mentor' at the school.

This sort of code has worked in the past and works in other

cultures, so there's no reason it shouldn't work in 21st century Britain. It just needs someone to start the ball rolling.

- You can't forge an alliance without allies. Many organisations would have an interest in joining such a discussion, e.g. the local Children's Centre, play organisers, Neighbourhood Watch co-ordinators, community police officers, social workers and local shopkeepers.
- There are as many ways to proceed with a project like this as there are neighbourhoods, but to get the local populace talking you could try:
  - sticking leaflets through doors
  - starting a campaign in the local newspaper or free-sheet
  - involving the local radio or TV station
  - a poster campaign in shops and supermarkets
  - manning an Adult Alliance stall at local fetes or other gatherings.

  The aim is to create a social climate in which all responsible adults join the alliance, and so return responsibility for rearing children to the real people who have a personal interest in their healthy development, rather than abandoning them to marketing influences. (See also Chapters 8, 9, 10)
- For many more suggestions for community involvement see *Making It Better for Boys* by Ali McClure (Network Continuum).

What can politicians do?

- We need root and branch reform of education, to create a system that prepares children for the challenges of the 21st century. Politicians could begin by reading Guy Claxton's book *What's the Point of School?* They also need to uncouple education from politics, e.g.
  - dissolving the many educational quangos that have grown up

in recent decades and setting up a single independent commission to advise on and monitor educational practice and national standards

- devolving much more responsibility to local authorities and schools
- encouraging the development of an independent professional body, to develop the professionalism of teachers, similar to the British Medical Council (the current General Teaching Council in England – unlike its Scottish counterpart – does not have the respect of the profession because it was initially too closely aligned with the government).

- Community cohesion must come from within the community itself. For instance, parents who are informed about the vital necessity of unstructured outdoor play for their sons' healthy development can provide the impetus for community action. Politicians can encourage this by:
  - supporting schools in providing the type of home-school liaison described above
  - supporting local councils and opinion-formers helping re-establish the 'adult alliance'
  - dismantling some of the excessive 'child protection' and 'health and safety' legislation (including the pointless insanity of CRB checking for all adults in contact with children) that militates against community involvement in children's lives.
- See also suggestions in the coming chapters.

Chapter 8

MOTHER NATURE'S SONS

How 21st century forces can
hijack human nature ... and why
adults have to help boys rise
above the quick-fix instinct

The struggle of parents and teachers to discipline the boys in their care is an ancient one. It's no easy task to respect boys' essential nature while simultaneously reining in behaviour that might damage them or the people around them. For the last couple of millennia, adults in most western countries have been helped out by the religious injunction to avoid the seven deadly sins. It was easier to point a boy towards self-discipline when pride, sloth, gluttony, lust, envy, anger and greed were generally frowned upon. The downside of course is that over-zealous application of such social rules (using scourges, whips or other authoritarian means of control) can break boys' spirits or turn them against adult society.

But now that competitive consumerism dictates the values of the western world, attitudes to the seven sins have changed. In a market-driven economy, 'sin' is not only acceptable, but positively encouraged – most advertising campaigns stress the desirability of at least one of the seven. In a social ethos that urges boys to indulge their baser selfish instincts and sneer at any suggestion of self-discipline, responsible parents and teachers swim against the tide.

And the discipline problem is even trickier when progress happens at electric speed. In the face of rapid technological change, how can you second-guess which new innovations might lead young human beings further astray? Or whether something that's great for adults might not be so great for developing bodies and brains? The 21st century guiding light is science, but scientists take time gathering and sifting evidence, and the world changes so fast that problems can spin out of control before the scientific message is clear. This happened with cigarettes (and the seemingly never-ending struggle to stamp out smoking demonstrates the power of entrenched market forces) and more recently when over-indulgence in junk food spawned the obesity epidemic.

Instincts that once stood a Stone Age tribesman in good stead can now hazard a boy's physical, mental or social well-being. But since these outdated drives still linger on in human DNA, responsible adults have to help 21st century boys avoid temptation and find ways of channelling natural drives into productive directions. As so often in matters of human well-being, it's all a matter of balance.

A question of taste

Take sugar for instance. Prehistoric man developed a taste for sweet foods because he needed all the energy he could get to keep his body up and running in pursuit of the prey. But when 21st century boys indulge this inherited sweet tooth with a diet of chocolate, sweets, biscuits and fizzy drinks, and then lounge for hours in front of a screen, they end up clinically obese and possibly toothless. They may also find themselves in trouble at school. Rapid sugar intake provides a rush of energy to the brain followed, as the sugar rush dies away, by a lowering of spirits which in many children causes problems with concentration.

Sadly, scientific knowledge often counts for little against the might of market forces. Information about the perils of too much sugar has been available for donkeys' years, but sugary products are still cheap, freely available and directly marketed to children. Encouraged by the cheery ads, boys naturally view anyone trying to reduce their sugar intake as a killjoy, and since most adults have a sweet tooth themselves and indulge in their own 'naughty but nice' moments, it's difficult to keep up the pressure.

The problem extends to many other foodstuffs. High levels of salt and fat in processed foods have long-term implications for physical health, while brain function may be adversely affected by specific cocktails of additives (so specific that they vary from child to child, so scientific guidance is difficult), manufactured trans-fats or lack of essential nutrients, such as zinc or iron. Basically, the further we stray from a balanced diet compiled from fresh ingredients, and the more highly processed treats we allow our children to eat, the more damage we do to developing bodies and brains.

One foodstuff we should be eating more of is fish – our prehistoric ancestors ate a lot of seafood, and the omega-3 fatty acids in fish oil appear essential to brain function. Studies have shown improvements in concentration and behaviour in children and young men given a fish-oil supplement. Since testosterone suppresses the beneficial effects of these fatty acids, supplements may be particularly helpful as boys reach adolescence. Sadly the strand of DNA that drove prehistoric man to devour fish doesn't seem to have been passed down to the present generation. Or perhaps it's just that no marketer has yet put his mind to making fish oil cool.

At present food advertising to boys tends to concentrate on the stuff that does them damage. As well as exalting the tastiness of these products, ads also emphasise the manly, cool qualities implicit in certain brands. One ad for burgers that appeared repeatedly while I was working on this chapter featured a young man and his girlfriend out Christmas shopping. Escaping from this boring female slavery, our hero was helped by other men into Santa's grotto, where he was ushered – à la *Great Escape* – down a tunnel, and emerged into the bliss of a burger bar. Sadly, before he could bite into a mouth-watering burger, the girlfriend arrived to tick him off. The message was clear: burgers are fun, boys love them, and men have to stick together to defeat the spoilsport motives of the women in their lives.

Sadly, it's not just adverts that tempt boys away from wholesome home cooking. Very few families nowadays actually cook at home on a regular basis: working parents have little time or energy to prepare meals from scratch, so they often find themselves relying on ready meals or takeaways eaten in front of the TV. If we're to avoid the experts' prediction that half of all boys will be clinically obese within 40 years, the adults who care for them must get together to fight back against the marketers. There are indications that this fight-back is beginning. Schools' healthy eating policies provide parents and teachers with a joint platform for action – if we're to improve diet for all boys (and girls), there are two broad courses to pursue.

The first is to work locally to change families' eating habits, perhaps finding 21st century ways to reinstate the celebration of food and communal eating: worldwide research shows that when children help produce and prepare food, and when they eat with the adults who care for them, their diet, health, learning and behaviour all improve. Since this aim also fits with the sustainability agenda, it's got the zeitgeist on its side.

The second is national action, as voters and consumers, in the short term to curb marketing of unhealthy products, and in the long term to persuade the food industry to sell us stuff that is good as opposed to bad for human health. A couple of years ago, McDonald's adjusted their policies in response to bad publicity in the film *Supersize Me*, and many manufacturers have quietly removed unhealthy trans-fats from their products before consumers could recognise their contribution to a range of health issues. If governments can be shaken out of their worship of market forces, they can make a huge difference. Part of Finland's enormously successful campaign to reduce the prevalence of strokes and heart disease was the nationwide substitution of salt with a salt substitute, while Sweden has banned all marketing to children under the age of 12. Nearly two-thirds of UK adults agreed in a recent survey that a ban on the marketing of unhealthy foods to children would help a lot. Since the current limited UK ban on TV advertising doesn't cover ads shown during 18 out of the 20 programmes most commonly watched by the under-12s, there's a clear role here for parent power to influence politics.

Mens sana in corpore sano

It's been known throughout history that, especially where boys are concerned, mental health goes hand in hand with physical exercise. The ancient recipe for 'a healthy mind in a healthy body' has been followed in almost all boys' schools since schooling began and during research for this book I found educational psychologists and neuroscientific researchers in complete agreement that sporting activities and outdoor pursuits are the best antidote to ADHD and boys' mental health problems. Yet in many schools today, pupils have only one or two 45-minute periods of physical education per week.

The reasons include a general climate of risk aversion, as described in Chapter 6; a reduction in the time available for PE due to a test-orientated curriculum, as outlined in Chapter 7; and a general decline in boys' own interest in outdoor pursuits as screen-based entertainment has taken over from first-hand involvement. This decline has coincided with the commercialisation and commodification of professional sport – many boys now prefer to support premier teams and collect sporting paraphernalia rather than play themselves. There are also far fewer opportunities for them to engage in the sort of informal kickabouts that traditionally inspired their interest. Instead, there are adult-run clubs with 'little leagues' where the emphasis tends to be on coaching and competition.

Paul Cooper, who started a campaign called Give Us Back Our Game to reinstate 'fun football', argues that many clubs and leagues not only put less able boys off playing, but can also destroy early talent. As a children's coach himself, he noted a growing competitiveness among parents attending matches with their sons, and a tendency for clubs to put more emphasis on training and winning matches than on the pleasure of taking part. His campaign has struck a chord not only with parents and teachers, but with professional coaches and sports psychologists who recognise that the contemporary preoccupation with product (winning) as opposed to process (gradually developing skills through commitment to the sport) is often counter-productive.

The pursuit of 'product' is, of course, what competitive consumerism is all about. Marketers want us all to believe that a product will solve our problems for us. And we've seen in Chapter 7 that they know the importance of 'mastery' to the male psyche. According to IT expert Ian Jukes, modern computer games are designed to reward the player every seven seconds, thus guaranteeing plenty of practice, and incremental mastery of skills. But just as junk food appeals to the taste buds while failing to nourish, many of the games boys play on the Xbox and other virtual playing fields are designed to hit deep psychological buttons without truly benefiting the body or mind. And while electronic gadgetry such as the Wii can provide enjoyable physical workouts (and, indeed, social interaction when games are played by groups of friends), these virtual activities are still no substitute for real-life engagement and first-hand experiences within real time and space.

Psychologists tell us that involvement in structured physical activity – including individual competitive sports, team games and endurance sports such as mountain biking or mountaineering – not only increases fitness, but also develops confidence, self-esteem and emotional resilience. Like the real play described in previous chapters, real sport and other outdoor pursuits build character (see also Chapter 9). Screen-based games satisfy a psychological itch – and the best ones build skills that are doubtless important for 21st century boys – but they don't fill the bill in rechannelling the Cro-Magnon drive for physical exertion, genuine sporting competition and personal achievement.

As well as encouraging healthy eating, schools and parents need to work together to lure boys away from excessive virtual activity and back into the great outdoors. Schools need parental support to escape from risk aversion and obsessive testing, and to provide a range of daily physical activity, introducing boys to team games, individual sports and other outdoor pursuits. Parents need the support of schools and the rest of their local community to help them limit the time boys spend in on-screen gaming and re-establish their right to roam, kick a ball about, and engage in 'everyday adventures' in their local area. And all parties could let political representatives know that unless communities have space for children and adults to move about in, future bills for physical and mental health problems will be astronomical.

A mind to learn

Poor diet and a sedentary lifestyle are often linked to problems with sleeping – and sleep problems are also commonly associated with learning and behavioural difficulties. According to the experts, today's children and teenagers get on average one-and-a-half hours' less sleep per night than required for healthy physical and mental development, and there's copious evidence that technological gadgetry is largely responsible. TV and computer games seem to speed up mental processing, creating a state of 'heightened alertness' that's not conducive to sleep, and older children and teenagers often stay up late engaging in electronic chat, or are woken during the night by beeping mobiles. If parents want to introduce sensible sleep schedules, the first step has to be to remove electronic equipment from their sons' bedrooms. Schools could support them through parent meetings, information drives, policy documents and home-school agreements that set out the scientifically recommended amount of sleep per night.

Like sleep, all the human needs mentioned so far in this chapter relate to aspects of 21st century boys' physical lifestyle. But all also have implications for mental functioning. One well-documented effect of poor nutrition, lack of exercise and/or in-adequate sleep is difficulty with concentration, which has obvious knock-on effects in terms of learning and behaviour at school.

Another reason for poor concentration is emotional distur-bance – most people know how difficult it is to keep their mind on a task when they're feeling anxious or distressed. There are many reasons why modern children may suffer from emotional stress, ranging from worries about family breakdown to viewing unsuitable material on their bedroom TV or computer.

In fact, when I researched *Toxic Childhood*, I found time and again that the same behavioural symptoms were listed for all children's emotional, behavioural or mental health problems. Whatever the apparent cause, the results boiled down to trouble in attending or focusing concentration, usually accompanied by impulsivity or lack of self-control. Indeed, problems with the conscious direction of attention are also central to the 'develop-mental conditions' described on pages 153–157, even though in different children with different genetic predispositions this lack of control manifests itself in different ways. At the same time, the success of intervention programmes – including diet-ary adjustments, outdoor activity projects, the introduction of consistent sleep schedules or highly structured classroom man-agement systems – always seems to be a function of improve-ments in concentration and children's ability to control the focus of their attention.

The capacity for controlled, focused thought is, of course, central to human progress. Being able to concentrate on the task in hand was as essential to a prehistoric hunter, a Greek philoso-pher, a medieval architect or a 21st century social theorist as it has been to schoolboys throughout the ages. Unless a boy can tune his mind to learning he'll not only have difficulty acquiring the basic skills, but he may also struggle to follow or apply reasoned arguments, to conform to the discipline of scientific method, or simply to pay attention to what his teacher tells him.

But this ability to control one's attention and behaviour is not inborn. It is *learned* through experience, and there are many human activities described in this book that help boys develop 'a mind to learn'. They include:

- an infant scientist's research into the workings of the material and social world (aided and abetted by a faithful personal assistant)
- the process of acquiring language through loving interaction with adults
- opportunities to focus intently on free-flow play throughout the early years
- tuning into human culture and social mores through enjoyable activities like singing, dancing and listening to stories
- self-directed, satisfying (and often social) learning during unstructured outdoor play
- a careful introduction to disciplined learning at school, by a teacher who's attuned to his level of understanding.

It also requires a consistent level of physical well-being, based on our species' need for good nutrition, healthy levels of exercise and the right amount of sleep. If some or all of these mental and physical preconditions are missing, a boy's capacity for self-control in thought and action might not develop satisfactorily. It's up to parents and schools to challenge the government policies and market forces that prevent them happening.

Thought control

Once boys start formal education, learning to read and write gives a hefty boost to the capacity for focused concentration. As the Canadian psychologist Professor Merlin Donald points out, '*literacy skills change the functional organisation of the brain*', introducing '*the elaborate procedural habits of formal thinking*'.

Donald explains that these formal habits of thought are not natural to human beings. They depend on our capacity to convert thoughts into symbols – words, numbers, pictures and so on – which does appear to be a natural human skill. Cro-Magnon man could speak, count and draw pictures, but his use of these symbolic tools was limited to the here and now – shared between a speaker and his listener at a particular time in a particular place. It was when humanity found a way of *recording* words, numbers, musical notes and so on, so they could be revisited, revised and shared across time and space, that we moved the potential for human thought on by several notches.

The 3Rs of reading, writing and arithmetic are unnatural acts that 'piggyback' onto the totally natural activities of listening, speaking and counting. Since they're unnatural, they '*have to be hammered in by decades of intensive schooling, which change the functional usage of certain brain circuits and rewire the functional architecture of thought*'. Literacy and numeracy are thus central elements of modern schooling – an externally imposed social discipline that's essential if boys are to survive and thrive in today's society.

But as Donald suggests, reading and writing are not just useful skills. In the words of American essayist Neil Postman, '*print means a slowed-down mind*', and a slowed-down mind helps children develop conscious control of their thought processes. For instance, in order to decode the word 'cat' a boy must focus his attention on a sequence of visual symbols and the sounds they represent, blend those sounds in a linear sequence, and come up with a meaningful word. Once he's learned this trick (44 sounds to learn, represented in a wide variety of ways by only

26 symbols), he can apply the skill to gleaning meaning from linear sequences of words, progressing over about ten years from 'The cat sat on the mat' to the works of Shakespeare. It's a long, hard slog, requiring well-honed attention skills. As pointed out in Chapter 7, motivation helps a lot. It does however pay off. Research shows that, at 16 years of age, the best indicator of future success is the amount of time a boy spends reading.

On the other hand, Neil Postman also points out that '*electronics speed up the mind*' and in a multimedia world, there are many quicker ways of accessing information and entertainment than reading. As we've seen in previous chapters, boys in particular are drawn to screens practically from the moment they're born. But TV browsing and the type of computer games that appeal to the under-tens require little focused mental effort. Rather than developing active conscious control of his own thought processes, a boy watching TV hands over control of his thoughts to the producer of the programme. When he plays a computer game his personal contribution is simply to watch and react rapidly to predetermined events, and his attention is maintained by frequent incremental rewards. Often this attention is partial. The Childwise survey quoted on pages 170–172 reported that boys particularly like to 'channel-skim', flicking between two or more shows, or to play a game while simultaneously keeping one eye on the TV.

So instead of enhancing self-disciplined conscious thought – as happens during the 'getting of literacy' – screen-based entertainment seems to encourage boys to relinquish conscious mental control. There's increasing evidence that too much early screen-based activity can contribute to learning difficulties. Researchers offer various explanations, but to me it's most likely that passive attention to rapidly changing visual stimuli is in direct conflict with the 'slowed-down' focused attention children need for reading and other complex learning activities. To develop the controlled conscious learning that underpins disciplined thought, Mother Nature's sons need a healthy lifestyle,

'natural' opportunities for brain development (as listed above)
and good structured teaching of the 3Rs. They don't need an
early diet of technological wizardry.

Digital natives, digital learners?

This is not an argument against information technology. It's
abundantly clear that the developments of recent decades are at
least as significant to human progress as the invention of the
printing press. We're at the dawn of a new Renaissance, as momentous as that 16th century rebirth of learning which propelled
Europe out of superstition and into the Enlightenment. Inspirational contemporary thinkers like Daniel Pink, the business
writer and author of *A Whole New Mind*, point the way towards an
infinitely creative – and productively empathetic – 'Conceptual
Age'. Merlin Donald, whose thoughts on the significance of literacy are quoted above, heartily agrees that computers offer a
massive extension to the mind's '*external memory field*'.

But if the values that drove the Enlightenment (and brought
humanity this far) are to survive, we must make sure all our children can use new technology effectively, not merely for entertainment but to learn and create. Democracy demands that
everyone has a mind to learn, not just a fortunate elite who can
manipulate the disempowered majority. To use computer technology effectively – accessing hypertext, diving in and out of
windows, holding a variety of multimedia information in the
mind while maintaining a logical train of thought – boys need
to focus their concentration just as efficiently as they do to read
and write. Probably more.

It's by no means easy to make (and retain) creative mental
connections while at the same time clinging on to the thread of
an underlying logic. In fact, it takes a lot of intellectual discipline.
Most experts I've met from the field of 'digital literacy' insist that,
in order to use computers well, children must be able to read and
write first. They intuitively feel that this 21st century way of using

the human brain 'piggybacks' on the logical, sequential processes of old-fashioned literacy.

If this is the case, it has enormous implications for education. Children, especially boys, are drawn to screens and screen-based learning from the moment they're born, and in a 21st century world it seems important that these 'digital natives' take their place as soon as possible in the digital world. There's pressure from all directions – media, marketing and government education gurus – to get them hooked into technology as soon as they can manipulate a mouse. Adults who've grown up through the digital revolution are understandably excited by the huge potential of the digital future and its exponential rate of development.

'*Kids today are not remotely the same as we were... their brains are different,*' said education expert Ian Jukes at a conference I attended recently. '*Children's brains are adapting to the digital bombardment... They are not teenagers but screenagers!*' His argument was that regular frequent exposure to digital technology rewires children's brains in ways that enhance their visual memory and processing skills, so that the current generation has learned to process information in a fundamentally different way from their forebears. '*Digital learners*' prefer to access information from multiple media sources (pictures, sounds, colour, video) rather than old-fashioned text, operating, as Jukes puts it, at 'twitch speed'. They use parallel processing and multitasking techniques, applying 'continuous partial attention'. Their expertise is in randomly accessing hyperlinked multimedia information, and their reward is '*learning that is relevant, active, instantly useful and fun*'.

This argument is reassuring for 21st century parents. But with a little reflection it's obvious that '*the elaborate procedural habits of formal thinking*' won't develop out of continuous partial attention, flicking here and there at twitch speed. It's learning, Jim, but not learning as we've known it throughout human history.

The success of the species so far has relied on application, focused concentration and the capacity to pursue long-term rewards rather than immediate gratification. As, thanks to literacy, more and more human beings acquired these mental strengths the more progress Homo sapiens made. As a woman, most of whose sex were allowed access to literacy and learning only a hundred years ago, I'm very conscious of the democratising power of formal thought processes ... and, on behalf of my daughter and future generations of women, very anxious that literacy should continue to work its magic on the minds of men.

But for most boys – whose nature doesn't fit them for sitting in a classroom, messing about with fiddly little symbols – the development of disciplined attention takes several years of determined effort. As Ian Jukes himself points out, if we encourage them to adapt to the digital bombardment too soon, *'the downside is that children may find it more difficult to follow a logical train of thought'*. Since logic underpins every aspect of education and civilisation, this is a serious downside.

In a multimedia world, it would be insane to suggest we keep little boys away from technology until they're literate – it's an integral part of their world and a source of fun and information. But there are many reasons to put sensible limits on its use. We've seen that tuning a boy into screens before he's learned to tune into people may well inhibit his development of human empathy. In the same way, tuning him into quick-fire 'digital learning strategies' before he's mastered the ability to read and write may inhibit his capacity to think clearly and logically. In these two very important respects, allowing a boy to turn into a dedicated screenager before he enters his teens may lead to an unbalanced brain.

The drugs don't work

As, over recent decades, many boys have found it more difficult to concentrate and control their behaviour at school, teachers and psychologists have sought explanations and solutions. In a fast-moving technological S-type world, few people considered that they might merely be suffering from lack of love, talk, song and play in their early years. And it sounds positively cranky to suggest the 'cure' might be real food, real play, time to mature and plenty of first-hand interaction with real-life human beings (including, around the age of seven, a teacher who's trusted to take them patiently through the process of learning to read and write). Instead we've looked for systemised answers to the problem.

Special Educational Needs (see also Chapter 5) has become a veritable industry. In the words of educational psychologist Sami Timimi: *'The more we've devalued motherhood, the more problems have emerged. We now have a whole army of professionals to deal with children and their problems.'* We also have a plethora of specialised teaching methods, endless quasi-scientific solutions (often with an institute to promote them), and a growing tendency to medicalise classroom problems. Having worked with children with learning difficulties, I don't by any means wish to trivialise their problems, and am only too aware of the need to explore every possibility to help them and their families. But it didn't take me long to work out that a Special Needs teacher's first course of action should always be to look at the child's lifestyle. For many boys I taught, preventative lifestyle choices in the early years would have been infinitely preferable to their long-term suffering and adults' attempts to find a cure.

For instance, around half a million prescriptions are now written annually in the UK for Ritalin or other psychotropic drugs to deal with the symptoms of ADHD, which is four times more common in boys than girls. These drugs do not cure attention problems – they merely calm children down, helping them concentrate for a while, so they can hopefully benefit from highly structured behaviour management techniques and teaching strategies. According to recent research, after about three years the medication ceases to have an effect: as one researcher put it: *'In the short run it will help the child behave better. In the long*

run, it *won't*.' What helps a child behave better in the long run is
the application of warm-but-firm discipline, which is much easier to apply when a boy is young than when he's acquired deep-
seated habits of uncontrolled behaviour.

I came across only one boy in my Special Needs career who
displayed high levels of attention deficit and hyperactivity despite
a loving, secure and highly structured upbringing. It was only
much later, when I read about the significance of omega-3 fatty
acids (found in fish) that I wondered whether his family's passionate vegetarianism might have exacerbated his problems.
Perhaps massive doses of flax seed (a vegetarian source of
omega-3) would have done the trick.

In my experience, pathologising children's behaviour is more
likely to add to their difficulties than alleviate them. An eight-
year-old boy in my local school who saved up his Ritalin for a
week and attempted suicide with an overdose explained to his
mother that it was: *'Because I'm too naughty. I'm just a nuisance to
everyone.'* Drug treatment for behavioural or learning problems
should be a last resort, as should any medical intervention,
which children – like any human being – usually find worrying
or at the least embarrassing.

Unfortunately, UK attitudes to learning and behavioural difficulties are increasingly influenced by trends from the USA,
where one in ten white school-age boys now take Ritalin and
drugs are now frequently prescribed for a wide range of 'per-
sonality defects' such as shyness and moodiness. Bipolar disorder, considered rare in children a decade ago, has become
'the new diagnosis du jour' and according to one professor of psychology, *'we are now prescribing antipsychotic drugs – with well-
established side-effects, that were initially designed to treat schizophrenic
adults – to children for an "illness" that is not even remotely well defined
or understood'*. A gathering number of US paediatricians believe
the educational and medical establishments are now engaged
in providing *'individually calibrated chemical solutions to what are
really predominantly social problems'*.

It is, of course, far easier to home in on some poor child's educational or behavioural shortcomings than to deal with problems inherent in the system as a whole. And as science increasingly dazzles us with shiny diagnostic possibilities, it's easy to forget that those shortcomings are enclosed within a small real-life human being, who's much more likely to prefer a human solution. Scientific innovations also open up many commercial possibilities in the field of Special Needs. A recent book from one of America's foremost authorities on boys' education recommends parents ask for a brain scan to help pin down certain learning difficulties. It can't be cheap.

The feel-good factor

Another recent educational development has been the growth of Personal, Social and Emotional (PSE) education. Teachers have been reporting a steady increase in low-level bullying and behavioural problems since the early 1990s. And this lack of social skills has a knock-on effect on educational standards, since the teachers are kept busy with crowd control. So in England the government now pays schools to put more emphasis on teaching PSE.

It's always been part of schools' remit to help children learn to get along together, follow rules and fit in with institutional life, and where current initiatives support these educational aims they're clearly helpful. But, just as Special Needs has begun to blur the distinction between education and medicine, Personal, Social and Emotional education has begun to include activities more readily associated with psychotherapy than education. In some schools, lessons may involve exercises to raise self-esteem, strategies for 'anger management', meditation or activities based on counselling techniques.

All these practices undoubtedly have value in the hands of skilled practitioners dealing with individuals whom they have time to interview and assess. But there are obvious dangers in asking teachers to apply therapeutic techniques for which they've had little or no training to whole classes of children. There's also the possibility that institutionalised approaches to emotional and behavioural problems may be counter-productive. Sociology professor Frank Furedi argues that rather than building resilience, over-emphasis on feelings and emotions in schools can encourage the notion of 'the fragile self' and thus fuel, rather than reduce, mental health problems. (One's reminded of the boy who would never have dreamed of putting beans up his nose until his mother warned him not to.)

There's gathering evidence, according to Carol Craig of the Centre for Confidence in Scotland, that ham-fisted attempts by parents and teachers to increase children's self-esteem in the USA have backfired. In some children they've contributed to inflated self-opinion, narcissism and an exaggerated sense of entitlement. In others, constantly trying to live up to a 'brilliant' reputation becomes oppressive and may lead to depression. Craig points to particular danger when attempts to raise self-esteem go alongside the sort of risk aversion described in Chapter 6 and adults begin to feel that their role is to protect children from *all* painful feelings, criticism and difficulty, leading to over-protection and hyper-control. As Scottish psychologist Sandy MacLean points out, focusing too much on the feelings of the individual can make young people '*think they are the centre of the world and blow out of proportion any setbacks or challenges in life*'. So instead of looking for ways to make children feel good, schools (and parents) should be helping them get problems in perspective and develop coping mechanisms.

This fits with the bluff approach of a boys' school head teacher I met in Essex who used his PSE money to fund two new members of staff: one to teach philosophy and the other to take outdoor pursuits. Since the time of the Ancient Greeks, schools' role in forming boys' character has been through the development of intellectual and physical discipline. The former was traditionally pursued through the study of philosophy, science, arts and humanities, all of which provide opportunities for discussion of the human condition, and the latter through physical education. In contrast with these tried-and-tested methods, specific lessons in Personal, Social and Emotional education might easily turn into another example of the 21st century preoccupation with product ('instant well-being') rather than the long, demanding process (nurture and discipline) required to achieve it.

This long, demanding process incorporates what parents and teachers have discovered over several millennia about raising and educating the next generation – and, indeed, what scientific 'happiness studies' (described on page 212) have found lead to authentic feelings of well-being. For children to thrive, they have to develop physical fitness, emotional resilience, social skills and intellectual competence. History suggests that these qualities are to a large extent caught (by example and experience) rather than taught. While children with clinically diagnosed mental health problems may benefit from pharmaceutical or therapeutic intervention under the supervision of a qualified specialist, for parents and teachers there are no quick fixes – they're in it for the long haul.

Laughing it off

According to Anon, laughter is the best medicine. And in terms of resilience, perhaps one of the greatest gifts any adult can pass on to the next generation is a sense of humour. Fortunately, this seems to come pretty naturally to boys, who typically use banter, joshing and joking to bond with each other and deflect difficulties. Males tend to see 'laughing something off' or 'smiling in the face of adversity' as commendable marks of toughness and courage, while quick or elegant wit are admired as signs of intellectual strength. But like most aspects of human nature, humour has both a light and a dark side. On the one hand, it can be used to lift the spirits and make creative leaps; on the other, jokes can be cruel, destructive and divisive.

While the adults who care for boys are generally concerned to develop the life-enhancing aspects of humour, the media and marketers often encourage 'gross-out' humour, pranks and hoaxes – the type of male humour women often find distasteful and dismiss as 'puerile'. There may be good reasons for young males to be attracted by these themes. Hunters and warriors can expect to be put through some pretty gross experiences over a lifetime, including perhaps a harrowing death. An early famil-iarisation with the cesspit and the boneyard may be a way to pre-pare themselves for such horrors, and turning grim themes into sources of hilarity might help defuse the terror they would nat-urally inspire. In this case, jokes about belches, farts and other bodily functions are an obvious starting point. As for pranks and hoaxes, it's not difficult to see their relationship to that other masculine craving for 'power' and 'dominion'. Practical joking is an excellent way for young males to score over their peers (or to bring their elders down a peg) without resorting to violence.

This type of humour does seem to be an area where there's a significant gender divide, as I found when telling adults about a children's BBC show called *Prank Patrol*. In one episode, a ten-year-old boy contacted the BBC asking for help in hoaxing his best friend, who he felt was getting a bit above himself. After discussion of how best to distress this friend, it was decided to convince him that he and his most treasured possession (his computer) had been infected with dangerous radioactive dust. The infant prankster's mother, the local fire brigade and around a dozen BBC personnel were brought in on this hoax, and a fair amount of money spent staging it. After the boy had been con-vinced of the danger by a false news bulletin, a team of men in full decontamination gear drove up outside. The terrified child's beloved computer was smashed (apparently) before his eyes, and he was ushered into a decontamination chamber ... to be doused in green slime. At this point, he was let in on the 'joke'.

Most women hearing this story are appalled that adults

should collude to publicly horrify and humiliate a young child, but men, even when they disapprove, seem unable to stop their faces forming into a smirk – it's almost as though they *have* to laugh at the thought of the boy's distress. Perhaps the innate need for dominion-inspired humour is too great to resist? However, whether the national public service broadcasting company should encourage it is another question. While boys (and some girls) clearly enjoy such cruelty, it might not be a particularly good preparation for a social existence.

Parents and teachers, in the quest to develop civilised behaviour, have always tried to steer a warm-but-firm course through humour as through everything else, encouraging enjoyment of the witty, uplifting and absurd, while steering away from the coarse, the callous and the cruel. But it's much more difficult to do this when marketers and media actively exploit grossness and dominion ... and when they add to children's repertoire of dark, edgy humour by introducing them at an early age to satire and irony. Both of these can be productive forms of wit in adult hands, but children under the age of about eight lack the maturity to see beyond their literal application.

Exposure to TV shows such as *The Simpsons*, *South Park* and *Little Britain* (which were not originally made for children, but soon acquired an under-age audience) has the effect of developing an early taste for cynicism. Boys who learn at an early age to laugh off not only adversity but also the possibility of human decency and altruism can be difficult to educate and inspire. The traditional schoolmarm's cry of 'It isn't clever and it isn't funny!' doesn't cut much ice with a boy who's been schooled since toddlerhood to value smart-arsed behaviour far more than kindness.

In the film *The African Queen*, a wisecracking ne'er-do-well played by Humphrey Bogart is thrown together with a typical schoolmarm (Katherine Hepburn), all starch and principle. The pair must combine forces to steer a rickety old steamboat down an

equatorial river, facing almost certain death. When Bogart explains that, in the circumstances, getting blind drunk of an
evening is 'only human nature', Hepburn's character draws herself up to her full height and replies: '*Nature, Mr Allnut, is what we
were put on this earth to rise above.*'

The human race has been rising above nature for countless
millennia, building cities and civilisations all over the planet.
We've proved conclusively that we don't need to accept biological limitations, and our achievements – including great works
of art, music, literature, science and philosophy – have shone
through history as evidence of the power of the human spirit.
Education is about passing on this inheritance, so each generation stands on the shoulders of those who went before. But before they can take advantage of education and continue
humankind's upward journey, children need physical nourishment for a healthy body and psychological nourishment for a
healthy mind.

In a fast-moving, high-tech world, it's tempting to think we
can bypass these time-consuming natural requirements and
fast-forward into the technological future. Boys particularly are
attracted by the lure of what neuroscientist Susan Greenfield
calls '*the quick fix of a laugh, a rush of adrenaline and the immediacy of
the next sensory kick*'.

So it's up to the adults in their lives to help them keep their
feet on the ground and develop 'a mind to learn'. Otherwise, instead of equipping the next generation to rise above nature, we
sentence them to a lifetime of quick fixes. And just as too much
junk food damages the body, and junk play can damage the
mind, an excess of junk culture is poisonous to the human
spirit.

Chapter summary

This chapter explores further the claim that a market-driven, 'product'-orientated economy is in direct opposition to many of a boy's natural needs, and looks in more detail at diet, exercise, sleep and their effect on the capacity to focus attention. It reveals the links between the ability to control one's thoughts and literacy – the 'slowed-down mind' required for decoding of print which appears highly significant in the development of logical, rational thought processes. It contrast this with the 'speeded-up mind' associated with electronics and computer gadgetry and the surrender of conscious mental control while watching screen-based entertainment.

It discusses whether the modern-day tendency to medicalise and pathologise classroom problems is helpful, suggesting that these are really social problems which, in the case of many boys, might be prevented by a healthy lifestyle and warm-but-firm discipline from an early age. Similarly, it suggests that the huge increase in Personal, Social and Emotional education is an attempt to teach qualities that are best acquired naturally – emotional resilience; physical fitness, co-ordination and control; social competence and intellectual curiosity. It concludes that there are no quick-fixes in child-rearing or education, and despite our culture's current S-type obsession with 'product' rather than human-scale 'process', there is no way of bypassing the time-consuming human business of bringing up boys.

Helping boys resist temptation

What can parents and teachers do?

In an electronic global village, where marketers aim to 'get at them early, get at them often, and get at them everywhere we can' (see

YouTube: Consuming Kids), parents need support to keep their sons on the straight and narrow. I've already recommended building a support group of other parents (see Chapter 1) but as soon as your son starts school, there are a range of other responsible adults – teachers and support staff – with as vested an interest in his healthy development as your own. The suggestions at the end of the previous chapter provide a basis for parents and teachers to work together on issues affecting children's physical and mental health, creating a community ethos in which healthy behaviour is considered the norm.

- Recognise that the major elements boys require for well-being (LOVE, LANGUAGE, PLAY, DISCIPLINE and LITERACY) are free. From the parental point of view, they are costly in time rather than money. Marketers are therefore unlikely to promote them, as it's in their interest to keep parents working as hard as possible to pay for products they advertise. This vital information therefore has to be passed on by word of mouth by the responsible adults in boys' lives.
- **Diet and social eating**
  Schools can take a lead not only in providing healthy food for pupils, but also in:
  - creating a pleasant, relaxed social environment in school in which to eat it – British schools are notoriously bad about this, so it's not surprising their pupils prefer to gobble finger food
  - providing a forum for busy working parents to investigate ways of providing 'family meals' in a 21st century world (e.g. through 'supper clubs' where several parents divide the responsibility of preparing a meal for the group once a fortnight – if you're stuck for something to talk about, try www.finkcards.com!)
  - circulating new scientific information about nutrition as it

comes through, subscribe to www.fabresearch.org
- bringing parents together to discuss such information and work out ways of assimilating it in their children's diets.

● **Outdoor activities and sport**

See the recommendations for parents in Chapters 3 and 6 about providing outdoor play. As boys grow older, schools could encourage and support a range of sporting activities:

- promoting outdoor activities and sports clubs for children and families, using school facilities and distributing details of other organisations in the area
- developing boys interest in sport (including its competitive element), for enjoyment and physical fitness, not merely the pursuit of 'excellence'– see, for instance, Give Us Back Our Game (www.giveusbackourgame.co.uk) and the Children's Football Alliance (www.childrensfootballalliance.com)
- recruiting parents – especially fathers – to organise and run sports clubs, field trips and outdoor pursuits, such as camping exhibitions and bushcraft courses
- involving adults in playing sport themselves.

And every parent would benefit from reading a new book by Fiona Danks and Jo Schofield called *Go Wild! Bushcraft Adventures for Teenagers* (Frances Lincoln), which made even this 60-year-old couch potato desperate to get outdoors, build shelters, light fires and cook with a billycan.

● **Sleep**

To help parents enforce bedtime routines as boys grow older, schools could publish and promote information on:

- the amount of sleep needed for healthy development at different ages
- the importance of sleep in learning
- the ill-effects of bedroom TV (and other electronic paraphernalia) and ways of getting the TV out of children's bedrooms.

Agreements on parental responsibility in this respect could be arrived at through open forum discussions (see page 220–221) and integrated into home-school contracts.

- **Technology**

Research is urgently needed into the effects of technology on children's brain development and potential to learn. My opinion, after reviewing recent research and connecting it with what I know of cognitive development and learning, is that to be on the safe side, boys should be:

- kept away from screen-based technology as far as possible in the first three years of life
- thereafter, allowed to watch TV – monitored and mediated by parents – as long as it doesn't interfere with real play and family life
- until the age of seven, and successful acquisition of literacy skills, given only restricted access (in school and out) to computer technology.

Once boys can read and write, they also need time and encouragement to develop and embed their 'old-fashioned literacy' skills alongside digital literacy skills, to take advantage of the complementary modes of thought.

The following websites may be helpful: www.cyberangels.org (international parents organisation), www.chatdanger.com (magazine approach to issues, including phones, chat rooms, social networking), www.kidsmart.org.uk (basic safety advice, user-friendly presentation), www.getnetwise.org (gives list of tools for blocking websites, etc.) www.childnet-int.org (international campaign helping to make the internet safe), www.thegoodwebguide.co.uk (a good first port of call for reviews of websites on any subject).

- **Music, art, drama**

While these are not discussed in Chapter 8, they have throughout history been important civilising forces for boys, and provide opportunities for active structured social involvement that often appeal more than sport to less competitive males.

- schools should celebrate these subjects as much as academic ones, and ensure boys of all ages are encouraged to develop their full potential in creative arts
- parents who encourage musical, artistic and dramatic activities at home can often use them as a focal point for family time (see *Happy Families: Insights into the Art of Parenting* by Steve Bowkett et al [Network Continuum]).

- **Special Educational Needs**

  If boys have difficulties with learning, parents and teachers should explore:

  - lifestyle issues such as diet, physical exercise and sleep routines
  - possible emotional factors, such as concerns about family breakdown or difficulties with social relationships.

  Before resorting to chemical or technological solutions, schools and other agencies should support parents in making lifestyle adjustments or dealing with the causes of emotional distress (see also *Happy Kids* by Alexandra Massey [Virgin Books]). Many schools now employ 'parent mentors' to act as mediators between home and school in this respect.

- **Personal, Social and Emotional education**

  As institutions, schools are well equipped to teach systemised academic knowledge, and develop physical fitness through systemised games and activities. Institutions are not designed to develop E-type skills, so for this they rely on the collaboration of parents and others in the community (see Chapters 1 to 6).

  - Parents have to recognise the limitations of school-based education, and their role in the enterprise.

  If attention is paid to prevention, rather than cure, of learning and behavioural difficulties, schools could save time and effort on 'remedial' PSE programmes and concentrate on providing the sort of systemised teaching that has proved effective in the past, e.g. teaching of art, sport, music, philosophy, the humanities and so on.

Parents and teachers can develop the suggestions in Chapters 7–10 for collaborating to create shared value systems and healthy lifestyles for children.

- **Having a laugh**
Although responsibility is a serious business, being a 'responsible adult' isn't about being po-faced or failing to enjoy life. It just means keeping adult humour, activities and privileges in the adult domain, so that children have a chance to grow up 'responsible' too, and keep society going.

What can the rest of us do?

The electronic global village has produced many miracles, making life infinitely more comfortable, convenient and entertaining for its inhabitants, and there are doubtless many more to be discovered through digital technology. But to ensure the next generation grows up bright and balanced enough to develop the miracles wisely – for the benefit of everyone, not just a fortunate elite – we all have to participate in determining the global village's values and direction.

- All adults (including young, old and childless adults) have a vested personal interest in ensuring that what's on offer to children – at different ages and stages – helps them grow up with optimum mental and physical health. They'll be the citizens who keep the show on the road as the current adult generation grows older and more dependent, and society will need their resilience and competence in the future. So watch how you behave around children and young people, and present the sort of role model that will help rather than hinder their development as responsible citizens.

- Community leaders and opinion-formers can join with parents and teachers in promoting the message that the vital elements for childhood well-being are those listed above. Every message given in the real-life 'villages' where children grow up should promote:
  - the enormous value of parental love and discipline
  - the importance of communication and language
  - the necessity for unstructured, loosely supervised, outdoor play
  - the civilising impact of literacy.

- Since media and marketing forces currently downplay these messages and promote consumption, 'products' and smart-arsed behaviour as the way to happiness, all real-life responsible adults in children's lives have to counter unhelpful media and marketing messages. This can be done by example and by challenging smart-arsed behaviour.

- In recent years, broadcasters have been forced to change tack on several occasions when the public were sufficiently angered to register mass disapproval. If you feel that a general 'coarsening' of society is exacerbated by bullying on TV programmes, gratuitously cruel or unsavoury humour, or the broadcasting of news items (before the watershed) that could be destabilising for young children, let the broadcasters know. You can contact them with praise for good programmes and complaints about those that concern you at these addresses:
  - BBC: www.bbc.co.uk comments: 08700 100 222 or online www.bbc.co.uk/complaints
  - ITV: www.itvplc.com comments: 0870 600 6766 or dutyoffice@itv.com
  - Channel 4: www.channel4.com comments: 0207 306 8333 or viewerenquiries@channel4.com

- S4C: www.s4c.co.uk comments: 029 2074 1458 or hotline@s$c.co.uk
- Five: www.five.tv comments: 0207 550 5555 or customerservices@five.tv
- BSkyB www.sky.com comments 0870 240 3000 or viewerr@bskyb.com
- Ofcom, the broadcasting regulator: 0845 456 3000 or contact@ofcom.org.uk

Make sure you have the following details:
- The title of the programme
- Date and time of transmission
- Name of TV or radio channel.

- Don't let them convince you that you're an old fuddy-duddy or a saddo. Maintaining authoritative communities is not the same as *authoritarianism*. But it does involve challenging excessively indulgent actions.
- As a society, we also need to engage in ongoing discussion about the ways scientific and technological advances which are fine for full-grown adults may present dangers for growing children. Susan Greenfield's recent book ID: *The Search for Identity in the 21st Century* (2008) includes neuroscientific analysis of the possible effects of contemporary culture on the developing brain. Just the thing for a book group.

What can politicians do?

- Put the raising of the next generation at the heart of public policy by recognising the limitations of systemised and institutional solutions in this respect:
  - backing off from micromanagement and everyday involvement in child-rearing and education
  - supporting parents, teachers and other childcare profession-

als in providing responsible role models and personal attention for the children in their care (for this they need time and freedom from red tape)

- putting in train the type of root and branch reform of education suggested in Chapter 10
- using regulation – and if necessary legislation – to rein in the worst excesses of marketers and other corporate organisations that make it difficult for responsible adults to raise and educate boys (and girls)
- facilitating democratic public involvement in deciding the direction of the global electronic village, e.g. by requiring Ofcom to support the opinions of responsible parents and teachers in terms of children's needs, rather than the opinions of corporate bodies
- giving up on current attempts to provide 'sticking plaster' solutions through educational strategies (such as SEAL) which have the effect of pathologising childhood. Instead support schools and other community-based organisations in working with parents to tackle 'toxic childhood syndrome' so that learning and behavioural problems are prevented (rather than looking for 'cures' that are likely to be costly and ineffective).

- Target public money on those families who cannot or will not work with schools and communities to ensure their sons are 'well brought up' (see Chapter 10).

LEO'S STORY: THE RISE AND FALL OF MUMMY'S BOY

Our third fragile male (see page 49) was Leo, born a little premature and 'fussy'. There's some evidence that irritable baby boys are more likely to end up in trouble in later life, so perhaps his transformation into a teenage tearaway was inevitable. Or perhaps he's just a casualty of a 21st century lifestyle and values, and the legacy of the gender wars.

Leo's early years were eventful. We left his parents struggling with an immature and demanding baby. Reluctant to sleep, feed or settle in his cot, he seemed to need constant attention and, since they lived in a small city flat with no family support or local friends, his mum Cary felt isolated and exhausted. Looking back on it later, she realised how obsessed she'd become with Leo, and how that probably contributed to Mike's infidelity. Not that this was any excuse, of course.

He started working late, claiming they needed the overtime. Cary reckoned he was just trying to escape from all the crying. She accused him of shirking responsibilities; he claimed she was only interested in the baby and had 'squeezed him out of the equation'. She didn't want to nag or squeeze him out, but she was so tired and lonely that all she could do was moan, and Mike was the only person to moan at. In fact, even when Leo settled down, she couldn't seem to snap out of it – life had changed so much she didn't feel like herself any more. When it turned out Mike was seeing a girl from the office, she packed her bags and took Leo to live at her parents'.

Cary was horrified to become a single mum – she'd always looked down on such people – but she coped. Within 18 months, she'd found a council flat, a nursery place for Leo and a job as a teaching assistant. Child support payments from Mike helped make ends meet, and Leo was her pride and joy. After all they'd been through together, they were very close – every penny she could spare went on clothes and toys for him. He was a good boy, too, helping her with chores and well mannered when they were out and about. As she told her friends, he might only be a little boy but he acted like the man of the house.

The area they lived in wasn't all that good – no park nearby, or anything. But Leo got plenty of play and exercise at nursery all day, so Cary reckoned he was OK watching TV in the evenings and at weekends. He had a little telly of his own, so could enjoy his programmes while she watched hers. Mike didn't keep in touch – after their relationship broke up he went a bit wild. But as long as the support payments kept coming she was relieved not to have to bother with him, and Leo didn't seem to mind.

Then when Leo was four – a bright, bubbly little boy doing fine in his reception class – she met Aaron. Cary reckoned once bitten twice shy, and insisted they took things very slowly. When the relationship started looking serious, they had long talks about her boy. Aaron fully understood that the two of them came as a package, and she saw his point that perhaps Leo did need a little more discipline. By the time Aaron proposed, she was sure they could make it work.

And for several years it did. Leo made a lovely pageboy, and really seemed to enjoy having a dad at last. They moved to a new house, not that far from Cary's parents, who had always made a fuss of him. It had a little garden and Aaron took him out there to kick a ball about, or down the park to play with the other dads and lads. And when his little sister arrived, six-year-old Leo took it in his stride. Of course, he was sometimes jealous that Cary had less time for him, but that was only natural. While on maternity leave, she always tried to make some time to spend each day with Leo, while Aaron looked after the baby.

But the new mortgage meant maternity leave couldn't last for ever, and once Cary was back at work, it was much more difficult to juggle all the balls. A teaching assistant's hours are more child-friendly than most, and her mum and dad helped out with occasional babysitting after their work, but she still struggled to combine a job, housework, being a supportive wife and caring for two kids. Fortunately, Leo's school had plenty of after-hours clubs so most days he was kept active and occupied till six, and a combination of Nickelodeon and Nintendo seemed to work the rest of the time.

But as time went on, she noticed him getting cheekier, and his run-ins with Aaron about behaviour grew more frequent. She was torn in two when they rowed. On the one hand, she loved Aaron and knew it was in Leo's long-term interests to put on a united front. On the other, she had these stupid guilty feelings that her marriage was a sort of betrayal of her son. Somehow, she could always see Leo's point of view.

Then she and Aaron began arguing about it. He said she didn't support him in disciplining Leo. She accused him of opting out of family life, spending all his time at work or the club, and losing touch with the kids – she felt a dim sense of déjà vu, but wasn't sure why. To begin with, they'd make up, and both promise to be better, try harder. But then her son would find another way to rattle Aaron's cage, he'd retreat to the pub and they'd be at each other's throats again. By the time Leo started secondary school, there was more war than peace in their marriage.

That's when the real trouble started. At 12, Leo fell in with a disreputable crowd, and Cary discovered that the 'school football club' where he claimed to spend all his evenings was a fantasy. He was out on the streets, getting up to goodness knows what with these older bad lads. There were terrible rows at home, and one night Aaron – her kind, decent Aaron – actually hit her son. She rushed to help Leo, screaming abuse, and Aaron fled. She couldn't believe it when he moved out – turned out there was a woman down the pub, a divorcee, who listened to him ...

Leo calmed down for a bit, helped her try and get sorted. There were horrific problems over money and Aaron's access to little Katie. Suddenly Cary was a single mum again, struggling to keep her head above water. Leo tried to be the man of the house, just like when he was little, but soon realised he couldn't really help. In fact, the more she struggled, the more he withdrew. He was growing up fast – put on about six inches in as many months – and it wasn't long before he drifted back to his mates.

Then he developed a hard face, a hard look in his eyes, and Cary was almost frightened of him. She knew he stole from her purse (What for? Drugs? Drink? – she lay awake at night panicking about it) but didn't dare confront him. That's when the letters from school started coming, then the complaints from neighbours and local shopkeepers, and finally the visits from the police. There was no one to turn to – her parents were as helpless as she in the face of Leo's defiance, and Aaron was only interested in Katie. The social worker seemed more concerned with Leo's rights than how to sort him out, and none of her neighbours would talk to her any more. She was a single mum with a delinquent son, and she wanted the earth to swallow her up ...

Chapter 9

BOYS AND MEN

Why boys need quests to pursue,
codes to live by and mentors to guide them ...
and why adults must get over their
fret about gender

Way back in Chapter 1, boys started being boys when their Y chromosomes kicked in, leading to the production of testosterone. That initial testosterone surge, between the second and sixth month in the womb, ensures that a child develops not only a male body, but the potential for a male mind. We've seen how Y-driven genetic traits, combined with the experiences of childhood, influence how boys learn and behave for the rest of their lives.

Around five months after birth, baby boys have another testosterone surge, but after that things settle down and during childhood most boys are relatively untroubled by the male hormone. They still have some testosterone in their bloodstreams, as we all do – it contributes to human verve, competitiveness and drive. But for most boys childhood is a relatively low-testosterone zone, allowing parents and teachers a dozen or so years to nurture, socialise, educate, and discipline them before it kicks in seriously again.

As the average boy heads into double figures, his testosterone levels build up again to trigger the physical changes of puberty. By around 14 years of age, they've begun to soar. Over the four or so years of adolescence, testosterone production increases tenfold as the average boy grows about a foot in height, puts on a stone of muscle and drops an octave in the pitch of his voice.

Testosterone also triggers a 40% increase in heart muscle and boosts the oxygen levels in his red blood corpuscles, preparing his body to pump extra energy to every extremity, in readiness for action.

The eternal quest

In early 2007, as I started work on this book, a 14-year-old boy hit the headlines for being the youngest person to sail single-handedly across the Atlantic. Michael Perham was taught to sail by his father, who was also his trainer for the 3,500-mile solo voyage (and, being a devoted dad, followed a mile or so behind in his own boat, just in case). Michael's voyage was demanding. In the mid-Atlantic, he encountered storms, sharks and technical problems – on one occasion he had to dive into the water, roped to his boat, to sort out a problem with the self-steering mechanism. On arrival in Antigua, he was feted as a hero.

On the same day, the *Daily Mail* carried a story about another 14-year-old boy famous for something very different. As he entered his teens, Dale Carter became the youngest child in the UK to be given an ASBO (antisocial behaviour order) for causing a string of disturbances in his local neighbourhood, throwing stones and insults, starting fires and so on. By 14, he'd graduated to theft and joyriding, and was now on remand in a young offenders' institution. His mother told the paper how he'd been a happy, sporty boy during his primary years, but spiralled down into criminality when he hit his teens.

Both these lads, as high-energy risk-takers moving from childhood to manhood, would have been in their element on the Stone Age hunting grounds. A 14-year-old male in prehistoric times was an undoubted asset to his tribe. He was approaching the peak of physical development and fitness, and primed by nature to pursue quests and face challenges. Even though, as a hot-headed, hot-blooded youth he still had much to learn and would need the calming influence of older, wiser hunters, this was clearly the time to initiate him into the world of men.

Ten millennia later, in a culture that no longer acknowledges the world of men (as in any way distinct from the world of women), our systems don't take account of the long – and extremely consistent – human tradition for channelling boys' energy during the turbulent teenage years. Instead, boys on the verge of manhood today are caged in school, treated like children and expected to prove themselves by sitting at a desk pushing pens around on paper. Until 2009, 14 was the age when English school pupils sat a petty-fogging test known as the Key Stage 3 SAT, which checked how far they'd progressed since the Key Stage 2 SAT three years earlier. Like all the SATs, this was primarily an exercise in teacher accountability – certainly not a meaningful or motivating task for a full-blooded, testosterone-driven male. It remains to be seen whether the current system can produce a useful alternative to keep boys' noses to its tests-and-targets grindstone.

If a boy has been well brought up and well educated, and if he's lucky enough to have parents and/or teachers catering for his personal needs and interests, then like Michael Perham he'll probably be well supported in steering through the storms, sharks and technical problems of adolescence. He'll be guided towards other lads with similar values and support systems, and the chances of his falling into one of the many pitfalls of 21st century adolescence are significantly reduced. But if his teachers are preoccupied with their own accountability and the other responsible adults in his life leave him to make his own way in a world of evercool market forces, he may, like Dale Carter, drift into 'bad company'. There's then a high chance that he'll start burning off the surplus energy coursing through his arteries in aimless antisocial sensation-seeking. Psychologists now recognise that the main cause of teenage misbehaviour is a potent mixture of testosterone and peer group pressure and researchers have found that even 'well-brought-up', privileged boys, when left to the mercy of the peer group, engage in antisocial activities to impress their mates.

After one joyriding expedition when Dale left a car wrecked and burning, his parents found him hiding, shaking and remorseful in an alleyway. They asked why he'd done it, and he replied: 'I don't know, Mum. I'm so sorry.' It's easy to brush off these protestations of shame as the typical response of a bad lad, and certainly, once he started his antisocial and criminal activities Dale put himself beyond sympathy and the law had to take its course. But if boys aren't offered quests worth pursuing by people they respect, they'll find their own. And if they've spent the last ten years absorbing marketing messages that self-indulgence leads to self-fulfilment, we can't be surprised when they indulge their evercool needs for power, dominion and 'edge' with acts of random destruction. Many of Dale's antics – smoking, drinking and driving – are activities officially denied to 14-year-olds, so his behaviour is clearly laced with a desire to be 'grown up'. But, as his response to his mum's question shows, once the red mist lifted even he realised how pointless it all was.

Some boys instead choose more sedentary 21st century quests, sublimating their need for excitement and action through computer games. A few hours a week of virtual questing is unlikely to do any harm (and some of the more cerebral games are almost certainly good for the S-type parts of the brain), but sedentary technological alternatives don't offer a satisfactory alternative to first-hand physical challenges. Boys' bodies and brains exist and grow in real time and space, so the eternal quest of the hunter requires real time and space too.

This leaves adults with an eternal quest of their own. How do we help boys channel this surge of male energy productively in the over-heated, over-crowded, supposedly 'unisex' culture they inhabit today?

Code of honour

The drive behind teenage boys' questing spirit is not only physical, but social. A Stone Age tribesman wouldn't get far on the
hunting ground or battlefield without the support of his peers.
So throughout the millennia, successful methods of channelling
male energy have involved teamwork. According to evolutionary
biologists, boys are naturally designed to be team players.
Across cultures, male friendship patterns are less intimate than
female ones – they're more group-oriented, and based on each
individual finding his own niche within the group. This means
that, while driven to seek as much status as possible on their
own terms, they're also able to accept an appropriate place in a
well-led hierarchy.

Almost all great human advances have been achieved through
teamwork, each man playing to his strengths and supporting
his colleagues, and even in our highly individualistic western
21st century culture, it's recognised as essential for progress. In
a modern context, team-building is at the heart of theories of
management. But for the hunter or warrior, the interdepend-
ence of the team was no mere management strategy. It was a
matter of life and death. And the rules for behaviour between
teammates on the hunt or in battle were more than just rules:
they were a code of honour.

The quests into which men channel their energies have always involved codes of honourable behaviour: the medieval code
of chivalry, the soldier's code among his comrades, the code of
Victorian gentlemen as they conquered and ruled an empire, the
universal code of 'sportsmanship'. Most male pursuits have also
involved written codes – rules and regulations, complex scoring
systems, policies and protocols – but these are legal niceties to
ensure everyone knows the ropes, the scribblings of systemisers. A code of honour is of a higher order, rooted in the deep E-
type understanding between human beings who strive together
on a quest. And a man's status among his peers has, in the past,

been closely linked to honour. It's been a male virtue across cultures and time. In countless stories from myth, legend, fact and fiction, a man's 'good name' matters at least as much as the trappings of worldly success.

Looking back through boys' development, the male code of honour probably has its origins in play. When a father plays with his son, throwing him up in the air or wrestling him to the ground, his mother may worry about potential risks, but the little boy trusts dad to keep him safe. A few years later, three- and four-year-olds allowed to play-fight with their pals learn (sometimes painfully) how to trust each other not to go too far – and how to avoid the company of those who do. During the course of childhood, this deep-seated emotional experience of trust among males is translated into consciousness via unstructured play, when boys learn to negotiate rules of behaviour between themselves, and discover the concept of 'fairness' that underpins all human ideas of justice. Honour and fairness are henceforth inextricably linked.

Anyone who works with boys knows how important honour can be. From an early age it underpins the unwritten 'boy code' that you never snitch on your mates. For adults dealing with recalcitrant youth this can be deeply irritating, but irritation is tinged with respect when a boy's loyalty to his friends clearly overcomes self-interest. Since society depends on mutual trust, good teachers recognise it as a 'childish' quality to nurture.

Part of each adult generation's task is to find ways of translating young males' primitive impulses into behaviour that fits the social structures of the day. So a code of honour, along with rigorous attention to 'fair play', has been an essential part of the organised activities devised over the centuries to channel male energy: the adult play of field sports, team games, athletic events, and so on. All of these offer not only an exhilarating physical workout, but also an opportunity for social contact and involvement in teams, clubs and so on, and the development of mutual trust between participants.

Schoolmasters through the ages have recognised that the discipline of organised sport helps teach boys about balancing rights and responsibilities, following rules, and displaying honourable, sportsmanlike behaviour to fellow players. Where adults collaborate to involve boys in this sort of activity, there's a pay-off in both personal and social development. Boys find out through the motivating route of play how to translate a primitive code of honour into their adult lives of work, home and citizenship.

Empire's sons and freedom's orphans

In the late 19th and early 20th centuries, a growing number of working-class boys were struggling to contain their adolescent demons in an industrial landscape, with little access to sporting or outdoor pursuits. Concerned adults devised new systems to draw them into organised teams. First came the Boys' Brigade, offering fellowship and discipline through brass bands and boxing. Then Baden-Powell devised the scouting movement, with its emphasis on the ancient male skills of living off the land and camp-fire camaraderie. And there were the army, air and sea cadet forces, teaching military skills, including the use of weapons. Since all were devised by sons of the British Empire, all drew on traditional trappings of systemised masculinity – uniforms, marching, flags and salutes – to help youngsters make the transition from the 'boy code' to disciplined manhood.

Then came two devastating world wars, the unspeakable evil of the Nazi Holocaust, and the invention of weapons of mass destruction. In the flickering light of countless newsreels, the trappings of systemised masculinity suddenly lost their appeal. The post-war recognition of man's inhumanity to man – and of his newfound potential to annihilate the species – spurred a reaction against masculinity in general. It was widely agreed that male aggression must be reined in before it destroyed the whole human race. Feminist thinkers (female and male) went further, claiming that male culture as a whole was at fault, and every aspect of 'patriarchy' should be questioned.

So post-war freedom has involved the rejection of traditional male values. Those newsreel memories meant many people now view uniforms, marching, flags and salutes with deep suspicion, so uniformed organisations for boys have fallen out of favour – most are only kept afloat by their preteen membership. And as feminist views spread via the schools and universities, all-male clubs and other organisations were condemned as sexist. But there was also a widespread collapse of self-confidence among men about their traditional strengths, especially in terms of raising boys. In a secular, sexually equal, anti-militaristic society, the ideals men urged boys to strive for – such as 'disciplined manhood' or a 'code of honour' – now sound faintly ridiculous. Feminist scorn for patriarchal values has transformed noble aspirations into a bad joke.

So in place of old-fashioned uniformed organisations, churches and social workers now set up easy-going youth clubs, welcoming both boys and girls. The very idea of extracurricular 'discipline' became laughable in an age of freedom, and as the century wore on the thought of older men helping adolescent boys channel their male energy began to seem quite suspect. Young people wanted to do things their way, and they had no shortage of support from media and marketers, who recognised the economic potential of the age group. It was marketing men who devised the unisex word 'teenager', and helped drive the growth of youth culture, defined by music and fashion, quite distinct from the adult world.

The influence of the culture of cool, described in earlier chapters, peaks during the teenage years, when guilt money and pester power give teenagers immense spending potential (according to one TV marketing executive, *'Teens run today's economy. There's an innate feeling for moms and dads to please the teen, to keep the teen happy.'*) So materialistic, 'evercool' messages are beamed relentlessly at the age group: teenagers in the US are believed to absorb around 3000 marketing messages a day. While parents are needed to pay for these purchases, marketers are otherwise anxious to keep teens away from the influence of parents and other responsible adults, who might want to spoil their fun.

Half a century of abandoning young people to the mercy of the market has not turned out well. There are problems with teenage misbehaviour across the developed world, but it's particularly bad in the USA and UK, where consumerism is particularly aggressive, and the influence of the family in many teenagers' lives has been almost completely eroded. According to a recent report by the Institute for Public Policy Research, many young people are now '*on the verge of mental breakdown, at risk from antisocial behaviour, self-harm, drug and alcohol abuse*'. In inner cities, peer pressure has resulted in a violent gang culture (see Chapter 10). Attempts to lure youngsters off the streets into unstructured youth clubs have proved worse than useless – according to US researchers, '*in terms of antisocial behavior, it may be better to be uninvolved than to participate in an unstructured activity, particularly if it features a high number of deviant youth*'. In the absence of clearly defined goals and plenty of firm adult guidance, deviant youth jostles for peer group status and trouble ensues.

The IPPR report, *Freedom's Orphans*, issued an urgent call for the UK government to act on this problem, suggesting that all teenagers should participate in regular '*structured, positive extra-curricular activities*', preferably with active community involvement, and probably requiring '*an element of compulsion*'. Authorities in other countries have come to the same conclusion, and politicians everywhere are looking for ways to introduce structured positive activities into the lives of disaffected teens.

But international reviews of youth projects in an age of choice and freedom show that the 'element of compulsion' is unlikely to have the desired result. In the words of one Australian research team: '*policies that compel individuals to contribute to society may actually weaken their citizenship identities*'. The teenage boys I've talked to are unanimous in their agreement: 'We get told what to do enough at school' was a typical response. 'We want to control what we do in our spare time.' So how can 21st century adults round up freedom's orphans and teach them to be good citizens?

Rights and rites

One possibility is give them more of the control they crave. In his book, *E.A: The End of Adolescence*, psychologist Philip Graham points out – as I did earlier in this chapter – that most cultures have initiated boys into adulthood at around 14 years of age. He argues that if we want our teenagers to learn how to balance rights and responsibilities, we should give them some rights and responsibilities to balance. At present, society treats adolescents as children, denying them access to the many adult activities they see celebrated all around them. They therefore act like children, challenging authority and running out of control. He suggests lowering the age of various adult rights – at present scattered confusingly through the later teenage years – to 14. Graham's list of rights includes smoking, drinking, legal sex, part-time paid work and, eventually, the vote. For consistency, he'd raise the age of criminal responsibility to 14 too.

An American psychologist, Robert Epstein takes a similar tack in *The Case Against Adolescence*. He too points out that in the past '*young people moved smoothly from childhood to adulthood as soon as they were able*' and that '*the more teens are infantalised the more psychopathology they show*'. His solution is to allow teenagers legal access to adult privileges as soon as they can demonstrate their competence on some sort of test. (This does beg the question of how one actually tests someone's competence to have sex,

smoke, drink alcohol, leave home or – most contentious of all
– vote.)

Both authors believe that giving teenagers adult rights is, in
Epstein's words, '*not about giving ... more freedom but about giving
them more authority and responsibility*'. Indeed, neither questions
the 21st century assumption that all teenagers should be in full-
time compulsory education, which leaves them economically
dependent on their parents or the state until the age of at least
16 (and, from 2015, 18). This is, in fact, also the case with the
patriarchal rites of passage that have always taken place worldwide around the age of 14. While marking a boy's transition into
the adult world – an important public statement for a status-
driven male – none confers economic freedom. On the contrary,
boys enter the world of men as humble apprentices.

The case made by Graham and Epstein is that many 21st century teenagers' problems stem from lack of status. Conferring
rights and responsibilities would be a modern-day statement of
enhanced status – a 'rite of passage' at the time when teenagers'
bodies tell them they're no longer children. But neither author
deals with the nitty-gritty of how this new 'authority and responsibility' would be exercised. Perhaps the answer is to give some
civic rights at 14 in exchange for some sort of civic responsibility.
How about a choice of 'positive structured activities' in community – or even global – projects?

An American review of youth projects found the most effective way to develop adolescents' civic responsibility was to provide activities '*aimed towards skill-building, rule-guided, led by a
competent adult*'. This is, in fact, exactly what adults have served
up to 14-year-old males through the ages. In Stone Age cultures,
the newly initiated tribesman would start at the bottom of the
male hierarchy and work his way steadily upwards by learning
from older, wiser hunters and warriors. In the same way in
medieval Europe, a high-born boy went at 14 to become a squire,
serving and learning from a knight until at 21 he was ready to
graduate to knighthood himself. Less wealthy lads left home at

14 to take up apprenticeships, living with their masters and learning the ropes over seven long years.

Perhaps, to turn freedom's orphans into willing apprentice citizens, society could grant them the ultimate 21st century right: choice. *Real* choices regarding the direction and content of their education from 14 onwards could acknowledge young people's graduation from childhood to apprentice adult. But to make this transition genuine, the range of adult skills on offer should include those that the boys themselves consider useful routes towards responsible citizenhood – not just subjects listed in a sterile national curriculum. They should involve, for those boys who need them, opportunities for outdoor adventure and supervised risk-taking. Perhaps most important of all, if youngsters are to feel committed and motivated, the person who supervises their activities and passes on the skills has to be someone *they* consider 'a competent adult'.

Learning to be men

The essential element during the transition from boy to man, as at all stages in a boy's life, is the attention of other human beings. We've already seen that human role models are important from the moment of birth, as parents unconsciously provide examples of social behaviour, language and life skills. And it's been argued several times (notably in Chapter 6) that boys need the consistent presence of a father figure, providing examples of acceptable male behaviour as they grow up. But as boys enter their teens, there may be tensions between father and son – hence the recognition across all times and cultures that adolescent boys need to move beyond the family and spend time learning from other men. Perhaps the most significant difference between the lives of adolescent boys in the past and teenage boys today is the company they keep. Until the second half of the 20th century, boys over the age of about 14 lived and worked with men.

This is probably why the two most widely respected international authorities on raising boys, Steve Biddulph in Australia and Michael Gurian in the USA, both firmly recommend that families find a male 'mentor' – not the father – when their sons enter the teenage years. It also accounts for the fact that many successful recent educational research projects have involved 'mentoring' schemes, where male teachers or older students counsel boys with educational or behavioural difficulties.

But on the whole, school today isn't the best place for a boy to find a suitable mentor. Apart from anything else, the majority of secondary teachers now are women. While boys growing up in a sexually equal world benefit from mixing with and learning from women as well as men, female teachers – for obvious reasons – can never act as male role models. But even male teachers seldom have the opportunity for the sort of personal relationship with pupils that characterises the relationship between master and apprentice. Secondary teachers teach specific subjects, covering many classes and working with maybe a hundred or so different pupils each week. And as described in Chapter 7, many now spend much of their time merely coaching pupils for exams or attempting to maintain order in a school system that's run out of steam.

Throughout *21st Century Boys* I've stressed that 'it takes a village' to ensure youngsters' healthy development. If adults want boys to act responsibly, they have to be prepared to act responsibly themselves, which means coming forward to act as role models. Twenty-first century 'villages' – real-life communities based around a locality or a specific task – must get involved again in civilising their young. To offer young people from the age of 14 a meaningful range of positive skills-based activities, we would have to extend the idea of education beyond the limits of school. The activities would have to run alongside – or perhaps in some cases take the place of – school-based learning, so other adults besides teachers would have to volunteer to pass on skills and act as role models.

Sadly, in a society low on trust and high on risk aversion, I can't imagine many British men being prepared to volunteer as a role model. Our society's growing 'fear of boys' (see Chapter 6) means most older citizens now steer clear of youngsters. According to the Good Childhood Inquiry, the British are more wary of children and young people than any country in Europe. This fear runs alongside another distinctly unhealthy and wide-spread 'fear of men'. A combination of feminist rhetoric and media obsession with paedophilia has turned every man into a potential child molester. In the words of one male interviewee who gave up running an athletic club, *'People think you're a weirdo if you want to hang about with boys.'* Indeed they do, to the extent that adults must now be cleared by the Criminal Records Bureau before even spending time in the same room as children. To this atmosphere of profound paranoia, add the facts that people are too busy to spare their time these days and that, in a society where kindness isn't valued, volunteering has gone out of fashion.

So, apart from frazzled teachers, the only adult male role models currently available to many 21st century boys are the ones they meet on screen. Decency and responsible behaviour aren't likely to be on show here, since these characteristics don't draw in the punters. Instead – along with the usual cool marketing fare – young viewers meet male celebrities illustrating the joys of nar-cissism and excess, actors modelling the full range of male anger, bullying and violence, and reality TV performers plumb-ing the depths of human misbehaviour. If they turn to a sports channel they won't find many lessons about sportsmanship: today's high-stakes commercialised sport is concerned mainly with ruthless self-interest and winning at any cost (professional fouls, performance-enhancing drugs, bribes, bungs and corrup-tion). As for male politicians and other figures in news pro-grammes, they're far less likely to be in the public eye for acts of heroism than for dishonourable conduct of some sort or ex-ploitation of power.

It's a strange way for a society to prepare its young men for manhood – depriving them of rights and status; ranging them round with temptations and restrictions; separating them from the daily influence of older, wiser men; leaving them to the mercy of their peer group; and exposing them on a daily basis to all the worst excesses of human frailty.

Me Tarzan, you Jane

We haven't even mentioned the topic usually uppermost in the minds of hot-blooded young males: sex. Here too, 21st century boys (and girls) have been largely cast adrift by the real-life adults in their lives. The seismic changes in gender roles at the end of the last century took men and women into uncharted waters, and many 21st century adults are still struggling, often painfully, to steer their own way through the flood.

Sex is now celebrated by marketing and media as a form of recreation, free of the pre-20th century hang-ups associated with procreation. But, as pointed out earlier, the yearnings awakened by an adolescent testosterone surge have emotional and social as well as physical implications. Love – though cool young men may deny it, and marketers would wholeheartedly support them – is perhaps the deepest of all human needs and, once sex hormones kick in, intimately connected with sexual behaviour. Sexual conquest is an important element of male status, so success or failure affects both self-image and social standing. And while courtship may no longer be a necessary preliminary to sex, the social and emotional drives that inspired it still linger in our psyches.

A questing beast like the human male is driven by ideals, and one of the most long-running ideals in western society is that of romantic love. We tend to associate it with the Age of Chivalry but I suspect this particular ideal arises from a much deeper male impulse. The quests that drove our tribal ancestors sprang from the need to feed, clothe and shelter not only themselves, but also their women and children. Hunters returning with the kill would be welcomed by their offspring and womenfolk, whose lives depended on them. So a man's status and honour were related not only to skill on the hunting ground, but to his success as a protector and provider. It's not just the archetypal knight on a white charger who seeks honour by protecting the vulnerable, but every man across time and cultures who's struggled to put food on his family table.

And honourable behaviour towards women and children, like that towards their comrades on the hunting ground or battlefield, can be a matter of life and death. Only a century ago when the *Titanic* hit the iceberg, the accepted code decreed that men help women and children first into the lifeboats, thus consigning themselves to almost certain death. Twentieth century feminist sneers at men's protective behaviour towards women (including condemnations for opening doors, carrying bags, and so on) were more than a graceless rejection of good manners. They were dismissing honour as stupidity, downgrading attempts 'to do the right thing' as old-fashioned claptrap, and writing off altruism as pointless human waste. Sisters may indeed be perfectly capable of doing it for themselves, but their breathtaking lack of grace has left the current generation of young men with no reason to behave honourably to women.

In terms of relationships between the genders, the removal of honour from male–female relationships is almost certainly implicated in what a high court judge recently called the 'meltdown' of family life. But there are wider implications in the stinging suggestion that men who behave honourably and altruistically are actually stupid. If society airily dismisses men's status-driven instinct to protect women and children, what happens to their sense of social responsibility?

At an intellectual level, there's no problem answering this question – there are sound rational, humanitarian and socio-economic reasons for responsible behaviour, reasons that apply equally to men and women. But human beings are not just brains on legs. Our capacity to reason is rooted in deep primitive drives, and the drive towards socially responsible behaviour is, for biological reasons, different in men and women. Successful human cultures have always recognised this, and celebrated it. Sadly, our confused society not only fails to celebrate the masculine virtues of altruism, honour and courage, we also allow media and marketing gurus to celebrate their most ignoble impulses. By the teenage years, cool culture increasingly plumbs the darkest depths of the male psyche, entertaining confused youth with the angry aggression, macho posturing and misogynist abuse of gangsta rap and 18-rated computer games.

Somehow, feminism has managed to collude with commercialism to create a culture of profound disrespect between men and women. Canadian political philosopher Waller Newell is probably right when he wearily inveighs against the feminist movement:

> Thirty years of stereotyping have equated manliness with macho, piggish, violent behaviour ... If you teach boys and young men that their gender is collectively disposed to be aggressive, mindless, and exploitative toward women, that's exactly how they will behave. It will become a self-fulfilling prophecy.

Sex and drugs and rock and roll

There's no doubt that masculinity (and femininity) must change to fit a changing world, just as men and women have adapted to fit social circumstances throughout the millennia. But the changes of the last 30 years have been extraordinarily profound and many contemporary adults, struggling to reconcile the lessons of the past with the reality of the present, simply have no idea what guidance to offer the next generation. Perhaps that's another reason why real-life role models are so thin on the ground.

As it is, teenagers are left to sort out the post-modern mess for themselves, under the twin influences of school and cool. And by the teenage years, cool has considerably more appeal for the vast majority of youngsters than an educational system bogged down in government prescription and paperwork. In a screen-saturated world, it's also constantly on tap and extremely inclusive, apparently uniting every teen – rich or poor, black or white, academic star or total illiterate – in a global democracy of youth. Its predominant theme, obvious from the very beginning of teen culture around the middle of the 20th century, is rebellion. This is to be expected in testosterone-primed boys, born to push boundaries. And of course it's fiercely encouraged by the marketers responsible for the whole phenomenon, who swiftly commodify each rebellious trend, then sell it back to their adolescent consumers.

But as youth culture evolved through the decades, teen rebellion has been fed increasingly by anger, disgust and despair at the hypocrisy of the adult world. And of course each generation of teen rebels has to ratchet up the levels of cynicism and anguish needed to fuel their passion and shock the adults they wish to punish. Marketers then pillage their psyches and wardrobes to usher in another wave of teen fashion. In the last 30 years, many youth movements have also tried to express disgust at this commercialisation, but the ad men just hoover up their anguish to add to the cool commercial brew. Over time, this dance of communication between tortured teens and responsive marketers has created a highly combustible cocktail of nihilistic fury and cynical contempt.

Teenagers' feelings about the world are mainly expressed in the same way human beings have always expressed their deepest emotions: music. During recent decades this has plumbed most depths. Sexual confusion, disillusion and perversion. Despair at a dishonourable world and disgust at its institutions. Anger and hatred of every kind, from racism to misogyny. Glorification of cruelty, criminality and violence. And, of course in a consumer society, constant celebration of products that might solve all problems – drugs, alcohol, weapons. For the musicians who bang out each teen generation's angst, there's the satisfaction of catharsis (and the possibility of being discovered by the cool merchants and integrated very satisfactorily into society). For its millions of consumers there's the opportunity to be consumed for a while by the throbbing bass and shared emotion. In a perverse way, marketers are – like the sons of empire who took urban ragamuffins off to Scout camp – offering a way to exorcise adolescent demons.

The majority of teenagers take what they need from teen culture and slough off the rest. Among the lucky ones with a future to look forward to, the painful realisation that one is being exploited (and will probably continue to be so for the rest of one's life) can often be laughed off with an ironic postmodern shrug. But in the words of Sandy Campbell, founder of the Working Rites project, '*Contemporary teen culture is peer-led, mixed-gender, and success at school is certificated. This hits the button for some boys, but by no means all.*' As time goes on and toxic childhood makes young people less resilient, more and more youngsters – especially boys – find it difficult to rise above the negative vibrations. For those with no possible future in a consumer-based society, despair increasingly breaks out in the form of antisocial behaviour, street violence and crime (see Chapter 10). Others may choose non-criminal ways of risk-taking – devoting time, money and energy to the quest for kicks through promiscuous sex, gambling, binge drinking, self-harm or computer gaming. And of course there's drug-taking, that glamorous symbol of the rock-and-roll lifestyle that morphs in the morning into misery, pain and squalor.

Most teenage boys flirt with some of these escape routes. Since they're born to be risk-takers, it would be strange if they didn't. And in a world generally devoid of adult mentors and guides, teenage misbehaviour is the nearest thing they have to rites of passage. What's worrying is that, rather than a quick kick or a 'weekend break' from a reality to which they're nonetheless prepared to return, some of them seem to be seeking something more. They seem actively to be pursuing what neuroscientist Susan Greenfield calls *'loss of the mind'* – the erosion of conscious identity through excessive use of chemical or technological fixes. She suggests that addictive escape into virtual worlds may serve the same function as drugs – choosing one's own cyber-tribe and living in a 'second world' in the form of an avatar frees a boy from the physical, social and emotional demands of real-life existence.

It seems that, the more cynical and nihilistic teen culture becomes, the more young men see 21st century 'freedom' as nothing more than the chance to get 'out of their heads' or 'off their faces' or to dissolve into cyberspace. When a sizeable proportion of a culture's young want to lose their minds, and social reformers find them *'on the verge of mental breakdown, at risk from antisocial behaviour, self-harm, drug or alcohol abuse'* I think it's fair to say that culture has seriously lost the plot.

It's time for the grown-ups to take over again.

It takes a village (reprise)

The teen culture to which we've all become accustomed over the last 50 years is based firmly on the principle of separating the men from the boys, the girls from the women. It's not in the interests of the market for teens to mingle with adults, who might influence them in the direction of responsibility and self-discipline. Keeping levels of consumption up depends on teenage self-indulgence, not the sort of sensible mature judgement a mentor might provide. So the relentless media and marketing message is that teens want no truck with the adult world ... and both teenagers and adults have come to believe it. Over 50 years, the chasm between youth and experience has expanded till it seems unbridgeable.

Yet when adolescent boys *do* have the chance to mix with men they admire – men prepared to give them some time and attention – it's soon clear that this marketing message is yet another lie. There are countless projects around the country where male role models make a difference to teenagers' lives – even the disaffected boys described in Chapter 10 change their view of what's cool when real people take an interest in them. Like boys on the verge of manhood throughout the ages, freedom's orphans are happy to defer to decent competent adults who'll initiate them into 21st century skills that seem worth having. And today's angst-ridden youngsters desperately need the influence of older, wiser men who've already negotiated their way through the Scylla and Charybdis of school and cool.

Throughout history, adults have collectively shouldered the responsibility of bringing up the next generation – it has never before been seen as devolving merely on parents or teachers. If a community is to survive, its members must get together to rear its young. In terms of dealing with the older boys, much of this responsibility must fall on men. They are the adults who know from deep within their own being that boys need quests to pursue, codes to live by and people to protect, an E-type understanding that's underpinned men's interactions with boys throughout the millennia. Of course, there have always been some perverse and perverted men who exploited the relationship, just as there have always been angry and aggressive men who twist the urge to protect and provide into an excuse for violence and destruction. But, on the whole, over time and cultures, so far the good guys have won the day and humanity has kept moving forward.

Women, their brains marinated in a different hormonal mix, can never really understand this masculine role in child-rearing. In a patriarchal society they had no option but to comply, so they gracefully took it for granted – just as men took motherhood for granted in the home. Women did their female E-type bit in the first few years of boys' lives, singing, talking and playing with their sons, and thus inadvertently laying the foundations for them to learn, reason and eventually – with the help of fathers and mentors – become the next generation of good guys. Eventually, this male/female collaboration helped move humanity on so far that people questioned men's 'right' to gender superiority. It seemed only fair and honourable that women should be accorded equal status with men.

This triumph of justice and reason is a wondrous testament to humanity's essential goodness. (Personally, I'm thrilled to have been alive when it happened. What a great species!) But the change was so seismic that it threw us off balance. We became obsessed with S-type thinking processes, which are common to both genders, and distrustful of that hormonally influenced E-type consciousness that makes men and women essentially different. But Spock-like devotion to reason can only take human beings so far – we need the motivation of our better natures to keep us on an upward trajectory.

For the sake of the next generation, it really is time to get over this fret about gender. Admitting that boys still need mothers, fathers and male mentors is not a denial of sexual equality. It's a recognition that men and women bring different strengths to the enterprise of raising their young. The achievement of sexual equality shouldn't make acting like a competent adult any more difficult than it ever was – 21st century men and women are still human beings with the DNA that makes them 'good enough' to take on their part of the task. But before they can get down to work and sort out the mess, men have to rise above the graceless feminist scorn and cynical commercialism that have made them doubt their better nature. And women have to recognise that, in terms of raising boys, there are some things sisters just can't do ...

There are some things systems can't do either. One of them is raising children. In a complex world, we need good systems to control the material, technological and scientific aspects of life and for economic, legal, political and social organisation. But applying systems to people's emotions is wrong. It's been tried many times across ages and cultures (and is currently in use on a global scale through marketing) and in the end it *always* causes problems. E-type thinking is a personal matter, so has to be real-life, upfront and human. As far as a boy's journey to manhood is concerned, it starts when his mum makes faces to attract his attention and his dad throws him in the air and catches him. And it ends when a competent member of the tribe looks him in the eye and satisfactorily answers three questions: *Who's in charge? What are the rules? And will those rules be fairly applied?*

One of the most inspiring boys I met during the research for this book was Brett. At 14, he was living in care, with far from great expectations. Then his teacher showed him some photos of poverty-stricken children she'd met on a trip to Ecuador. 'That's bang out of order!' said Brett. He and a group of friends persuaded her to defy the health and safety vultures, negotiate through all the bureaucracy, and take them to Ecuador to do something about it. They raised the money for the expedition themselves, stayed in the shanty town for a month, and under the guidance of competent adults, built a nursery school. Brett's pride about his contribution was evident when he spoke about the project at a conference on 'Creating Confidence'.

The key to Brett's transformation from disaffected teen to confident young adult was a real-life quest and the interest and guidance of real-life adults. They trusted him to work as part of a team, and he trusted them to lead the expedition and teach him the skills he needed. His teacher was a woman; the craftsman who organised the building work was a man. Both of them were more than 'good enough' to give this group of teenagers the confidence, competence and belief in humanity to confront any challenge the 21st century might throw at them.

Chapter summary

The chapter considers how, historically, the pubescent energy of boys at around 14 was channelled by their leaving the family home on some type of quest, either as hunters or warriors, or later as apprentices. Nowadays there is only test-and-target-based school achievement to satisfy this teenage need for risk-taking, so many boys create their own quests and often, influenced by 'evercool culture', these can lead to conflict with authority.

The chapter looks at the importance to boys and men of teamwork and codes of behaviour, and at how groups designed to provide these the last century fell out of favour after the Second World War as part of a general backlash against systemised masculinity. It considers the contribution of feminism to a devaluing of male honour and courage, leading to disrespect between the sexes and a confused attitude to love and sex.

It discusses various proposals to recreate the rites of passage that previously led boys more seamlessly into responsible adulthood and concludes that any solution must involve male mentoring for teenage boys. This involves an E-type understanding between boys and men, when a man satisfactorily answers the three key questions: *Who's in charge? What are the rules? And will those rules be fairly applied?*

Turning boys into men

What can parents and teachers do?

The advice by the prophet of Islam quoted in Chapter 5 (page 140) extends to cover the teenage years as well as childhood. It was translated to me in full as:

'*The first seven years are for play; the second seven are for discipline and education; the third seven are for* keeping with the adults.'

Times may have changed, but eternal truths don't. When boys reach adolescence, they need the influence of other adults beyond their family, to ease them gradually into responsible adulthood themselves.

- In his books *Raising Boys* (HarperThorsons) and *Manhood* (Vermilion), Steve Biddulph wisely suggests that parents should seek out other male 'mentors' for their teenage sons – other family members, friends and men in the local community.
- Teachers can act as role models for their pupils during school hours, but their professional responsibilities prevent them from taking a personal mentoring role in boys' lives. And many secondary teachers are women, who can't act as male role models for testosterone-driven young men.
- One way to tackle this problem is for parents and teachers to work together for the introduction of contemporary *rites de passage*:
  - genuine student choice about the direction, type and related assessment of educational provision from the age of 14
  - involvement of all students, from 14 onwards, in community (or global) projects, directed by appropriate professionals and volunteers who can act as mentors
  - in these projects, every boy has a key mentor who is male.
- Parents and teachers can also begin the fight-back against the destructive aspects of cool culture. As the adults boys know best, they can demonstrate that E-type values are at least as important as S-type sytems, status and success. This includes the implicit and explicit recognition that:
  - honour is still important among men
  - women (even the most equal of women) can recognise and respect honourable behaviour, and other ways that men communicate E-type ideals
  - casual sex, substance abuse, and other forms of self-gratification may bring immediate short-term satisfaction,

but (a) it tends to be short-lived and (b) in the long term it may damage mental and physical health

- nurturing genuine relationships and doing something you feel is worthwhile with your life increases individual well-being, enriches society, and adds greatly to the sum of human happiness.
- nurturing E-type values does not mean quashing youthful verve or creativity, or trying to resist change. But it does mean holding fast to eternal truths.

What can the rest of us do?

- Hold fast to eternal truths (see above, and below), and pass them on to the next generation through word and deed.
- If you're male, accept special responsibility for passing on E-type values and socially responsible attitudes to boys. You can do this informally in everyday life, but if you have time on your hands, you could also become a volunteer mentor (see the Mentoring and Befriending Organisation www.mandbf.org.uk). And if education can be redirected as suggested above, become involved in community projects.
- Recognise that systemised codes of behaviour are inadequate for promoting personal and social responsibility – there are always 'legal loopholes' that can be exploited for selfish gain or gratification. Honour, trust and care are *personal* qualities, and the personal responsibility of every individual to others around him (and her).
- Refuse to be impressed by smart-arsed manipulation of the rules. Express your disdain for people who behave dishonourably or carelessly, and help create a social climate in which cheating, lying, cruelty and exploitation are no longer acceptable.

- Challenge aspects of a manufactured 'culture of cool' that lead boys into self-destructive or antisocial behaviour.

We're all in this together, and the prophet of Islam's advice on page 284 holds good for all of us. So does another piece of ancient advice, summed up on the side of an Edinburgh building as

> *'Love God above all, and your neighbour as yourself'*

(in a secular society, it helps to translate 'God' as 'what's good for the world').

What can politicians do?

- Revise the secondary education system to create a 'lively educational culture' that values students' personal qualities as much as their potential to pass academic exams. Give equal weighting in curriculum design to the development of:
  - emotional resilience
  - social competence and responsibility
  - physical and mental health
  - intellectual curiosity and creative potential.
- To further these aims:
  - Give young people the right to influence their own educational destiny from the age of 14.
  - From 14, include community (and global) projects as a serious, highly valued aspect of the curriculum, with adequate time devoted to them. Involve young people in the design of these projects.
  - Look for ways of assessing students' success in this aspect of the curriculum that doesn't depend on tick-lists, written tests or systemised judgements of any kind (perhaps you could simply trust the personal judgement of students and

mentors?).

- · Ensure that the projects are *real*, not cosmetic attempts to tick a box called 'social responsibility'.
- To involve the community in secondary school projects, revise health-and-safety and child protection legislation so that it acts as a safety net *if* something goes wrong, rather than a brake on social interaction and innovation. Write trust back into public discourse.
- In reining in market and media influences (see suggestions for Chapters 7 and 8), bear in mind the effects of celebrity culture and dishonourable behaviour by public figures in influencing – and demotivating – young citizens.
- Try to behave honourably yourselves, e.g. if you make a horrible mistake in the service of the public or of parliamentary democracy, resign immediately. (You'll feel better for it.)
- Ensure that the legal and benefits systems support families in staying together, wherever possible, to rear their sons.

Chapter 10

LOST BOYS

Why some boys are born to lose ...
and how those born to win
add to their troubles

'I've been in so much trouble it's unreal. GBH, ABH, knives, assault, public disorder ... most of my arrests are for fighting.' Joe, aged 15, is talking to a reporter. 'A lot of the fighting's to do with boredom. And the
excitement of being in a gang.' Joe's been in care homes for the last
few years, constantly moved about because of his uncontrollable
behaviour, but able to find trouble wherever he goes. 'It usually
starts outside McDonald's,' says another lad to another reporter.
'You might go with one mate, then you get a phone call. Give it an hour,
there'll be ten people there, with nothing to do. Intimidating people is
something to do, a way of getting kicks. Like, "Oh my God, did you see
how they ran?"'

The media are full of such interviews these days. We hear so
many tales of violent and abusive youths that pushing a quarter
of Britons prefer not to go out at night and in 2008 a London
Cabinet minister touring her constituency wore a stab-proof
vest. Meanwhile Time magazine regaled the world with tales of
'Britain's mean streets', including a quote from the prime minister himself that: 'Kids are out of control... They're roaming the streets.
They're out late at night. There's an issue about gangs in Britain and an
issue about gun crime as well as knife crime.'

Britain's mean streets

I have to report that all the lads I met 'roaming the streets' as I researched this book were perfectly amiable when approached (even if some of them did wear hoodies). As pointed out in Chapter 6, when adults exaggerate the problem, normal law-abiding boys can be denied the leisure time freedom they need. According to the Chief Constable of the West Midlands Police, *'When you ask [adults] what they are worried about, it's not young people committing crime or young people committing criminal damage... It's actually young people just being there. Young people simply existing is now a source of concern for people.'* In summer 2008 the children's commissioners for the four countries of the UK condemned this negative attitude to youngsters, pointing out that it's beginning to impinge on their human rights. As argued throughout this book, negative media coverage combined with adults' lack of personal engagement in boys' lives has led to a nationwide 'fear of boys'. We all need to get out more.

But while exaggeration doesn't help, it's just as dangerous to ignore or attempt to minimise the problem. In the inner cities, many youngsters are indeed out of control – lost boys for whom violence and intimidation have become a way of life. Until their growing gang culture is dealt with, the mean streets they inhabit are indeed a no-go area for responsible citizens. And the more negative coverage they generate, the more copycat behaviour we can expect. Camilla Batmanghelidjh, who works with neglected and abused young people in South-East London, talks about 'initiators' and 'imitators'. The initiators are seriously damaged souls, devoid of empathy, and naturally aggressive. They set the standard for violent behaviour. The imitators are disaffected or bored lads, following the leaders in pursuit of thrills and spills. This is how a gang is formed, but it's also how gang culture – unless it's checked – can spread like a virus.

It's possible that an initiator's lack of empathy is inborn. But imitators' lack of concern about their victims' distress or pain is often the result of neglect and abuse (see 'Born losers' on page 292). Boys who cover their own pain with a hard outer coating have learned by the time they reach their teens to switch off any feelings of compassion. They regard the 'soft' approach of 'do-gooders' with contempt and instead find social solace in gang culture, where hardness is appreciated. The gang becomes a surrogate family, where younger boys look up to and learn from the older ones, acquiring the discipline that will one day render them similarly cool. It provides, says one researcher '*all the threads that hold a community together – a common identity, role models, a sense of safety… Our research suggests that young people are creating their own gangs in search of the influences that could once have been found in a traditional community*'. The result is a tribal identity, with strong territorial links – gangs often define themselves by clothing, other types of fashion statement or musical taste.

There's nothing new about all this – gangs have existed wherever youngsters are left to their own devices – but 21st century gangs have taken on a sharper edge. Today's gang members have been entertained from birth with a TV diet of coarse, casual cruelty and angry aggression. They've listened since they were small to gangsta rap, with its celebration of hard drugs, conspicuous consumption, gratuitous violence and rampant misogyny. And they've had plenty of practice of virtual murder and mayhem through their 'play' as the heartless macho heroes of X-rated computer games. Lost boys' understanding of life is based firmly in the cold male values identified by marketers – power, dominion, grossness, mastery, cynical callous humour and 'edgy' risk-taking.

There's little tribal trust or 'boy code' here. Life in the mean streets is based largely on fear and dominion ('*You've got to be a bully or you may as well own nothing because you just get robbed all the time*'). Respect and reputation depend on hardness, and boys who've never learned the art of social contact see disrespect in every inadvertent glance, upping the need for gang membership ('*If I join a gang I'm 50% safe; if I don't join a gang I'm 0% safe*'). In this world, weapons are essential – even if only for defence – and suddenly damaged, pain-ridden boys are transformed, in the words of a recent newspaper special, into '*knife-wielding, gun-toting, pit-bull-packing hoodies*'.

Media reports on gangs inevitably focus on killings and serious injury and at the time of writing knife crime dominates the headlines. In mid-2008, a spokesman for the Association of Chief Police Officers noted '*both an intensification in the severity of offending, and a worrying change in the age profile of offenders and victims, which has decreased from mid-late teens to early twenties down to early to mid-teens*'. Over a four-year period, researchers noted a 30% increase in hospital admissions as a result of serious assaults, and in 2006–07 admissions for serious stab wounds increased from around 3000 to 5000. In response to the perceived threat of violence, more children and young people began carrying blades for defence, ratcheting up the likelihood of violence. In the inner cities the death toll rose steadily, reaching a high of 27 in London in 2007 (despite a massive police crackdown, the London tally in 2008 was still 23). Gun crime, always comparatively low in Britain, reached a peak around 2003, but declined thereafter as police resources were targeted on guns.

But focusing on this week's weapon of choice is a distraction from the real issue. The worrying subplot is that gang membership is increasing, especially among younger teens. Researchers in London and Birmingham in 2008 found that the number of under-16s involved in gangs had roughly doubled in the past five years. Imitators are being drawn into violent copycat behaviour younger, and the virus of callous cruelty is spreading.

Society really does have to sort out this problem. If you've managed to read this far, you'll know only too well how boys get lost. In a world where women's work has always been low status and usually unpaid, the well-brought-up men and women who form social policy take all the most important aspects of child development for granted.

Born losers

In the vast majority of cases, boys are lost because their parents are poor. There's now a mountain of evidence to show that poverty breeds school failure, leading to antisocial behaviour, leading to youth crime. And it's scarcely surprising. From the moment of conception, a boy whose mother has a poverty-stricken diet and lifestyle is likely to be even more fragile than the average fragile male. Once he's born, if his parents are struggling with money worries, living in substandard housing in run-down neighbourhoods, and beset by fears of crime and violence, they're unlikely to provide the stable, secure home a little baby needs to thrive.

Members of poor families are statistically more likely to be depressed, have physical or mental health problems, fall into alcoholism or drug abuse or get in trouble with the law. Any of these factors can lead to anger and frustration, spilling over into domestic rows or violence. Research proves that early experiences of violence or abuse cause long-term damage to mental health.

It doesn't even have to be that dramatic. Neglect alone is enough to start a child on the road to failure, and a combination of depression, ignorance about babies' needs and constant distraction by daytime TV is a fine recipe for neglect (see Chapter 1). Researchers have found that, by the age of two, children in poor families are generally more passive, less engaged with the world around them and know fewer words than children from wealthier homes. They're less likely to be able to draw a circle, stack up a pile of bricks, point to parts of the face when asked, or put on their own shoes. If you've read Chapter 2, you can put two and two together: when these mini-scientists cried out for first-hand experiences of their world and the attention of loving adults, their cries went unheeded.

So when our poor boy arrives at nursery, he's already trailing behind the rest of his age group in the development stakes. He probably has trouble relating to other children and finds himself on the wrong side of the teacher from the beginning. What's more, nurseries in disadvantaged inner city areas are more likely to have a high turnover of poorly trained staff than in the leafy suburbs. They seldom have much outdoor space for boys to run about. So the chances of helping our little lad to deal with aggression and learn to play co-operatively, as recommended in Chapter 4, are low.

As time goes on, his school is more likely than average to have poor behavioural and educational standards – its intake is mostly children like himself, so it starts from a very low baseline. The law nevertheless requires that poor boys start formal schoolwork at the same early age as everyone else, so without the linguistic, social and emotional foundations he needs to learn, the 3Rs remain a mystery to him (see Chapter 5). Living in a poor neighbourhood, he's also wide open to every aspect of 'toxic childhood', including junk food, junk play, plenty of exposure to the culture of cool, and little parental support in developing habits of self-discipline (Chapters 6 to 8). In these circumstances, the current school system is little more than an irritating distraction – it certainly offers no hope of escape.

At home, the effects of poverty continue to blight his childhood. The family stresses listed earlier don't bode well for long-term domestic harmony, and the malign sociocultural cocktail described in Chapter 9 makes things worse. Lack of trust and commitment between sexual partners and lack of social pressure for fathers to 'protect and provide' make all 21st century relationships fragile. Poor parents often live together rather than marrying, and cohabiting couples are more likely to split than married ones, so the chances of both our fragile male's parents being around throughout his childhood are worse than the one-in-three average.

The repercussions of family breakdown in poor families are even more profound than in others. According to a 2005 government report, boys from poor lone-parent families are more likely to suffer from mental health, developmental or behavioural problems than any other group of children. So chances are they'll end up in the criminal justice system: UNESCO records that 70% of young offenders (who are, of course, predominantly male) are raised in single-parent homes and more than half have, at some point or another, been through the care system.

The poverty trap

Amid the mass of depressing evidence and statistics, it's easy to assume that poverty is a trap from which boys can never escape. Perhaps society should just throw in the towel? Yet, in the comparatively recent past, they did escape. Until the late 1970s, the gap between rich and poor in the UK grew steadily narrower. This spurred many poor parents, determined to give their sons the chances they'd been denied themselves, to put time and effort into raising them. Throughout the first three-quarters of the 20th century – despite the devastating fall-out of two world wars – a happy combination of nature, nurture and culture meant these parents' efforts were often rewarded.

Part of this success story was people's very belief in the possibility of a better life. Hope is the essential driver of change. Hopeful mothers are less likely to become depressed; hopeful fathers move heaven and earth to put food on their family's table. But there was another significant element – the stuff people took for granted. Before all-day TV and video, mothers who wanted to calm or entertain their babies had no option but to talk or sing to them, inadvertently developing their language skills. Before the build-up of traffic and generalised fear, all children played out and learned to get along together, inadvertently developing their social skills. So no matter what their background, a growing number of children had the chance to develop the linguistic, social and emotional foundations they needed to succeed at school. With a generally less driven start

to primary education in the post-war years, there was also considerably more chance of a lad from the mean streets learning
to read and thus setting his foot on the ladder to educational
success.

When I became a teacher in the early 1970s my generation
genuinely believed we were on the way to eradicating poverty
and all the social evils it drags in its wake. We could see that, by
teaching children to read and write, we gave every one of them
the chance to be master of their own destiny. And then in the
1980s, unintended side effects of rapid social and cultural
change transformed the early childhood experiences of poor
children. Nature and nurture stopped working together to create those sound foundations for education. Schools went
through various educational fads and fancies to end up in their
current parlous state. The toxic influences of a booming consumer culture – poor diet, lack of sleep, an indoor sedentary
screen-based lifestyle – reduced children's chances even further.
Hope receded ... and social mobility ground to a halt. Despite
Britain's economic success during the last 25 years, by 2005 we
had the seventh widest poverty gap in the European Union, a
gap that appears to be growing year on year. So there are steadily
more born losers about, and the streets of the inner cities grow
meaner by the day.

Yet it's no more inevitable today that the rich should get
richer and the poor poorer than it was 30 years ago. In other
economically successful parts of Europe – notably the Nordic
countries – the poverty gap doesn't yawn anywhere near as wide.
It's no coincidence that these countries have chosen for over 50
years to pursue a child-friendly economy, rather than encouraging the growth of 'economy-friendly families'. Parents are celebrated for their contribution to society, and mothers (or fathers)
encouraged to stay at home for the first few years. There's
tremendous emphasis on childcare and early education services,
with plenty of outdoor play, song and stories in the nurseries
and not a TV or computer screen to be seen. No child is forced

to start on the 3Rs till they're seven, and play is valued. This positive cultural attitude permeates society, so parents in poorer families still have hope for their children's future. Finland and Sweden also do well in international comparisons of educational achievement, as well as scoring highly in the 2007 UNICEF review of children's well-being – the one in which the UK came bottom.

Their crime figures are impressive too. While recent figures for the UK show 141 out of every 100,000 people are in prison, the numbers in Nordic countries range from 73 to 59, well under half our total overall. In fact, Britain has the highest number of incarcerations in Europe and in 2008 the government announced plans to develop several super-prisons, suggesting they expected things to get worse rather than better.

Tough on crime

If a born loser ends up in prison, his chances of retrieval are slight – a tragic outcome both for the bad lad himself and for society, which loses a potential taxpayer and gains a huge drain on the public purse. But if a teenage hoodlum breaks the law and gets away with it, it encourages all his mates (and their mates, rippling outwards through society) to think they can get away with it too. It also sends a message to law-abiding citizens that the government is not 'tough on crime', that the criminal justice system can't be trusted to protect them and that boys – all boys – are potential criminals, so should be removed from the streets. As gang culture and youth violence proliferate, justice has to be seen to be done, to prevent the situation spiralling any further out of control.

Enter the Youth Justice Board, with its vast array of non-custodial sentences, orders and programmes for young offenders – ASBOs, ISOs, CROs, ISSPs and many other acronyms administered by the YOT (youth offenders team), usually combining some sort of restriction on individual liberty with positive help – drug treatment, anger management courses, literacy lessons, restorative justice processes and so on. It's a very proper attempt to be 'warm but firm', and bring a little discipline into lost boys' lives. But, despite the best efforts of many good people, the older and colder boys grow, the less effective a 'soft-looking' systemised solution is likely to be. Discipline, like love, is personal. What bad lads need more than orders and programmes is the influence and interest of authoritative men whom they respect more than their gang leaders.

Shaun Bailey, who runs a youth project called 'My Generation' in West London, reckons he was saved from a life of crime by joining a cadet force at the age of 12. He went along for the sport, drill and camping expeditions, and thinks two factors helped him keep out of trouble. The first was discovering that there were ways to succeed *'that didn't involve beating people up or making money by hustling'*. The other was learning to accept orders from *'role models who were not from the street'*. He points out that fatherless boys don't take kindly to being told what to do but *'when a big hard man tells you to shut your mouth, you do it. Once you've learned to accept discipline from an adult, you can carry that through to school and home.'*

His story reminded me of one I heard from a high court judge at a conference. She told us about an ex-marine who ran a centre for young offenders, whose success rate with bad lads was the best she'd come across. His method was quite simple: *'He ran 'em about a bit ... ran 'em about a bit,'* she told us, *'and then he listened to them.'* It's the same recipe used by sergeant majors since the year dot: show the lads you're a hard man, give physical challenges, establish your authority ... and then – if you're man enough yourself – move into a mentoring role. Not so much 'warm but firm' as 'firm, then warm'. It's the masculine version of the S/E child-rearing balance, and once lost boys have hit puberty it may well be the only way to retrieve them.

Ray Lewis, a former prison governor and ordained minister, takes on the role of 'big hard man' for boys referred to him by parents, teachers and social workers who have run out of options. His academy for disaffected lads scoops them up during out-of-school hours to develop discipline and self-respect with a diet of marching, PE, extra lessons in the basic skills and – when they need it – a listening ear from the burly ex-prison guards he employs as mentors. Lewis is a charismatic hard-edged character: *'In many ways I'm the biggest gang leader in London.'* He has no truck with political correctness, stating categorically that women teachers can't inspire respect in lads raised on gangsta rap and expressing contempt for 'ologists' who dole out diagnoses but no solutions.

The sort of male persona who can command the respect of bad lads doesn't always tick all the boxes of a liberal unisex establishment. Ray Lewis discovered this when he accepted the post of London's deputy mayor for young people, only to resign a few weeks later amid rumours of financial, sexual and other scandals in his past. Interestingly, the 'listening ex-marine' was drummed out of his job too, because he managed to alienate everyone in the local youth justice department. Big hard men are likely to be forthright, combative, possibly arrogant, and inevitably risk-takers – it would be surprising if their cupboards didn't contain a few skeletons. But if society allows boys to reach the teenage years without becoming at least partially civilised, their only hope of re-engagement is a male mentor who can impress them.

Alf Hitchcock, the police chief chosen to advise government on youth crime, recommends that jobless youths should take part in a non-military version of national service, helping others in their own communities or working on overseas aid programmes: *'It should be something where they can learn skills and help people. It would give them a sense of responsibility and achievement – and some discipline. It should not be seen as a punishment, or a pressurised duty like conscription, but as an opportunity to go forward into a successful adulthood.'* This sounds very similar to the *Freedom's Orphans* recommendations for all teenagers, or the mentor-led rite of passage I suggest in Chapter 9. But a system is only as good as the people who work in it. The organisers of programmes for disaffected boys would have to admit that they need tough, authoritative mentors, the sort of 'big hard man' whom testosterone-driven young males deem worthy of respect, but who might not go down too well with females and ologists. And if they want them to be authoritative, they have to trust them to get on with the job. Alternatively, of course, we could just build lots more super-prisons.

Tough on the causes of crime

In the long term, prevention has to be better than cure for both lost boys and society, and it certainly makes good economic sense. Investing at the beginning of a poor child's life may actually bring in a return by turning out a responsible citizen, whereas present policies just lead to never-ending expense once they hit adulthood. As one recent report put it, '*the dividend is 12–16% per year for every £1 of investment – a payback of four or five times the original investment by the time the young person reaches their early twenties*'. The way to avoid the need for excessive firmness at the end of the child-rearing process is to put in more warmth at the beginning.

In the last ten years, scientific evidence has mounted that the best antidote to poverty and crime is good mothering. The most critical period for brain development is the nine months before and three years after birth, so if a mother looks after herself well during pregnancy, then looks after her baby well when he's born, his chances of growing up to be a responsible citizen are much greater. If she doesn't, and things start going wrong, it becomes progressively more difficult to sort out the mess.

The trouble is that poverty-stricken women are seldom well placed to look after either themselves or their babies. They're usually poorly educated, often have drug and/or drink problems, may well be depressed or abused by a partner, and have scant idea of a little baby's needs. Mothering skills are passed through the generations by example, and the odds are that this mother's mother wasn't up to much herself. The unfortunate lass is unlikely to have the support of a partner either: over the last couple of decades there's been a huge rise in the number of young single mothers living in poverty.

The most recent government solution has been to urge single mums into work or training, so that they acquire some skills (and a stake in society) while their sons can be properly cared for in a nursery. But the critical input in the early years is mother-love, not available in an institution. So another strategy is to try and teach poverty-stricken mums how to relate to their babies. A decade ago, a number of Sure Start projects were set up in disadvantaged areas, with drop-in centres and special courses. Sadly, the neediest mums, wary of authority, failed to drop in. While Sure Start has now expanded across the country, offering 'integrated services' to all young families, the ones who most need its services remain stubbornly 'hard to reach'.

These are young women desperately in need of mothering themselves, which is probably why the only project that's had consistently good results is the Nurse Family Partnership programme designed by Professor David Olds of the University of Colorado. Olds had the idea of matching vulnerable expectant mothers with experienced nurses who could become their friends and mentors during pregnancy and the early months of their baby's life. This neatly combines impersonal S-type organisation and personal E-type engagement. The system identifies the mums, provides the nurses and keeps them up to date with scientific findings about child development. The nurses build a relationship with the young women based on mutual trust. They help them establish a healthy lifestyle during pregnancy, then show them how to look after and interact with their babies.

Over 25 years the Olds project has been shown to make a real difference to mothers' and children's prospects in extremely disadvantaged areas of the USA. But trained nurses don't come cheap and it takes time to forge a fruitful relationship with a young mother, so it's an expensive option. It's being trialled in the UK but there's already concern that our version, using health visitors, will fail because the case loads are too high – Britain has a long record of attempting to provide childcare solutions on the cheap. It does seem, however, that if politicians want to influence children's very earliest years, they're better off investing in highly targeted, one-on-one, human intervention, rather than wasting money on institutions and systems that don't hit the button.

Education, education, education

With the help of a properly funded Olds-type mentor, a poor young mum might ensure her son gets off to as good a start as possible. But as Professor Leon Feinstein, the UK's major researcher in the field of childhood poverty, points out, a good start is only the start. The child still faces a childhood with all the problems listed in 'Born losers', on page 292, and to ensure he continues to prosper, society has to offer the right sort of support throughout his childhood. His family will probably need targeted help in terms of health care and parenting skills on and off throughout his childhood. And they'll need it from professionals who – like an Olds nurse – are able to relate to them long term on a personal level. This means Sure Start projects and children's centres must offer outreach workers who can build a personal relationship with families.

But this sort of people-intensive provision isn't sustainable indefinitely. Somehow, society must help born losers break out of the cycle of poverty altogether. So in the end we come back to the oft-repeated mantra 'education, education, education'. And sadly, the word needs saying thrice because our education system – in England at least – manages to fail poor boys three times over.

The first failure is that it starts too early. In Chapter 5, we saw how 'too much too soon' means that poor boys often fall at the first fence in the literacy stakes. The government's own figures show that 50% or more of the children in disadvantaged areas of the country arrive in their reception class with significant language delay. Learning to read and write is pretty difficult if you can't talk and listen first. 'Born losers' need time to talk, sing, listen to stories and play with the other children to acquire the spoken foundations of written language.

Failure number two was described in Chapter 7. We saw how, throughout the school system, over-testing and bureaucracy lead to bland, boring teaching and problems with pupils' behaviour. Poor boys who fail to thrive in the classroom (which in inner-city areas can be just about all of them) are very often behind these behavioural problems. Instead of learning to control and discipline their minds at school, they reject their teachers' values and abandon themselves to the self-indulgent pursuit of 'cool'. Researchers have found that marketing influences are greater on poor children than others. These boys – perhaps more than any others – need teachers with authoritative control of their classroom, and the freedom to create a rich and lively 'school culture'.

Education's final failure happens, as illustrated in Chapter 9, when 'born losers' reach puberty. By this time, the pursuit of cool has led them inexorably towards gang culture – the only cool substitute for the family structure they've always lacked – and hormonal changes drive them to seek action and status. Their main hope lies in finding a male mentor who can lure them away from cool cultures, teach them some useful skills and initiate them into responsible adulthood. There's little chance of interesting them in a school system that's entirely focused on pencil-and-paper work for exams they're destined to fail. Indeed, their very presence in the classroom simply makes it tougher for teachers to reach the other pupils.

Born winners

How does a society manage to lock itself into systems that, instead of levelling the playing field, seem to create problems and perpetuate poverty? It isn't as if it's in anyone's interests to have a yawning gap between rich and poor. In *The Impact of Inequality*, public health expert Professor Richard Wilkinson shows how, in societies where income differences are smaller, community life is stronger, violence rarer, health better, life expectancy longer, prison populations smaller and educational attainment higher. Everyone – even the rich – benefits when society as a whole is going well. Professor of Economics Richard Layard comes to the same conclusion in his book *Happiness*, where he argues that inequalities of wealth lead to fear, stress and mental health problems, not just among the poor but among the wealthy.

This is where we came in. It was Professor Layard who, at the end of the Introduction, suggested we all should give less prestige to smart-arsed behaviour and more to kindness – that is, to try and redress the balance in our society between S- and E-type thinking styles and values. Until we do, we'll not only fail the 'born losers', but we'll go on promoting a certain type of 'born winner' – high-functioning systemisers who often seem to suffer from an empathy bypass. These boys (and an increasing number of girls) tend to be a dab hand with data, but not much cop at working out how people tick. It makes them susceptible to economic and political theories that emphasise the power of data above human input. Such born winners have come to dominate our political classes.

In a way, they are victims of the system too. There seems to be no doubt that they all genuinely want social justice but, ironically, their low E-type thinking style helps perpetuate inequality. Since the early 1980s, many UK politicians – like bankers and the heads of big corporations – have been in thrall to a political philosophy known as 'game theory'. Its underpinning principle is summed up by documentary-maker Adam Curtis in his BBC series *The Trap* as '*Human beings will always betray you; only trust the numbers.*'

High-functioning born winners easily absorb this mind-set. Since many of them have problems understanding people (at least, people from outside their own social circle), it's comforting to translate human beings into stick figures on a graph. Computers can crunch the most amazing sorts of data these days, turning almost anything into numbers, and once the untrustworthy human element is removed from the equation, policy decisions are much easier. The stick figures stand for abstract commodities, which can be 'lifted out of poverty', 'educated' or 'provided for'. And the political spotlight can be trained exclusively on the systems needed to deliver this utopian state of affairs, the data to drive procedures, and the targets to measure success.

So we end up with top-down control of Stick People Land, co-ordinated from the centre. Our born winners devise sophisticated performance targets based upon measurable outcomes. Then they create highly prescriptive strategies and initiatives complete with long-, medium- and short-term plans and objectives, backed up with sheaves of risk assessments and regulatory tick-lists. To someone who's abandoned (or possibly never experienced) E-type thought, all this must seem infinitely preferable to providing frontline workers with high-level training, then leaving them to get on with the job. Human beings are fallible, so it would be dangerous to let them take responsibility, exercise judgement or show initiative. But all a stick figure has to do is 'deliver' services by carrying out procedures and filling in the forms that allow the numbers to work their magic.

In the paranoid world of 'game-theory' politics, the non-professionals in children's lives – parents, other family members and adults in the community – can be trusted even less than professionals. Since they're not employed by the state, there's no way of controlling their behaviour through regulation and target-driven incentives. And anyway the human qualities they supposedly bring to the business of child-rearing (such as love, talk, song, play and tolerance) can't be counted and measured. So our born winners' aim is gradually to move responsibility for child-rearing away from parents and community, and towards professionals who can be controlled by centralised authority.

The end result is a society that trains people to distrust their own judgement and the judgement of others – a society with no place for E-type strengths or common sense. Parents feel incapable of bringing up their children, people in the local community think the local children are no concern of theirs, and demotivated 'professionals', drowning in paperwork, find themselves constantly watching their backs – if anything goes wrong in this system, the obvious reaction is recourse to the law. It's also a world in which the adult population has been taught to value worldly status and material success – as summed up in shallow celebrity lifestyles – over real-life human relationships, and to rely increasingly on systems to substitute for kindness and honour.

Inevitably, the people who suffer most from this lack of faith in humanity are those at the very bottom of the pile: the poorest children. Despite the Every Child Matters window dressing (or perhaps because of it), a child protection expert in 2008 claimed that serious neglect is now so widespread in disadvantaged areas that exhausted teachers, social workers and others don't even notice it: *'They get so used to seeing low-level parenting. Then it starts to look average. They fail to appreciate how much harm it's doing.'* My impression is different: the thousands of frustrated professionals I meet every year are well aware of the neglect around them and the harm it's doing. But they're so deskilled, disempowered, and bound up in red tape that they have no idea what to do about it.

Over the last ten years, the UK government has invested billions of pounds to eradicate child poverty, and devised innumerable S-type strategies and initiatives for the purpose, with targets, outcome duties, league tables and tick-lists galore. And since 1997 well over half a million children have indeed been technically transferred from one side of a poverty balance sheet to the other. Sadly, out in the real world it's gradually become clear that the change happened only on paper: poor children's lives had not got noticeably better. By summer 2008 a *Guardian* columnist was complaining that '*Evidence, reality, consequences, the classroom failures of struggling pupils – none of these matter. The statistics, however flawed and unreliable, are all that count.*' Several high-profile child protection cases later in the year graphically demonstrated the inadequacy of red tape and regulation in protecting vulnerable children.

The 21st century challenge for high-functioning politicians is to spot the difference between stick people and real-life human beings. Numbers and systems are important, but so are ancient, immeasurable human qualities. The critical ingredients of good childcare can't be conjured up by government policies, controlled by watchdogs or turned into numbers for computers to crunch. They're human qualities, and they'll only reappear if we value them. Albert Einstein, one of the highest-functioning systemisers of all time, used to have a sign hanging over his desk at Princeton that read: '*Not everything that counts can be counted, and not everything that can be counted counts.*'

Levelling the playing field

Lack of empathy is not 'natural' in either gender. As Einstein and other great human minds have illustrated, it's possible to excel in both S- and E-type thought. Jesus Christ, William Shakespeare, Abraham Lincoln and Nelson Mandela spring to mind. The rest of us may not have the genetic material to attain these dizzy heights, but the overwhelming majority of us are born with the capacity for both S- and E-type thought. Both types are developed through our experiences, especially in the early years of life. I've attempted throughout this book to explain why boys may find it slightly harder to develop E-type strengths than girls, and how the tumultuous social changes of the last few decades have made it harder still. In the final two chapters, I've suggested that social pressures now make it even more difficult for men to display E-type skills in ways that come naturally to them. And that, in a world where it seems safer to trust numbers than people, both men and women have learned to rely on the objective S-type analysis than to trust to subjective E-type insights which may not be understood by the other gender.

The escape from S/E imbalance is to some extent – as Professor Layard suggests – a simple question of changing mind-sets. If everyone in the country were to stop celebrating the smart-arses and start showing appreciation of kind behaviour, the UK would at a stroke become a friendlier, happier place. Even if only a few people made that decision, deciding to trust and be trustworthy to their fellow men rather than operate on fear, there are S- as well as E-type reasons to believe their influence should eventually triumph. In his 2008 book *The Logic of Everything*, economist Tim Harford describes the Hammond computer model in which a few honest citizens sprinkled among a population of dishonest crooks eventually creates an 'outbreak of honesty'. The crooks work on the assumption that everyone else is dishonest, but if they personally meet enough examples of honest behaviour to start fearing other crooks will act honestly, they do the same.

> *After a long period of pure corruption ... suddenly, very quickly, everybody in the world decides to be honest. The moment the process starts, it's impossible to stop: offering a corrupt deal becomes irrational and suddenly the world is full of crooks who have decided that honesty is the best policy. It is a self-fulfilling decision. The cascade of tiles on the computer screen changes colour abruptly as honesty breaks out everywhere.*

As a cock-eyed optimist, I'm delighted to discover this S-type vindication of my E-type conviction that it'll all work out all right in the end. But we could help it along by creating an educational system that ensures the next generation of born winners are not only bright but also balanced thinkers. At present, the three failures of 'education, education, education' damage the born winners as well as the born losers.

E-type failure for a born winner starts with the encouragement to be too clever too soon. You may remember that back in Chapter 5, I suggested that an early start to formal education could be just as bad for high-functioning S-brainers as for children from disadvantaged homes. A carefully structured kindergarten stage up to the age of six or seven, with an emphasis on play, song, dance, stories, art, drama and opportunities to 'mess about' outdoors, is important for all children. These activities – as old as humanity itself – work at a deep emotional level, building on *all* children's natural strengths and interests. They provide opportunities for combining S-type learning and natural E-type understanding of oneself and others, laying the foundations of balanced thought processes.

The UK tradition of pushing high-functioning systemisers towards formal learning as soon as they are able (which is often very early indeed) not only robs them of enjoyable childhood experiences, it also steers them towards S-type and away from E-type thought. This is particularly damaging for bright boys, who are less likely than girls to be natural empathisers. Many of them end up as educational high-achievers, but socially and/or emotionally out of sync. So it's no wonder that when these little professors grow up to become their society's leaders and opinion-formers, the social ethos of the nation is thrown off balance too.

As they move through the school system, high-systemising, low-empathising born winners may have trouble in the playground, where there's a very reasonable fear of bullying by born losers. This, of course, reinforces the message that human beings can't be trusted, whereas pencil-and-paper tests can. So as time goes on, the experience of school convinces another generation of born winners that S-type status and success are infinitely preferable to grubby humanity. Hence the second failure of education – over-reliance on tests, targets and bureaucracy that, as recorded in a 2008 OECD report, *'seems to perpetuate rather than break the cycle of inequality'*.

The third failure of education is now inevitable. A born winner couldn't possibly see how today's bright youngsters might benefit from human-led community-based rites of passage. After all, they would have hated it themselves! Imagine being dragged from the security of the examination room to mix with non-academic people teaching low-level practical skills and values that can't be quantified? So secondary education retains its academic bias, and schools keep looking for ways to furnish non-academic pupils with paper qualifications, which are – in a born winner's world – the only ones that really matter. Life's Little Ironies hit new heights when earnest attempts to iron out elitism actually create it.

Colder, sadder, meaner

Allowing *all* children the chance to develop their social and emotional skills as well as intellectual ones benefits everyone in the long run. If the smart-arsed 'masters of the universe' behind the current financial crisis had spent more of their childhood learning the ropes of human interaction and acquiring a little common sense, perhaps E-type alarm bells would have sounded before the world's financial systems began to collapse.

Sadly, most corporate bosses, media and marketing men appear to have been reared with the same S-type bias. They simply don't recognise that brainwashing babies, hijacking playground culture for corporate profit, and driving a wedge between angst-ridden adolescents and the adults who care about them have serious long-term consequences for society. In terms of 'lost boys' these commercial tactics hugely ratchet up levels of 'toxicity' throughout childhood. Since most poor parents don't or can't take responsibility to raise their sons in an authoritative way, they're left to marinate from birth in a screen-based stew of evercool marketing messages, shallow celebrity culture and media violence.

I've said little about screen violence in earlier chapters because responsible parents do still struggle to restrict their sons' access to such stuff. But common sense and scientific research are in accord that exposing children to scenes of cruelty can either desensitise them to its effects on others or make them more timid and wary of their fellow humans. At the beginning of this century, the American Medical Association, American Psychological Association and American Academy of Pediatrics got together to issue a joint statement on these ill-effects: '*At this time well over* 1000 *studies… point overwhemingly to a causal connection between media violence and aggressive behaviour in children.*' There have been many more studies since, but it hasn't made any difference to the levels of violence readily available for children's consumption. Indeed, they appear to be getting worse.

As I write, the 2008 summer box office hit is *Batman: The Dark Knight.* Marketing for this film was brilliant and relentless, with endless toys and collectables, junk food promotions ('Feed your dark side'), website treasure hunts, TV tie-ins, ringtones and other merchandising tricks that go right under most adult radar. The playground peer pressure to see the movie was immense, especially among boys, and translated in the home into massive pester power. Unable to compete with this onslaught, the British Board of Film Censors gave the film a 12A certificate. This allowed parents to assume it must be OK for children under 12, as long as they are accompanied by an adult.

But social commentators across the political spectrum didn't agree. '*With its numerous shootings and knifings, persistent atmosphere of nihilistic morbidity, and the terrifying appearance and speech of Heath Ledger's Joker, this is as surely a* 15 *as the last shirt on a rugby team,*' said *Guardian* columnist Mark Lawson. In the *Daily Telegraph,* Jenny McCartney complained that the '*sustained level of intensely sadistic brutality*' at the very least '*taints children's world view*'. Neither questioned the critical acclaim for the film (which is a disturbing vision of a desperately corrupt society) and Ledger's remarkable performance. Their concern was whether such stuff should be shown to children, whose world view and social attitudes develop in response to the experiences adults provide.

For boys whose lives are already tainted by the misery of poverty, the film graphically reinforces the message that life is bleak, soulless and cheap, and the Joker's throwaway, calculating cruelty lends 'evercool' support to the opinion that '*intimidating people is something to do, a way of getting kicks*'. When society encourages its young in these beliefs from an early age, we can't be surprised that Britain's mean streets grow meaner by the year. But *The Dark Knight*'s success can be counted in billions of pounds (some of which pour into the Exchequer and are needed for the never-ending quest against social injustice), so the high-functioning systemisers of the corporate and political world happily close their eyes and ears to its potential ill-effects on children's minds.

A Department of Health report on child protection describes 'emotional abuse' as '*the persistent emotional ill-treatment of a child such as to cause severe and persistent effects on the child's emotional development*'. It goes on to say that:

> It may involve conveying to children that they are worthless or unloved, or valued only insofar as they meet the needs of another person. It may feature age or other developmentally inappropriate expectations being imposed on children. It may involve causing children frequently to feel frightened or in danger, or the exploitation or corruption of children.

In the light of the research quoted throughout this book, I believe that children growing up in poverty in the UK – especially the more fragile male children – are victims of state-sponsored child abuse. In addition to the natural disadvantages of their birth, school now condemns them to an early-start, tests-and-targets culture, while the extracurricular culture of cool feeds them a constant diet of media violence and marketing messages. Since the real-life adults in their lives are unwilling or unable to protect them from either of these malign influences, it's not surprising if they grow up emotionally, socially and cognitively stunted.

But it's not just born losers who suffer in a society where systems, status and worldly success are valued far above personal relationships and empathetic understanding. It's everyone. As competitive consumerism gained ascendancy over the last quarter-century, the cynical exploitation of others (including children) has become acceptable, and the importance of kindness forgotten. Care has been sidelined, selfishness celebrated and the breakdown of trust that drives lost boys into gangs now pervades society. In economist Richard Layard's words, *'Our fundamental problem today is a lack of common feeling between people – the notion that life is essentially a competitive struggle. With such a philosophy the losers become alienated and a threat to the rest of us, and even the winners can't relax in peace.'* Until we do something to challenge this culture, all 21st century boys – and girls – will grow up in an increasingly divided land.

Chapter summary

This chapter looks at the rise of gangs in modern culture – the lost boys whose understanding of life is based in the cold male values identified by marketers – power, dominion, grossness, mastery, cynical callous humour and 'edgy' risk-taking. It looks at the causes of crime and concludes that poverty, and all the social ills that accompany it, is the single most important factor, since it leads to poor child-rearing. It discusses why in the not too distant past education was able to lift children out of poverty, and why the poverty gap has grown so much larger in Britain than in other European countries.

It then discusses the failure of systemised solutions to youth crime and suggests that the best solution might be 'tough' programmes run by authoritative male mentors. However, the best long-term antidote to crime is good mothering, which research suggests requires very early intervention by authoritative female mentors. In general, however, the problem of 'born losers' will not be solved until society's 'born winners' (in government, commerce, finance, education, etc.) begin to recognise the importance of E-type strengths, so they stop relying on smart-arsed systemised solutions and start believing in the possibility of human kindness.

Bringing lost boys into the fold

What can parents and teachers do?

- Work together to bring up and educate bright, balanced boys, as described in previous chapters.
- Acknowledge that – even if you do a wonderful job – the boys for whom you're responsible live in the same world as those who haven't been so fortunate.
  - In the short term, make sure responsible teenage boys are streetwise
  - The best preparation is outdoor play and opportunities to be 'free-range' in the preteen years
  - Share commonsense advice (e.g. download the Kidscape 'Street Sense' leaflet for teenagers from www.kidscape.org.uk).
  - In the long term, work to ensure that society's born losers (and winners) grow up as bright and balanced as the boys in your care – see below.

What can the rest of us do?

- Support the concept of professional support for families incapable of taking responsibility for their own sons (and daughters) – especially 'mothering the mothers' of children born into severely disadvantaged homes.
- This means accepting that solving entrenched social problems costs money – taxpayers' money.
- It also means ensuring that our political representatives use the money productively – not just to create and sustain systems that fulfil the requirements of Stick People Land.
- So when voting for political representatives (at all levels) look for candidates with experience of the real world, who are clearly as interested in human values as in systemised solutions. Challenge them about the things that really matter, and don't let them bamboozle you with a load of systemised claptrap.
- Accept that, in our daily dealings, human beings are not, and never will be, perfect. We can only ever be 'good enough', and attempts to achieve perfection through complex accountability procedures generally lead to bureaucratic confusion, paralysis and fear. Since this usually makes things worse rather than better, we need to return to a social ethos where adults trust each other to act in the common good, rather than constantly watching their backs.
- As a citizen, ensure that you always try to be 'good enough' and assume that everyone else is trying too, e.g.
  - take responsibility for your own actions (and mistakes)
  - expect others to take responsibility for theirs
  - when something goes wrong, try to sort it out at a human level, exercising tolerance and consideration
  - use recourse to professional bodies or litigation only as a last resort.

- Be sceptical about 'top-down' systemised solutions to human problems. Where your personal experience suggests that institutions and regulations are causing more problems than they solve – so that taxpayers' money is being wasted – challenge them:
  - discuss the matter with colleagues and friends
  - point out the problem, perhaps in a letter to a local or national newspaper
  - make use of web-based reporting and consultation procedures (see 'What can politicians do?' below)
- In daily life and personal interactions, increase the amount of trust in the world by:
  - acting honourably yourself, and expecting others to act honourably in return
  - valuing honourable or kind behaviour in others
  - avoiding knee-jerk reactions to other social groups, e.g. if there are young people 'hanging out' in your neighbourhood, don't assume they're up to no good unless that's clearly the case.
- But if they *are* causing distress or disturbance, it's your civic duty to report them to the police before their boundary-pushing gets out of control. The Home Office definition of antisocial behaviour is 'any activity that impacts on other people in a negative way'. Since this is so wide as to be meaningless, it requires common sense in interpretation and, in the case of young people, a degree of tolerance.
- Support changes to the educational system that will improve the S/E balance in society in the future.

What can politicians do?

- Recognise that there's a limit to what politically inspired

systems can achieve. The (rather obvious) lessons of recent
systems failures are that:

- top-down targets distort human behaviour
- tick-lists and paperwork distract frontline workers from the
  job in hand
- excessive regulation and accountability procedures stifle initiative and encourage a jobsworth mentality.

- Recognise the limitations of legislation in creating a healthy
  society. While the law provides a safety net to protect citizens
  from deviant behaviour, it can't regulate every aspect of
  human behaviour:
  - a healthy society depends on individuals exercising social
    responsibility
  - social responsibility depends on recognising other people's
    needs as well as your own, which involves the capacity for
    E-type thought.

- The capacity for E-type thought is 'caught' during childhood,
  through children's relationships with caring responsible
  adults. So for a society to flourish, it must balance S-type solutions (such as a legal system) with provision for E-type engagement. The political challenge is to achieve this balance.

- Get really tough (warm but firm) on the causes of crime and
  antisocial behaviour. Use public funds to provide specific, targeted support for children born into families that can't care
  for them adequately themselves, e.g.
  - mothering the mothers
  - intervening where necessary with health and parenting
    support
  - helping boys who fail to develop self-discipline during child-
    hood by using the education system to provide structured ac-
    tivities (chosen by them and providing personal support
    from *male* mentors) from the age of 14.

- Level the playing field for *everyone* by changing the education system along the lines suggested in previous chapters:

- revising early years policy along the lines of well-established developmental educational systems (such as Montessori, Steiner-Waldorf, or other successful European models), for children from three to seven
- ensuring swift and efficient teaching of literacy skills in the early primary years
- pursuing the sort of educational philosophy recommended by Professor Guy Claxton (which does not in any way preclude academic rigour or essential subject knowledge)
- reforming post-14 education to include structured community engagement for all pupils, as outlined in Chapter 9
- giving all youngsters the right to choose their own educational destiny at 14, with practical and vocational routes valued as highly as academic ones (and assessed appropriately)
- creating a well-trained teaching force, then granting teachers authoritative control of their own classrooms, monitored by school and local management teams, and a national professional body
- dismantling the present system of testing up to the age of 14, and substituting the simplest possible methods of checking schools' efficiency and pupils' progress.

- Get really tough (firm, then warm) on antisocial behaviour and youth crime. For trust to flourish, responsible adults must know that society's systems support ethical behaviour, so
  - tackle problem behaviour immediately, through proportionate corrective facilities (including personal *male* support and mentoring)
  - since 'lost boys' are usually stuck at an earlier stage of development, ensure they get what they've so far missed out on:
    - lots of routine and regularity
    - a simple, healthy, natural diet (plenty of vegetables and *fish*)

- plenty of physical activity and challenge, followed by lots of sleep (in a quiet, darkened room)
- productive outdoor activities (e.g. working on the land or with animals)
- opportunities for music, art, spoken language activities (check out the work done with young offenders by the English Speaking Board) and drama
- exposure to good role models and NO exposure to bad ones
- help them learn to read and write, and in the meantime keep them well away from electronic entertainment of all kinds.

- Ensure that all systems instituted by government are designed to support the professionals who work in them, rather than hobble them with red tape. This will probably mean devolving more financial responsibility to local government, which can be more responsive to local needs than the centralised sort.
- Avoid initiative-itis. Short-term, knee-jerk initiatives just keep everyone pointlessly occupied in:
  - dealing with the bureaucracy involved in change
  - looking and bidding for funding to keep key workers in place.
- The type of personal professional engagement described in this chapter requires long-term contact to build real trust within a community.
- Look for ways of using the web to draw on the personal experience and knowledge of professionals and other responsible adults and to extend democracy in productive ways, e.g.
  - consultative plebiscites on matters of public interest
  - opportunities for individuals to report on failures and abuses within systems.
- But make any such provision genuinely responsive, not merely 'consultative window-dressing', which diminishes trust in politicians.

- Require all institutions, businesses, corporations, media and marketing to:
  - put the mental and physical health of the nation's children before any other considerations, including convenience or profit
  - support parents and other responsible adults in raising bright, balanced, healthy children.

This may be the biggest challenge of all, since the UK is not known for its love of and interest in children. Yet, if society's to flourish, it's a nettle some brave politician has eventually to grasp.

KEVIN'S STORY: WHEN DID YOU LAST SEE YOUR SON?

So we're left with Kevin, the last of our four, possibly fragile males. Why, at 16, does he end up lost in cyberspace?

During his first thousand days, Kevin seemed the least fragile boy of the lot – a contented baby with two doting parents, including a mum who'd already reared two boys and was happy to stay at home to look after him. He ate well, slept well, grew well, and eventually turned into a low-tantrum toddler, then a cheery chubby little boy. He enjoyed TV, but Stephanie made sure he played out in the garden too, and often took him along to the park.

She waited till he was three years old and settled in at nursery before doing what she'd planned for years – setting up 'PC Angel', a computer troubleshooting company for small businesses. After more than a dozen years of childcare, Steph reckoned it was her turn to make something of her own life. She could work from home so keep the domestic front going for the boys. And since his dad worked school hours, Kevin would never be short of a parent to pick him up or mind him during the holidays.

But Steph's business took off like a rocket, and within three years she had two offices and a staff of 12. Everyone said how amazing she was to juggle three lads and keep the firm going from strength to strength. People wrote articles about her in the local press and she was featured in a glossy IT magazine. Despite James's working hours and his professional interest in kids, she still shouldered most of the childcare and domestic duties – if she left it to her rather dreamy husband, it might never happen. Fortunately, she could now afford plenty of help, including a cleaner and an excellent childminder for Kevin. They moved house too, to a part of town they could never have afforded on James's teaching salary, and had some wonderful foreign holidays with the boys.

Meanwhile Kevin settled into primary school, brought home good – if unremarkable – report cards, and never seemed to get into trouble. But he wasn't one for joining clubs or teams, and seemed to lose interest in playing out. At the end of the school day, he liked to come home, watch a bit of TV, play on his Game Boy and annoy his brothers. The boys all had their own rooms, with all the latest gear – Steph got lots of great deals through the business – and were real digital natives.

Actually, she was glad her youngest son was a homebird, because even in their little town the traffic was building up. She had let the elder two boys out to the park when they were about ten, but there was no way she'd let Kevin. Things had changed in less than a decade, and the boys you saw on the street now were just cheeky little beggars or hoodies up to no good. She couldn't shut the stable door on Kev's brothers, because they'd already bolted (as it were), but she'd do everything possible to protect her youngest. Grumblers on TV and in the press said kids should get out more, but Steph felt a lot better knowing where he was. Even if he did sometimes play his brothers' X-rated games, it seemed that all lads did that nowadays. He was still her little boy when she popped in to say goodnight or when he mooched around the kitchen snaffling titbits while she cooked.

By the time Kevin reached secondary school, his brothers were both off at university. The house felt very empty. Steph and James were up to their eyes with work – they didn't see much of each other these days. She was opening a fourth much larger office in a nearby town, and he had a heavy teaching load as well as his management duties. In fact, sometimes a week would go by without the family ever sitting down to eat together. Kevin became an expert with the microwave, picking his own meals from a selection Steph left in the fridge, but he professed himself happy enough. His school reports were still nothing special – the general opinion seemed that he was bright but lazy. They tried talking to him, but he just shrugged and said there were plenty of lazier kids than him.

He was 14 when people started making jokes about 'needing to talk about Kevin'. Apparently there was some American book out about a college killer, like the Columbine murderers. Steph got a copy and thought it was horrible. James read it and made a few caustic comments about 'the high-achieving mother'. For the first time it occurred to her that he might not be utterly thrilled about her transformation from stay-at-home mum to successful businesswoman. He'd been trying for promotion for several years and getting nowhere while she just seemed to go from strength to strength. Could that be bad for Kevin?

In fact, when did she last see Kevin? She tended to avoid his room because it was such a tip – the cleaner fumigated it once a week. But now she went and tapped on the door. Kevin had one eye on his widescreen TV (*Buffy the Vampire Slayer*) and the other on his Nintendo game console – it looked like Mortal Kombat. He looked up briefly, said 'Hi!' and returned to his game. 'Wanted to talk about holidays,' said Steph. 'Your dad and I fancy Thailand. What d'you think?' 'Fine,' said Kevin. She sat for a couple more minutes while he clicked away and Buffy screamed in the background. At last, she said 'Bye then' and left.

They didn't go to Thailand. Steph promoted one of the office managers to take temporary charge of PC Angels while she took indefinite leave. She summoned her two big boys back from university for the weekend, and called a family conference. After apologising for spending so much time on the business she asked what they needed to do to get the family back on track again. The four men in her life sat in embarrassed silence. 'I'm fine, Mum,' said Kevin. 'We're OK, sweetheart,' said James. 'Everything seems OK to me,' mumbled Number One Son.

In the end, they arranged to have a family meal at least three times a week, to have Kevin's big brothers back once a month, and to look for things they could do as a family.

The resolutions petered out after a month. Nobody seemed to have anything to say to each other any more. Steph threw herself back into the business, James into his marking, Kevin painted his room black and added a Wii and a social networking site to his virtual repertoire. He managed to scrape five not-very-good GCSEs and agreed to go to college to study website design – not that he seemed to have much enthusiasm for it.

Steph felt pretty sure he wasn't going to become a campus killer. He simply didn't have the energy, or the commitment. He didn't really seem to have anything. He was a rather pasty, slightly overweight boy with no conversation, no ambition and no future. He went to school every day without any enthusiasm and came home every afternoon to return to his lair. He hadn't been out with friends or had anyone round to visit for years, and she couldn't imagine there ever being any romantic interest in his life. She really wished that she and James had talked about Kevin long long ago …

THE POWER OF THE PERSONAL

It's only in the last few decades that science has begun to confirm what wise parents have always known about child development. Fortunately, however, there have been enough wise parents to keep the species moving onward and upward and, over the millennia, responsible adults have found humane ways to equip young males to survive and thrive in a wide variety of environments and cultures.

This ancient wisdom has been adapted as cultures evolve and change, and the more we discover about the development of the human brain, the clearer it becomes what is needed to rear balanced young men who are well equipped to thrive in a high-tech, urban, sexually equal society. The basic recipe is described on pages 15–16 of the Introduction, and the details fleshed out, with suggestions for taking things forward, at the end of each chapter.

The four pen portraits interwoven through 21st Century Boys are necessarily specific stories. Each is a composite picture, based on boys and men I've met or heard about over the last ten years or so. They illustrate various ways that side effects of 21st century culture combine with human evolutionary influences and misguided nurture to lead boys into trouble. So poor little Dylan, born to run, struggles against imprisonment in his ideal home and smart new school uniform. Ozzy, the hot-housed 'brain on legs' – brilliant at adult games but bewildered by children's play – faces a future of social and emotional illiteracy (although he might get a very good job in a hedge fund or government office). Meanwhile, the over-indulged, under-disciplined Leo roams the streets in search of kicks, and Kevin – whose busy parents have inadvertently deprived him of the will and confidence to be a real-life contender – listlessly loses himself in cyberspace.

But on page 14, I also describe another typical modern boy based on interviews with parents and sons. He's Adam, the teenager whose upbringing ensured he grew up well prepared to meet the challenges of a 21st century future. I've met and heard about many such boys in the last ten years or so, boys reared by 'good enough' parents and other responsible adults, who've found 21st century ways of balancing S- and E-type thought and values. In fact, in the early months of writing *21st Century Boys*, a real-life Adam entered my own life, so I was able to check out at first hand how a 'good childhood' can develop the personal qualities needed to see boys through modern life.

Madam, I'm Adam

He didn't look at all as I imagined him. Bookish old ex-headmistresses like me don't expect a bright, balanced young man to be wearing earrings and dreadlocks, or to have arms and legs covered in tattoos and a face festooned with hardwear. We're even more taken aback when we notice pink eyeshadow and skilfully applied black eyeliner.

It was my daughter who found Adam, working in the pub round the corner. She'd convinced me we needed someone to look after her dog while she was away for a while, and since I travel a lot on speaking engagements it was either that or losing Fosbury completely. Adam was, she told me, a delightful person, a dog-lover who was conveniently between homes and would make the perfect lodger. So a meeting was arranged and

– just like my fictional Adam in the introduction – this appari-tion grinned, looked me straight in the eye, proffered a hand and said 'Hi!'. What's more, Fosbury adored him on sight.

And my daughter was right: he is the perfect lodger. He doesn't smoke, drink, take drugs or play loud music – or, at least, he only plays it through his iPod, so it never disturbs. He's unfailingly cheerful, honest and polite, keeps the kitchen tidy (mostly) and takes the rubbish down without being asked. What landlady could ask for more? Even when I no longer needed a dog-sitter and Adam moved on to live nearer his girl-friend, he stayed in touch, kept an eye on the flat when I was away, and carried on helping this 20th century woman try to make sense of aspects of male psychology that to someone of my gender and generation are frankly unfathomable.

For instance, I find it impossible to understand Adam's need to go once a week to the local boxing club, where he removes all the metal from his face and tries to beat seven bells out of some other bloke while the other bloke cheerily tries to damage him. But he explains that the need for physical competition (in-cluding a degree of pain) is just something in his genes that he has to cope with. He copes with his other pressing need to take physical risks – completely beyond my female mind-set – with extreme sports, nearly killing himself snowboarding, not to mention the fire-juggling (don't ask). And as a 21st century man, he supplements these real-life activities with virtual ones that presumably help deal with some ancient bloodlust. He and his girlfriend spend hours playing bloodthirsty computer games or watching blood-curdling movies. (I hope to check with Tanya exactly what she gets out of this when I write my book on girls.)

From the moment I met him, I struggled to understand Adam's dramatic 'modern savage' appearance. Are his tattoos, metallic adornments, hairstyle and face-painting another way of reconciling primitive impulses with 21st century existence? Since he's such a nice young man, it seems a shame that our neighbours scurry away when they meet him on the stairs. But apparently he just likes that kind of look … and when you work in a city-centre pub a fearsome exterior often comes in handy. Still, he happily agrees that if his parents' generation had lived through a real war (as mine did) rather than a gender war, he may have chosen different fashion statements.

Obviously, the major question is how this highly intelligent, extraordinarily self-disciplined, socially competent and (under the metal and gunk) very handsome young man ended up serving behind a bar. He reckons it's choice – he doesn't fancy office jobs, and barwork is a way of using his organisational skills and social intelligence (indeed, over the last 18 months, he's risen through deputy manager to manager of the pub, and his employers are clearly blessing their good fortune that he wandered their way). But I reckon there's more to it, which is where his resilience comes in. As I worked on the book, it seemed pretty obvious how nature, nurture and culture had combined to make Adam the person he is.

Nature, nurture and culture (reprise)

There's no doubt about his E-type skills. His social confidence, self-knowledge and the deep satisfaction he feels from defusing difficult situations in the pub without aggression are testament to that. To some extent these skills may be innate, but from my work on Chapters 1 and 2 I assumed he must also have been well mothered. And yes, it turned out that as a tiny baby he'd spent endless contented hours engaged with his mother and father in a satisfying dance of communication. As he grew to toddlerhood, that same mum and dad clearly did a wonderful job of balancing warmth and firmness, bringing up a natural learner – intellectually curious and fascinated by any new challenge.

Familial good fortune was compounded by geographical luck. Growing up in a Yorkshire village meant Adam had the freedom to get out and about with friends from an early age, and an infant school that resisted pressure to rush children into formal work too soon. So he thrived in the early stages of schooling and learned to read and write without difficulty (his spelling is excellent, which is deeply gratifying to an old literacy specialist like me). Indeed, he seems to have led a fairly charmed childhood: his competence in domestic matters is a testament to his parents' well-ordered home life, and his capacity to rise to challenge bears witness to long hours playing out with his mates.

The responsible adults in his local community were presumably warm enough to tolerate most antics of growing lads, but firm enough to nip antisocial behaviour in the bud – if a boy's well reared and known to his neighbours, a sharp word or a withering glare is far more powerful than an ASBO. So Adam's parents had the support of their village in raising a boy with self-confidence and emotional resilience. Which was just as well, because his glory days ground to a halt when he started at secondary school and was told to sit down and submit to the interminable boredom of a test-based curriculum.

It's clear from the boxing, snowboarding and so on that Adam is a high-testosterone male. Once adolescence kicked in, he'd need help to contain his lust for action. Perhaps if there'd been a more 'lively school culture' at his local comprehensive, he would've managed to direct his boundless energy and undoubted S-type skills into study. Or if someone had taken him to Ecuador to build a nursery, it might have been the start of a life of altruism.

Unfortunately, he suffered the fate of far too many young people in UK schools and colleges. A selection of bored, browbeaten teachers showed him how to jump through pointless hoops and tick endless boxes in order to keep the government's 'educational' record on track. As there was no way he'd bring shame on his family by opting out, Adam put his head down and slogged miserably through SATs, GCSEs, A/S and A levels and finally a degree in Business Studies.

None of it stimulated his naturally enquiring mind, fed his

spirit, or suggested there was anything to look forward to in the adult world of work. So by his late teens he escaped to the distractions of evercool culture and, eventually, into losing his mind for long periods through consumption of any mind-altering substances that came his way. For several years he existed in a stupor of boredom, drugs and alcohol. It must have broken his parents' hearts.

I reckon the piercings, tattoos and other fashion statements were Adam's way of demonstrating his contempt for the soul-rotting social orthodoxy life seemed to offer. They also, of course, signalled his hyper-cool credentials and since piercings and tattoos involve a degree of pain, perhaps they helped remind him he wasn't actually dead. Another invigorating sign of life is sex, of which Adam also took advantage, eventually falling in love and moving in with a girlfriend. When that relationship hit the usual 21st century confusion, his personal Chapter 9 came to a miserable end.

Fortunately he didn't proceed to Chapter 10. The girlfriend debacle shocked him into summoning up reserves of resilience laid down in childhood. He decided to cut out drink and drugs, eschewed meat for good measure and started living again. By the time I met him, he'd thrived under this self-imposed discipline for several years and was completely back on track. His present girlfriend – a thoroughly 21st century young woman – seems to suit him perfectly.

Adam's transformation from fallen angel to reinvented man is a heartening affirmation of the power of nature and nurture – I'm sure he's a now a worthy member of the 'transition generation' described by James Martin, ready to help the human race face the challenges of the new millennium. And I could point to many other young men in my notebooks who, through whatever serendipitous combination, seem to have achieved similar levels of self-discipline, control and respect. Some haven't yet found a way to contribute to a society in which they have little faith. Others are academically or creatively inclined;

one's destined for the business world; one's a talented sportsman; another's about to join the police.

But always, when I dig deeper into their experience, it's the
power of the personal that's kept these boys on track. Every boy
needs loving human input throughout his childhood, and the
real-life involvement of responsible adults as he grows to adulthood himself. Usually his family provides the necessary warmth
and firmness to begin with, handing the responsibility gradually
over to the rest of the community as time goes on.

Happily ever after

'Please give your book a happy ending,' a young friend urged
recently, and as a cock-eyed optimist I'm delighted to oblige.
After all, this is certainly not the first time a culture has swung
out of balance, and things have always sorted themselves out in
the past. Since human progress tends to be driven by status-
obsessed, go-getting, high-functioning systemisers – the sort
of people who naturally resist the restraining hand of E-type
thinkers – societies have been losing the plot since time immemorial. But every time we go off course, something happens to
reawaken E-type sensibilities and re-establish equilibrium – a
spiritual rebirth perhaps, an enlightened philosophical or political movement, or the influence of art or literature. Through
the centuries men and women have found many ways to redis-
cover their better nature.

Britain's last period of serious imbalance happened a couple
of centuries ago, in the industrial revolution. Rapid social and
cultural change (driven then, as now, by new technology and the
forces of greed) had left poor children slaving long shifts in fac-
tories, working down mines and up chimneys, suffering and
dying at the behest of an economic system. Such obvious physical abuse of young human beings was clearly not acceptable in
a civilised society, and on this occasion the power of the written
word helped redress the balance.

'*Dead!*' thundered Dickens over the corpse of Jo the crossing sweeper in his novel Bleak House. '*Dead, your Majesty. Dead, my lords and gentlemen. Dead, right reverends and wrong reverends of every order. Dead, men and women, born with heavenly compassion in your hearts. And dying thus around us every day.*'

Dickens had the luxury of speaking personally to every one of his readers, because – through the miracle of literacy, which had just caught on in a big way – his story unfolded inside their heads. Good novels can integrate E-type passion with carefully crafted S-type narrative. The story and characters are symbolically encoded by one human brain and decoded by millions of others. Literacy changes lives (and minds) so, although philosophers, philanthropists, religious leaders, educators, trade union activists and politicians helped drive social change during our 19th century fall from grace, I suspect it was Eliot, Dickens, Gaskell, Kingsley and the rest who reawakened 'heavenly compassion' in the hearts of Victorian men and women. And once that happened, the cascade of tiles on a heavenly Hammond computer model clattered into the colour of E-type action.

Today's obesity crisis has alerted society to ways that modern life can sentence children to ill-health and an early death. Official reports like the Good Childhood Inquiry should help nudge the nation's conscience about the threat posed by a screen-based sedentary hyper-consumerist lifestyle to young people's mental health. Physical and psychological abuse of the nation's children is clearly not acceptable in a civilised society, so history suggests something will soon trigger the personal human communication needed to set compassion alight. Perhaps this time blogs or YouTube will save the day? Perhaps it will be some other development on the web that helps people start making human contact again? Whatever it is, the challenge confronting our society is to devise social systems that support 21st century child-rearing – systems that empower all adults to act *responsibly* towards the next generation, systems based on hope rather than fear, care rather than greed.

*

A happy ending is always within our grasp. And it's a matter of personal choice. The tipping point happens when enough of us start valuing kindness again, and stop setting such store by the words of smart-arses and cynics. Tiles start cascading when we all remember that personal relationships are as important to human well-being as material comfort – and that children, like all human beings, thrive on love, time, warmly applied discipline, respect and trust.

And as the great day finally arrives when every adult in the 21st century global village acknowledges his or her personal responsibility to the next generation, the problems of Dylans, Ozzies, Leos and Kevins will swiftly be solved – along, I imagine, with many other inconvenient truths that keep us all awake at night.

NOTES AND REFERENCES

INTRODUCTION

Dylan, Ozzy, Leo and Kevin, whose stories unfold at more length later in the book, are not case studies. They're composite characters based on children I've met or heard described by teachers, parents and others.

Do we need to talk about boys?

UNICEF report: UNICEF Innocenti Research Centre: *An Overview of Child Well-being in Rich Countries: A Comprehensive Assessment of the Lives and Well-being of Children and Adolescents in the Economically Advanced Nations*, (UNICEF, 2007),
http://www.unicef.org/media/files/ChildPoverty Report.pdf

Teenage behaviour: see Institute of Public Policy Research, Margo, J., Dixon, M., Pearce, N. and Reed, H., *Freedom's Orphans: Raising Youth in a Changing World* (IPPR, 2006)

Teachers' concern about deteriorating behaviour/'toxic childhood syndrome': see Palmer, 2006

Boys' school achievement: see http://www.standards.dfes.gov.uk/research/themes/gender/challengingunderachievement/

Numbers of male/female students in higher education: see UNESCO Institute for Statistics, 'UIS Statistics In Brief: *education in United Kingdom*' (2005), http://stats.uis.unesco.org/unesco/TableViewer/ document. aspx?ReportId=121&IF_Language=eng&BR_Country= 8260&BR_ Region=40500.) Recent figures: in 2006, 47% of girls went into higher education and only 37% of boys 'Worry over girls' dominance in higher education', *Sunday Telegraph* Henry, Julie, (7 July 2007)

Incidence of 'developmental disorders': see Office of National Statistics, '*Mental Health of Children and Young People in Great Britain*', (2004) http://www.statistics.gov.uk/downloads/theme_health/GB2004.pdf

ADHD/dyspraxia four times more common in boys: see Forbes, F., 'Behind the medical headlines: Attention Deficit Hyperactivity Disorder', *Journal of the Royal College of Physicians*, Vol. 36 (2006); Boon, M., *Helping Children with Dyspraxia* (Jessica Kingsley, 2000)

Asperger Syndrome nine times more common: in *The Essential Difference*, Professor Baron-Cohen estimates AS is ten times as common in males than females, but in subsequent interviews has settled on nine times, e.g. Lane, Megan, 'What Asperger's syndrome has done for us', BBC News Online (2 June 2004)

Reading problems twice as likely: see Rutter, M. et al.: 'Sex differences in developmental reading disability: New findings from four epidemiological studies', in *Journal of American Medical Association*, Vol. 291, No. 16 (2004)

Mental health statistics: see British Medical Association, *Child and Adolescent Mental Health: A guide for Healthcare Professionals* (2006), http://www.bma.org.uk/ap.nsf/AttachmentsByTitle/PDFChildAdolescentMentalHealth/$FILE/ChildAdolescentMentalHealth.pdf

Four out of five criminal offences committed by males: see National Statistics Online, '*4 in 5 Offenders are Male*' (http://www.statistics.gov.uk/cci/nugget.asp?id=442)

'Criminologists agree that the gender gap in crime is universal: Women are always and everywhere less likely than men to commit criminal acts', quoted from Steffensmeier, Darrell, and Allan, Emilie, 'Gender and crime: toward a gendered theory of female offending' (*Annual Review of Sociology*, Vol. 22 (1996)

Dr Sami Timimi quote about boys externalising problems: personal interview, summer 2007

The role of nature

The major text on sex differences and evolutionary biology is Geary (1998). Debate still rages and will probably continue to rage on the subject, but it's now widely accepted that differences exist. My summary of major differences is taken from Stephen Pinker's well-argued case in the

Harvard Mind/Brain/Behaviour debate on 22 April 2008. ('*The Science of Gender and Science: Pinker vs Spelke – a debate*': The Edge: The Third Culture, http://www.edge.org/3rd_culture/debate05/debate05_index.html)

From Stone Age to city limits

More people living in cities: in May 2007, the United Nations Population Fund claimed that the tipping point would occur sometime in 2008. See UNFPA '*Urbanisation: a majority in cities*', http://www.unfpa.org/pds/urbanization.htm

Teenage gang culture has become increasingly violent of recent years – see Chapter 10 notes

See Chapter 8 notes for 'The drugs don't work' (page 239)

Systems, status and success

The Essential Difference – Baron-Cohen, 2003. His main argument is summarised in 'The male condition' by Simon Baron-Cohen, *New York Times* (8 August 2005) http://www.nytimes.com/2005/08/08/opinion/08baron-cohen.html?_r=1&pagewanted=2&oref=slogin

Too much of a good thing?

Ten-fold increase in ASD diagnoses: see Baron-Cohen, 2003. Latest estimates between 1 in 200 and 1 in 58 due to variations in diagnosis: Baron-Cohen quoted in *The Times*: Aluja, Anjana, 'Autism: the truth' (12 August 2007)

Biological basis for autism and Asperger's: see Frith, 1991

Nature and nurture

Recipe for rearing a son – discussions with many parents, backed up by research cited throughout the rest of this book.

The S-type/E-type balancing act

Quote from Lord Richard Layard: personal interview, 2005, cited Palmer 2006 (Chapter 10)

CHAPTER 1: THE FRAGILE MALE

Quote about 'flaw line of biological weaknesses' and information about ratios of male:female embryos; prenatal damage; statistics

on developmental conditions: see Kraemer, Sebastian, 'The fragile male', British Medical Journal, Vol. 321 (December 2000). I'm en-
debted to Dr Kraemer for correspondence on this subject and
many of the references in this section

What are little boys made of?

General background with thanks to Constance Fozzard, retired consultant obstetrician

X and Y chromosomes: Bradman, Neil and Thomas, Mark, 'Why Y?
The Y chromosome in the study of human evolution, migration
and prehistory', Science Spectra, Vol. 14 (1998)

Damaged chromosome quote: attributed to Germaine Greer at a
book launch in 1991

Decline of the Y chromosome: see Jones, 2002 and genetist Brian
Sykes quoted in Dowd, 2005

Must try harder

General background to brain development in the womb: see Gilbert,
2000 (Susan Gilbert is a science journalist who specialises in
child development). Also Kimura, Doreen, 'Sex differences in the
brain', Scientific American (May 2002)

Female is default mode: see Jones, 2002

Sebastian Kraemer quote: personal communication.

'Insurance policy' see Pinker, 2008

Mothers who took cocaine: see Delaney-Black, Virginia M.D. et al.,
'Teacher-assessed behaviour of children prenatally exposed to cocaine', Paediatrics, Vol. 106, No. 4, [pp. 782–791] (October 2000)

Improving medical care means premature babies who would have
died 20 years ago are now surviving: see 'Fear over "premature babies
rise"', BBC News (21 April 2006),
http://news.bbc.co.uk/1/hi/health/4928282.stm

Prematurity: one in four born before 25 weeks have severe
mental/physical disability; one in three born before 32 weeks have
educational/behavioural difficulties at seven: see Shennan, A.H.
and Bewley, S., 'Why should preterm births be rising?' British Medical Journal, Vol. 332 [pp. 924–925] (April 2006)

Strong, silent and slow

Effects of testosterone on development: see Baron-Cohen, 2003

General background on brain development: see Gilbert, 2000

Foetal mouth movements: see Hepper, P.G., Shannon, E.A. and Dornan, J.C., 'Sex differences in fetal mouth movements', *Lancet*, Vol. 350, 1820 (1997)

Not so big and bouncy?

Poorer development of senses in newborn males reported in Livingstone, 2005

Boys more 'emotionally reactive': see Tronick, E.Z. and Weinberg, M.K., 'Depressed mothers and infants: failure to form dyadic states of consciousness', in Murray, L. and Cooper, P., (eds) *Postpartum Depression and Child Development* (Guildford Press, 1997)

Boatella-Costa, E., Costas-Moragas, C., Botet-Mussons, F., Fornieles-Deu, A. and De Cáceres-Zurita, M.L., 'Behavioral gender differences in the neonatal period according to the Brazelton scale' *Early Human Development*, Vol. 83: No. 2, [pp. 91–97] (February 2007)

Behaviour problems: see Linnet, K.M., 'Gestational age, birthweight and the risk of hyperkinetic disorder', British Medical Journal's Archives of Disease in Childhood (2006)

Premature baby boys fail to catch up in brain size: see Reiss, Allan L., Kesler, Shelli R., Vohr, Betti, Duncan, Charles C. Katz, Karol H., Pajot, Sarah, Schneider, Karen C., Makuch, Robert W. and Ment, Laura R., 'Sex Differences in Cerebral Volumes of 8-Year-Olds Born Preterm', *Journal of Pediatrics* (August 2004)

Boys' poorer response to parents' humming reported in Sax, 2005

Less eye contact: see Simon Baron-Cohen above; research collated by Gurian Institute: see Gurian, 2001

Parental perceptions about boys and girls: see Karraker, K.H., Vogel, D.A. and Lake, M.A. 'Parents' gender stereotyped perceptions of newborns: The eye of the beholder revisited' in *Sex Roles: A Journal of Research* (November 1995)

Knowing me, knowing you

Attachment theory: major sources for this extensively documented area of psychology: see Gerhardt, 2004, Sunderland, 2006. I am also indebted to Sir Richard Bowlby for personal interviews about his father's work, 2006/7

Colwyn Trevarthen's 'dance of communication' – personal interview

2005. See also summary of Trevarthen's work in David, Tricia, 'Child development pioneer', *Nursery World* (16 June 2005); also Trevarthen, C. and Marwick, H. *Review of Childcare and Development of Children from Birth to Three: Research Evidence and Implications for Out-of-home Provision* (Scottish Executive Education Department, 2002)

Royal College of Paediatrics and Child Health, 2002

The dance of communication

Differences between boys and girls in communicatory dance: see Trevarthen, C., Kokkonaki, T. and Flamenghi, G., 'What infant imitations communicate: with mothers, with fathers and with peers', in Nadel, J. and Butterworth, G., *Imitation in Infancy* (CUP, 1999)

Cambridge study: see Baron-Cohen, 2003

'Scientists studying babies in the first three months of life... ': Leeb, R.T. and Gillian, F., '*Here's looking at you, kid! A longitudinal study of perceived gender differences in mutual gaze behaviour in young infants*', quoted in Brizandine, L. *Sex Roles: A Journal of Research*, Vol. 50 (2004)

Six-month-old babies: see Malatesta, C.Z. and Haviland, J.M. 'Learning display rules: The socialisation of emotion expression in infancy', *Child Development*, Vol. 53 (1982)

Stevens and Gardner research: see Stevens, G. and Gardner, S. *Separation Anxiety and the Dread of Abandonment in the Adult Male* (Praeger Publishing, 1994), available online at http://www.questia.com/PM.qst?a=o&d=24470410

Fragile parents

Thanks to Dr Sami Timimi for discussion on the background to this section.

2007 survey about young mothers for *Mother and Baby* magazine reported in the *Daily Telegraph*: Womack, Sarah, 'Babies destroy social life, say new mothers' (18 October 2007)

Statistics on postnatal depression: Royal College of Paediatrics and Child Health, 2002

Depressed mothers 'out of sync': see Goleman, 2007

The technology trap

See also Chapter 4 , 'It's good to talk' in Palmer, 2006

Baby Einstein range of DVDs is now owned by Disney. See www.baby-einstein.com

Study of babies and mothers using video link described by Colwyn
  Trevarthen at Early Years Educator Conference, New Lanark, 9
  September 2006

' … fascinated by changing patterns on a brightly lit screen': According to paediatrician Dimitri Christakis, TV programmes for
  children exploit the 'orientation reflex': see Linn, 2008

American Academy of Pediatrics: see www.aap.org. See also Vande-
  water, E.A. et al., 'Digital childhood: Electronic media and technology use among infants, toddlers, and preschoolers', *Pediatrics*,
  Vol. 119, No. 5 (2007)

For summary of research linking early screen-based activity to developmental conditions, see Sigman, Aric, 'Visual voodoo: The biological impact of watching TV', *Biologist*, Vol. 54, No. 1 (February
  2007). The two key studies are Christakis, D., Zimmerman, F.,
  DiGiuseppe, D. and McCarty, C. 'Early television exposure and
  subsequent attentional problems in children', *Pediatrics*, Vol.113
  [pp. 708–713] (2004) and Waldman, M. et al., '*Does television cause
  Autism?*' Study presented to National Bureau of Economic Research health conference (23 October 2006)

French ban on TV programmes for under-threes: see Olliver, Christine, '*France bans broadcast of TV shows for babies*', Associated Press
  (20 August 2008), http://ap.google.com/article/ALeqM5jNXX-
  uQkaIdgBV1UwbslQwlJQvnAD92M89Joo

Kraemer quote from 'The fragile male', *British Medical Journal*, Vol.
  321 (December 2000)

FOUR FRAGILE MALES

The four boys described on page 48 may or may not have a genetic
  predisposition towards a developmental condition or a mental
  health problem. I'm working here on the assumption that they
  didn't. But all four were born into late 20th century families, and
  their lives have been influenced by the sociocultural cocktail described throughout this book. These fictional accounts of their
  progress are intended to illustrate how environmental factors can
  interact with general male characteristics to lead them 'off the
  rails'.

CHAPTER 2: A MIND OF HIS OWN

The lust to learn

Attachment theory: major sources for this extensively documented area of psychology: Gerhardt, 2004, Sunderland, 2006. I am also indebted to Sir Richard Bowlby for personal interviews about his father's work, 2006/7

The image of a baby as a scientist is taken from Gopnik, Meltzoff and Kuhl's 2001 book *The Scientist in the Crib: What Early Learning Tells us About the Mind*. This also provides the cognitive development for the following two sections

Urie Bronfenbrenner quote: see National Scientific Council on the Developing Child, 'Young children develop in an environment of relationships', Working Paper 1 (2004) from University of Harvard, available at www.developingchild.net

S-type learning: the material world

See above

E-type learning: the social world

See above

Infant recognition that he's 'attached but separate': see Hobson, 2002

Significance of mind-mindedness summarised in Chapter 4, 'It's good to talk', Palmer, 2006

The parental balancing act

'Warm-but-firm' parenting: the large body of research about this 'authoritative' parenting style (as the most successful in raising self-regulating children) is summarised in Martin, 2005

Thanks to Cordelia Fine for permission to use the quote from Fine, 2006

How to thwart a scientist

Children's early learning is rooted in movement – see Goddard Blythe, 2008

Smart rats experiments of the 1960s: see Diamond, M.C., Krech, D. and Rosenzberg, M.R., 'The effects of an enriched environment on the rat cerebral cortex', J. Comp. Neurol. Vol. 123, pp. 111–119 (1964)

Smart rats researcher's quote: Marian Cleeves Diamond, Professor of
  neuroanatomy at the University of California, addressing the Department for Health and Human Services Conference, Television
  and the preparation of the mind for learning', (1992). Quoted in
  Winn, 2000

How to dumb a scientist down

Boys slower to talk: see Law, 2004

Boys three times as likely to suffer from a language disorder – (reference thanks to Alex Hall of I CAN): see Robinson, R. 'Causes and
  associations of severe and persistent specific speech and language disorders', *Childhood Developmental Medicine and Child Neurol-
  ogy*, Vol. 33, No. 11 (1987)

Quote from cognitive psychologists: see Gopnik et al., 2001

Phonological basis of language: see Snowling, 2000

Babies born able to speak any language: see Gopnik et al., 2001

A dance to the music of time

The communicatory triangle and the significance of attachment and
  communication skills for thought: personal interview with Professor Peter Hobson, 2005, and his 2002 book *The Cradle of
  Thought*

Quotations re speaking to small children: see Hobson, 2002

Who cares?

Madonna getting tearful: *I'm Going to Tell you a Story*, Channel 4
  (11 December 2005)

Mothers would prefer the childcare option: see 'Mothers denied flexible working', 10 September 2007, *BBC News Online*

Mothers who can afford to stay home often do so: see 'High flying
  mothers who would rather stay at home', Doughty, Steve, *Daily
  Mail* (17 June 2004). A study published in August 2008 by Professor Jacqueline Scott of Cambridge University showed that a majority of both men and women have begun to feel that the family
  suffers when mothers have to work: Carvel, John, 'Two into one
  won't go', *Guardian* (6 August 2008)

Complex accountability procedures for nurseries: the requirements
  of the Early Years Foundation Stage became statutory in September 2008 for all children in England cared for outside the home.

See www.standards.dfes.gov.uk/eyfs/

Official reports: huge surveys such as the NICHD survey in the USA have concentrated on children's cognitive development because this could be measured on tests.

'Small but significant difference in a large group of children': the Effective Provision of Preschool Education (EPPE) Project, *final report* (Institute of Education, University of London, 2004)

Raised cortisol levels in infant brains: there are now a number of studies to support this observation, including Ahnert, L., Gunnar, M.R., Lamb, M.E. and Barthel, M., 'Transition to Child Care: Associations with Infant-Mother Attachment, Infant Negative Emotion, and Cortisol Elevation', *Child Development*, Vol. 75, No. 3, pp. 639–650 (2004)

Steve Biddulph quote: Biddulph, 2006

The power of the personal

National Childbirth Trust: see http://www.nctpregnancyandbaby-care.com/home

Mothers feeling inadequate: 'Celebrity yummy mummies make the rest feel failures', *Daily Mail* (28 February 2008)

Unresolved separation anxiety: see Stevens, G. and Gardner, S. *Separation Anxiety and the Dread of Abandonment in the Adult Male* (Praeger Publishing, 1994) available online at http://www.questia.com/PM.qst?a=o&d=24470410

CHAPTER 3: GOOD HABITS AND BAD INFLUENCES

The child is father of the man

What happens to us before three or four isn't recorded in ways that can be consciously accessed: see Donald, 2001

Interaction of genes and environment: see Ridley, 2004

James McNeal quote: McNeal, J. and Yeh, C. 'Born to shop', *American Demographics*, 34–39 (June 1993)

'Don't just think juice' quote: Lindstrom, 2003

Quote from President of Kids R Us: see Clark, 2007

The electronic cradle

Background on research on sleep, naps, etc: see Palmer, 2006; the research on poor sleep and napping habits leading to 'non-adaptable' or hyperactive behaviour is summarised in Weissbluth, 1998

Background on movement of electronic equipment into children's bedrooms: see Palmer, 2006; see also National Consumer Council report *Watching, Wanting and Wellbeing* (2007)

Quote re *Baby Einstein* video: Thomas, 2007

40% of under-fours with bedroom TV: see Close, Robin, *Television and Language Development in the Early Years: A Review of the Literature* (National Literacy Trust, 2004)

They are what (and how) we feed them

Government prediction for 2050: see Campbell, Denis, 'Half of all boys will be obese, warns leaked report', *Observer* (29 July 2007)

Mother's diet in pregnancy: see Bayoll, S.A., Farrington, S.J. and Stickland, N.C., 'A maternal "junk food diet" in pregnancy and lactation promotes an exacerbated taste for "junk food" and a greater propensity for obesity in rat offspring', *British Journal of Nutrition*, Vol. 98, pp. 843–851 (2007)

James McNeal 'cradle-to-grave' quote in Spurlock, Morgan, 'The Truth About McDonald's and Children', *Independent* (22 May 2005)

Study about food wrappings: see Robinson, T.N., Borzekowski, D.L.G. et al., 'Effects of Fast Food Branding on Young Children's Taste Preferences', *Archives of Paediatric and Adolescent Medicine*, Vol. 161 (August 2007)

Quote from Dr Diane Levin in Tanner, Lindsey, 'Study shows marketing shapes toddlers' taste buds', *Associated Press* (8 July 2007)

Quotes about use of child-friendly characters in food marketing are by Dave Siegel of Wondergroup Marketers, quoted in Thomas 2007

US report on 100% of parents influenced by their children affecting food purchases: see Griffin Bacal ad agency survey cited in 'Preschoolers: an emerging consumer set', *Kidscreen: Reaching children through entertainment* (1999), www.kidscreen.com

UK survey: see OFCOM, *Childhood Obesity – Food Advertising in Context: children's food choices, parents' understanding and influence and the role of food promotions* (July 2004)

Potential for parents to use natural pickiness (neophobia): see Wardle, J. and Cooke, L., 'Genetic and environmental determinants of children's food preferences' in *British Journal of Nutrition*, Vol. 99, pp. 515–521 (2008)

Poor diet at three linked to poor school performance: research by Dr Christine Emmett for the Institute of Education and the Bristol Children of the Nineties study (12 August 2008): see press release at http://www.bristol.ac.uk/news/2008/5849.html

The relentless rise of 'toy consumption'

Bob the Builder quote and 'how to get into kids' psyches' quote (by Norman Crossfield, President of 4 Kids) both in Clark, 2007

James McNeal quote from McNeal, 1992

Teletubbies profit figures and other information about money to be made from marketing: see Clark, 2007

Colwyn Trevarthen quote: see Smith, Kay and Harrison, Jody, 'Don't give a child toys, says expert: handing children the latest craze is neglectful', *Mail on Sunday* (15 July 2007)

Anything that gets the kids to read, huh?

Information on supermarket selling of books and the quote about *Thomas the Tank Engine* from Gregory, 2007

Thomas website: http://www.thomasandfriends.com/uk/index.asp

Money can't buy me love

Dr Tanya Byron: see Byron, 2007

The tyranny of choice

The advice given at the end of this section – like the advice throughout the book – is based on scores of interviews with experts on various aspects of child development, during and since my research for *Toxic Childhood* (Palmer, 2007)

The White House report *From Neurons to Neighbourhoods*: see Shonkoff and Phillips, 2000

CHAPTER 4: ONE OF THE BOYS

Child's play

Mark Berkoff quote from 'Taking play seriously' by Robin Manantz Henzig *New York Times* (17 February 2008)

Everything to play for

Surprisingly few links seem to have been made between children's free-flow play – and its importance in motivation and healthy development – and the concept of flow. Professor Mihaly Csikszentmihalyi of the University of Chicago explains the significance of *Flow: The Psychology of Optimal Experience*, which most adults recognise as the experience of 'losing themselves' in an enjoyable experience. True excellence seems to be a blending of flow (which sportsmen often call 'being in the zone') and training, as described in the famous coaching book series *The Inner Game* by Tim Gallwey.

When the mollycoddling has to stop

Learning the ropes of social encounters: see Sax, 2005

Footnote: It's obvious that children from violent and neglectful homes are likely to need help learning to play. They have learned before coming to nursery that the adults in their lives can't be trusted, which affects their behaviour. In boys this can result in aggression, and real rather than play fighting. Many schools now withdraw such children to a 'nurture group' – see www.nurture-groups.org – to help them learn social skills within a 'warm-but-firm' quasi-domestic setting.

Socialisation by the peer group: see Harris, 1999 and 2007

Panksepp, Jaak, 'Can play diminish ADHD and facilitate the construction of the social brain?' *Journal of Canadian Child and Adolescent Psychiatry*, Vol. 16, No. 2 (May 2007). His ' *urge to play is particularly insistent*' quote from Henzig, Robert Manantz, 'Taking play seriously' *New York Times* (17 February 2008)

Jerome Kagan quote from Chapter 6 of Kagan, 1994

Boys' toys and adult obsessions

There were innumerable studies of gender difference and the extent to which gender is socially constructed over the second half of the 20th century. They were comprehensively surveyed by Professor Eleanor Maccoby in *The Psychology of Sex Differences* (with Carol Najy Jacklin, 1974) and *The Two Sexes: Growing Up Apart, Coming Together* (1998). Boys' interest in construction toys, cars, trucks, etc. is discussed in Baron-Cohen, 2003.

David Reimer's story was summarised shortly after his death in *The* boy who lived as a girl, CBC News Online (10 May 2004)

Quote from his mother: *The Boy Who Turned into a Girl*, BBC2 Horizon (7 December 2000)

We don't play with guns here

Department for Children, Schools and Families: *Confident, Capable and Creative: supporting boys' achievements* (2007)

Nursery worker Gina is quoted in Penny Holland's 2003 book *We Don't Play With Guns Here*, which provides much background information for this section

Violent play peaks at around seven: Blatchford, P., Baines, E. and Pellegrini, A, 'The social context of school playground games: Sex and ethnic differences, and changes over time after entry to junior school', *British Journal of Developmental Psychology*, Vol. 21, No. 4, 481–506 (4 November 2003)

Boys versus girls

Male primates deprived of the opportunity to fight and expert opinion on play-fighting and empathetic engagement: see Sax, 2005

Importance of rough and tumble play in boys' upbringing: see Biddulph, 2003

Quote re nursery staff: see Holland, 2003

Vivian Gussin Paley's *Boys and Girls: Superheroes in the Dolls' Corner* is a delightful account of a sensitive kindergarten teacher's response to gender differences in her class

Boys' and girls' artwork: psychologist Donna Tuman sums it up as 'girls draw nouns, boys draw verbs': see Sax, 2005

Quote re 'perceived sexist patterns': Holland, 2003

Band of brothers

Boys' greater interest in construction play than girls is mentioned in practically every text on young children and gender, and obvious in every nursery setting.

Talk through construction: see Paley, 1986

Males communicating more easily side by side: personal interview with Sandy Campbell of Working Rites, 2007

Boys' preference for group play: see Benenson, J.F., Duggan, V. and Markovits, H., 'Sex Differences in Infants' Attraction to Group Versus Individual Stimuli', *Infant Behavior and Development*, Vol. 27,

No. 2 (May 2004)

A hard core of perhaps a quarter for whom a too-structured approach is anathema: Gurian, 2001, reckons between 20 and 30%, Holland, 2003, about 25%

Gary Wilson quote – personal interview, 2008. See also Wilson 2006 and 2007

Rallying round the flag of 'not being girls' – Maccoby (see above) concluded that children's group gender identity is more significant than individual feelings of gender. Peer pressure is particularly powerful in terms of gender.

Researchers find more integration through free play: see Holland, 2003.

Screenplay for the future

Computer games for babies and toddlers: see Clark 2007

Urgent calls for research: in the USA, Strasburger, Victor, 'First do no harm: Why have parents and paediatricians missed the boat on children and the media?' *Journal of Paediatrics*, Vol. 151, No. 54 (2006); Vanderwater, E.A. et al., 'Digital Childhood: Electronic Media and Technology Use Among Infants, Toddlers and Preschoolers', *Pediatrics*, Vol. 119 (May 2007) http://www.pediatrics.org/cgi/content/full/119/5/e1006. In the UK, Aric Sigman 'Visual voodoo: the biological impact of watching TV' in *Biologist*, Vol. 54, No 1, Febuary 2007

ADHD research: see Christakis, D., Zimmerman, F., DiGiuseppe, D. and McCarty, C., 'Early television exposure and subsequent attentional problems in children', *Pediatrics*, Vol. 113 (2004)

Daniel Anderson quote in Strasburger article cited above

Susan Greenfield quote: *The Scotsman* (14 September 2006)

CHAPTER 5: UNWILLINGLY TO SCHOOL

Nature article: Lonsdorf, E.V., Eberley, L.E. and Pusey, A.E., 'Sex differences in learning in chimpanzees', *Nature*, 428 (2004)

Documentary: see 'Why Men Don't Iron' by Ann Moir (1999), see also Moir and Moir, 1999

Passing on the culture

Thanks for background to this section to Dr Sami Timimi – personal interview, 2007. See also Timimi, 2005

The consciousness studies theorists (mostly in California) are trying to reconcile science and spirit. In *The Biology of Belief* (2005), Dr Bruce Lipton, a former molecular scientist, provides evidence to support his claim that children do not develop conscious control of their thoughts till they are six or seven. I'm grateful to William Murtha for drawing my attention to this theory. It accords with the beliefs of many educationists over the last century or so, including Maria Montessori and Rudolf Steiner, with the developmental theories of Jean Piaget, and with the majority of European education systems, which don't start formal work till children are six or seven.

Why literacy matters

This section is informed by my own work in literacy between 1984 and 2004, which was greatly influenced by the work of Professor Margaret Donaldson of Edinburgh University (summarised in her pamphlet *Sense and Sensibility: some thoughts on the teaching of reading*, 1989). The first person I heard use the expression 'changing the architecture of the brain' was Professor Usha Goswami at Cambridge. Recent findings about 'the getting of literacy' are summarised in Blakemore and Frith, 2005 and its effects on our thinking processes are discussed in Greenfield, 2008.

The foundations of literacy

For background on this and the following section see Palmer and Bayley, 2008.

'Sustained shared thinking': see the Effective Provision of Preschool Education (EPPE) Project: *Final Report* (Institute of Education, University of London, 2004)

Development of balance and control: see Goddard Blythe, 2004 and Mcintyre and McVitty, 2004

Tuning the mind

See Sheppard, 2005

Worlds of words

Background on the significance of stories in human development:

Pink, 2005

The importance of storytelling in engaging children's attention: see Coleman, 2007

Pie Corbett quote – personal interview, 2007

Vygotskyan learning theory and practice: see 'Story grammar' in Dolya, 2008

Too much too soon

At the time of writing, controversy rages around the literacy targets for five-year-olds, enshrined in law in 2008 by the Early Years Foundation Stage Guidance, despite advice to the contrary by expert government advisers. Two of these have now been sent for review. Updates on the issue are available on www.savechild-hood.org

Government report re achievement gap: Department for Education and Skills, *Gender and Education: the evidence on pupils in England* (2007), http://www.standards.dfes.gov.uk/genderandachieve-ment/pdf/7038_DfES_Gender_Ed.pdf?version=1

The most successful European country in terms of literacy is Finland – descriptions of kindergarten practice are based on what I saw there on a visit in 2004

Explanation of the increasingly early start to formal education in England: Palmer, S., 'Reclaim reception', *Child Education* (September 2005)

US research on over-formal learning and creativity described in Honoré, 2008

On long-term effects of an early start by High/Scope Foundation: see Sylva, Kathy, 'Early childhood education to ensure a fair start for all' in Cox, Theo (ed.), *Combating Educational Disadvantage* available on http://www.ioe.ac.uk/lll/pdffiles/ksylva.pdf

Ofsted report: *The education of six-year-olds in England, Denmark and Finland*, Ofsted 2003

Four- and five-year-old boys exclusion figures from *The Trouble With Boys* by Chris Skidmore for the Bow Group, 2008 http://www.bowgroup.org/harriercollectionitems/BoysASchool-Report%5B1%5D.doc

Too clever too soon?

The Patterning of Complex Behaviour was the title of a 1974 book by the

New Zealand reading expert Dame Marie Clay. Learning to read requires a mixture of spoken language capacity, which children develop naturally given the input of articulate adults, and visual and auditory systemising skills.

The Flynn Effect, described in Ridley, 2004 and Johnson, 2005, charts the improvement in S-type thinking skills over the course of the 20th century.

For further argument about the 'too clever too soon?' issue, see Chapter 10.

'Their home background may ensure they get on well with adults': see Jerome Kagan's work on social development, referenced above in 'When the mollycoddling has to stop'.

Can't read, won't read?

Labels propelling boys into Special Needs: see Timimi, 2005 and Olfman, 2006

CHAPTER 6: BATTERY-REARED BOYS

Out to play

Quote from Cunningham, 2006

Quote re 1970s childhood: Collins, 2003

Children's Society research cited in Moss, Lyndsay, 'UK parents most protective in the world', *Scotsman* (18 July 2008)

Age at which most adults think children should be allowed out alone is 14: Good Childhood Inquiry, 2007 – see http://www.childrenssociety.org.uk/all_about_us/how_we_do_it/the_good_childhood_inquiry/1818.html

Survey of ten-year-olds at www.rights4me.org.uk in Cunningham, 2006

Information on home zones and safer streets: see Palmer, 2006, Chapter 2

Helping children grow up city-streetwise: see Advice of Parliamentary Advisory Council for transport and safety in Malkin, Bonnie, 'Let children cross road alone', *Daily Telegraph* (11 September 2007)

No increase in 'stranger danger' crimes: Silverman. J and Wilson, D., *Innocence Betrayed: Paedophilia, the Media and Society* (Polity 2002), quoted in Gill, 2007

Effects of TV coverage on parental perceptions: Restak, 2004

Cotton-wool kids

The background for this and the next section draws heavily on the work of Tim Gill, through personal interviews, conference addresses and his 2007 book *No Fear: Growing Up in a Risk Averse Society*. Unless otherwise stated, references are taken from this book.

As long as reasonable safety procedures are observed there is no legal cause for concern: at the Halifax Early Years Conference (March 2008) David Ball, Professor of Risk Management at Middlesex University cited the Health and Safety at Work Act, 1974 in which the words 'so far as is reasonably practicable', referring to provision for safety, are repeated seven times. The same applies to public playgrounds, where the whole point of play equipment is to allow children to develop their physical skills and to learn how to take 'safe risks'. Play by its very nature includes an element of risk, e.g. learning to balance, judge distances: see 'Managing risk in play provision: A position statement' from the Children's Play Information Service, cpis@ncb.org.uk

'... If we were always to look at the world...' quote: Tim Gill – personal interview

Boys engaging in risky activities: Sax, 2005

Sir Digby Jones: see Paton, Graeme, 'The danger from our cotton-wool kids', *Daily Telegraph* (7 July 2007). The problem of risk-aversion has also been aired by Simon Woodruffe, founder of Yo Sushi, who fears that 'children will grow up expecting to be looked after throughout their lives, and expect corporate reasonableness for their entire working life'. 'Children need risk to thrive as adults, says Dragon's Den judge' *The Times* (10 July 2008)

Sir Richard Branson's autobiography: *Losing My Virginity* (Virgin Books, 2007)

Educational dumbing down: Adey, Philip and Shayer, Michael, *Report to the ESRC: Have the Norms for Volume and Heaviness for Year 7 changed since the Mid-70s?* (January, 2006), and personal interview with Michael Shayer

Fear of boys

'adult alliance': see Palmer 2006, Chapter 10

Frank Furedi quote: see Johnson, Andrew, 'Do we worry too much about the safety of our children?', *Independent on Sunday* (24 October 2004)

Virtual freedom

Roger Louv quote: Louv, 2005

Childwise survey: see Ward, Lucy, 'Life through a lens: how Britain's
    children eat, sleep and breathe TV', *Guardian* (16 January 2008)

'technocreep' quote: Coleman, 2007

Hugh Cunningham quote: Cunningham, 2006

Robin Moore quote in Louv, 2005

Family values

Further background on significance of family: Palmer, 2006 and
    2007

Vicious cycle of parent/child/TV social deterioration described by
    Professor Agnes Nairn in presentation to *Toxic Childhood* confer-
    ence at Exeter University, December 2007

One in three marriages ends in divorce:
    http://www.lawontheweb.co.uk/basics/family.htm

Womack, Sarah, 'One child in four lives in a lone-parent family', *Tele-
    graph* (12 April 2007)

The single parent website says 83% of lone parents are female:
    http://the-single-parent.com/single-parent-statistics

Battery-reared bullies

Effects of greenery on ADHD: see Taylor, A.F., Kuo, F.E. and Sullivan
    W.C., *Go Out And Play: Nature Adds up For ADD Kids* (University of
    Illinois, 2001) and Taylor, A.F. and Kuo, F.E., 'Children with atten-
    tion deficits concentrate better after a walk in the park', *Journal of
    Attention Disorders* (August 2008)

Effects of home routine (sleep schedules) on ADHD: see Dahl, R.E.,
    Pelham, W.E. and Wierson, M., 'The role of sleep disturbances in
    ADD symptoms', *Journal of Pediatric Psychology*, Vol. 16 (1991) and
    Gozal, Dr David et al., 'Sleep and Neurobehavioural Characteris-
    tics of 5- to 7- Year-Old Children With Parentally Reported Symp-
    toms of ADHD', *Pediatrics*, Vol. 111, No. 3 (March 2003)

Peer socialisation: Harris, 1999 and 2007

Canadian research into effects of play on prefrontal cortex: see
    Sergio Pellis at the Canadian Centre for Behavioural Neuroscience
    at the University of Lethbridge http://ccbn.uleth.ca/people/pri-
    mary/pellis.php. Quote from Henzig, Manantz, 'Taking Play Seri-
    ously', *New York Times* (17 February 2008)

Quote from Valerie Besag in Gill, 2007
Quote from Brian Sutton Smith in Henzig, 2008 article above
Hugh Cunningham quote from Gill, 2007
Byron Review: *Safer Children in a Digital World* (DCSF, 2007)
    http://www.dcsf.gov.uk/byronreview/index.shtml

It takes a village

ESCR report: Weller, Dr Susie and Brugel, Professor Irene, *Children play key role in forging close communities* report by the Families and Social Capital ESCR research group (ESCR April 2007),
    http://www.esrcsocietytoday.ac.uk/ESRCInfoCentre/PO/releases/2007/april/children.aspx?ComponentId=19628&SourcePageId=17700

CHAPTER 7: SCHOOL VERSUS COOL

A question of discipline

85% chance of primary teacher being female: the latest figures I could get from the Office of National Statistics were from 2001/2002 when 85% of nursery and primary teachers in the UK were female: see 'Full-time nursery & primary and secondary school teachers: by sex', *Social Trends*, Vol. 34 (2004) (http://www.statistics.gov.uk/STATBASE/ssdataset.asp?vlnk=7322)

Focused concentration, self-control (and including the ability to defer gratification) and working memory – along with high neural interconnectivity, which is gained from a variety of early experience – are key aspects of 'intelligence': see Geake, John, 'Net Working', *Times Education Supplement Magazine* (8 August 2008)

Keeping the boys on board

Among the many recent research projects on boys' learning in the UK are:
Raising Boys' Achievement, Mike Younger and Molly Warrington, (DfES, 2005), http://www-rba.educ.cam.ac.uk/report.html#story2
Raising Boys' Achievement, Gary Wilson (DfES, 2003), http://www.standards.dfes.gov.uk/genderandachievement/nhss_boys_achievement2.pdf?version=1

Teachers' series on TV *Raising Boys' Achievement*, http://www.teachers.
    tv/video/4911
Raising Boys' Achievement in literacy, Eve Bearne and Dr Molly War-
    rington (National Literacy Trust website, 2003),
    http://www.literacytrust.org.uk/Pubs/bearne.html
    Database of research on boys and literacy,
    http://www.literacytrust.org.uk/Database/boys/west.html
The story of the Scoutmaster is told by Steve Biddulph (Australia),
    Finton O'Regan (UK) and Jean and Don Elium (USA).

The trouble with systems

Background on the bureaucratisation of English education and its
    assessment system: see Mansell, 2007
In 2007 fewer than half of 16-year-olds gained the acceptable base-
    line and a third of businesses send staff on literacy/numeracy
    courses: see Claxton, 2008
11% of 16- to 19-year-olds are now classified as NEETs: see Henry,
    Julie and Goslett, Miles, 'Meet the Neets' *Sunday Telegraph* (14
    April 2007)
Independent academic criticism of primary education for the Alexan-
    der Review: see Tymms, Peter and Merrill, Christine, *Standards and
    Quality in English Primary Schools Over Time*, Research Briefing 4.1,
    www.primaryreview.org.uk
Nuffield Review quote: University of Oxford press release, *Nuffield Re-
    view warns that 14–19 education and training is not a business* (14 Feb-
    ruary 2008)
National Audit Office report *The Use of Sanctions and Rewards in the Pub-
    lic Sector* (September 2008),
    http://www.nao.org.uk/publications/nao_reports/07-08/sanc-
    tions_rewards_public_sector.pdf
Quote from head of QCA: see Claxton, 2008
McKinsey report: *How the world's best performing school systems come out
    on top* (McKinsey, 2007)
    http://www.mckinsey.com/clientservice/socialsector/resources/
    pdf/Worlds_School_Systems_Final.pdf
Institute of Public Policy Research report: Sodha, Sonia and Margo,
    Julia *Thursday's Child* (IPPR, May 2008)

Don't mention the gender wars

Statistics on boys' achievement from Skidmore, Chris, *The Trouble with Boys* (Bow Group, 2007)

Quotes from Chris Ford and John Geake from Wilce, Hilary, 'Complex tales of the males', *Times Educational Supplement* (7 August 2006)

Girls progress: UNESCO Institute for Statistics, *UIS Statistics In Brief: Education in United Kingdom* (UNESCO 2005), http://stats_uis.unesco.org/unesco/
TableViewer/document.aspx?ReportId=121&IF_Language=eng&BR_Country=8260&BR_Region=40500

In 2001/2, 55% of secondary teachers were female: 'Full-time nursery & primary and secondary school teachers: by sex', *Social Trends*, Vol. 34 (2004) (http://www.statistics.gov.uk/STATBASE/ss-dataset.asp?vlnk=7322)

Ratio of females to males among newly qualified teachers: see 'Feminising education is of benefit to no one', *Daily Telegraph* (11 August 2007)

Comment on Celia Lashlie's research attributed to Chris Keates of the NASUWT: see Milne, Jonathan, 'Women, step back and shut up', *Times Educational Supplement* (20 June 2008)

Single-sex classes: the summary of projects at http://www-rba.educ.cam.ac.uk/report.html#story2 reports that pupils are almost always in favour of this approach, but research has so far been inconclusive as most have been short-lived – the main reason being lack of staff commitment

'the peer police': see Wilson, 2006

Life on Jupiter

Defining evercool qualities: see Del Vecchio, 1997

Life is short – play more!

Mark Crispin Miller quote from *The Merchants of Cool* broadcast on PBS (27 February 2007) full transcript at
www.pbs.org/wgbh/pages/frontline/shows/cool/etc/script.html)

Eric Clark quotes: Clark, 2007

Pursuit of happiness

Sean Brierly quote: Clark, 2007

Cool is not a static phenomenon: see *The Merchants of Cool*, above

Brands quote: see Lindstrom, 2003

Boys concern about brands: see Mayo, 2005

Marketing executive quote from *Campaign*: see Clark, 2007

Happiness studies: information taken from Professor Felicia Huppert's address to Baroness Greenfield's all-party House of Lords committee: '*Well-being in the classroom*', Portcullis House (23 October 2008)

Redrawing the battlelines

Hilary Wilce quote: personal interview, 2005 (see also Wilce, 2004)

Lucinda Neall quote: personal interview, 2008 (see also Neall, 2007)

Professor Guy Claxton's recipe for 21st century education: see Claxton, 2008

CHAPTER 8: MOTHER NATURE'S SONS

A question of taste

Information about nutrition and eating habits in this section: unless otherwise stated, see Chapter 1 of Palmer, 2006

The omega-3 studies with young offenders were described by Professor John Stein of the Department of Physiology, University of Oxford at the *Feeding Young Minds* conference, Edinburgh (5 March 2008). They relate to the Wellcome Nutrition Prison Study by Bernard Gesch: 'Omega-3, vitamins and mineral supplements reduced offences in Young Offenders by one third', *British Journal of Psychology*, Vol. 181 (2002) and a recent, as yet unpublished, Dutch study: 'Ontwikkeling aantal incidentregistraties per 1000 detentiedagan voedingssupplementen- versus placebogroep'

Experts' prediction for 2050: see Campbell, Denis, 'Half of all boys will be obese, warns leaked report', *Observer* (29 July 2007)

Supersize Me by Morgan Spurlock, 2004

Removal of transfats: 'Hidden fats removed from foods', *BBC News Online* (17 October 2006)

Finland's salt-substitute policy quoted by Dr Paul Clayton at *Feeding Young Minds*, Conference, Edinburgh (5 March 2008)

Adults wanting a ban on marketing unhealthy foods to children: Children's Society – Good Childhood Inquiry, paper on Health (February, 2008). See http://www.childrenssociety.org.uk/re-

sources/documents/good%20childhood/7081_full.pdf
Current limited ban on junk food advertising: see Children's Food
    Campaign, run by Sustain:
    http://www.sustainweb.org/page.php?id=29

Mens sana in corpore sano

Information about the decline of exercise: unless otherwise stated,
    see Chapter 2 of Palmer, 2006
Paul Cooper's Give Us Back Our Game: http://www.giveusback-
    ourgame.co.uk/index.php; see also Children's Football Alliance:
    http://www.childrensfootballalliance.com/
Preoccupation with product as opposed to process: with thanks to
    Dr Jenny Wright for many interesting conversations about sports
    science
Computers reward every seven seconds: Ian Jukes, speaking at the
    Bridging the Gap conference, at the International School of Yoko-
    hama, Japan (29 October 2007)
Structured physical activity affects personal and emotional develop-
    ment: see Craig , 2007

Mind to learn

Background information about sleep: see Chapter 3 of Palmer, 2006
Electronic equipment in bedrooms: as well as above, see Sigman,
    Aric, 'Visual Voodoo', *Biologist*, Vol. 54, No. 1 (February, 2007)
Difficulty in controlling one's focus of attention: Professor John
    Stein of the Department of Pharmacology at Oxford University
    pointed out that this an underpinning feature of all the major '
    developmental conditions' at *Feeding Young Minds* conference,
    Edinburgh (5 March 2008)

Thought control

Merlin Donald quotes: see Donald, 2001
Neil Postman quotes: see Postman, 1994

Digital natives, digital learners?

Daniel Pink reference: see Pink, 2005
'External memory field': see Donald, 2001
Experts in the field of digital literacy: I've been lucky enough to dis-
    cuss these issues with a number of such people, notably Dr Chris

Yapp, now Head of Public Sector Innovation at Microsoft, and the delightful young researchers at Futurelab in Bristol, which I visited in 2007 and 2008.

Ian Jukes: Bridging the Gap conference, International School of Yokohama, Japan (29 October 2007): see also http://web.mac.com/iajukes/thecommittedsardine/Home.html

Fascinating video link from Ian Jukes' website relating to hypertext on http://www.youtube.com/watch?v=rDqGQ59jw_Y

The drugs don't work

Sami Timimi quote: personal interview, 2005

In 2007, there were 461,000 Ritalin prescriptions in 2007 to children under 18 in full time education in England, compared with 199,000 in 2003: 'Massive Variation in Ritalin Prescribing', *Health Service Journal* (17 August 2008)

Prescriptions of Ritalin in Scotland have risen from 30,276 in 2003 to 48,739 in 2007: the Scottish Parliament Written Answers (26 March 2008) (http://www.scottish.parliament.uk/business/pqa/wa-08/wa0326.htm) In September 2008, the National Institute for Health and Clinical Excellence (NICE) recommended that Ritalin should be prescribed as a last resort, if behaviour modification techniques had proved ineffective. See http://www.nice.org.uk/Guidance/TA13

'In the short run... ' quote from Professor William Pelham, of the University of Buffalo, on 'What Next for Craig?' *Panorama*, BBC (14 November 2007)

'One in ten white school-age boys now take Ritalin': paediatrician Lawrence Diller in *The Rise of Ritalin* in Olfman, 2006.
'... drugs are frequently prescribed for ... such as shyness and moodiness', see Lane, 2007 and Olfman, 2006

Quote re drugs for bipolar disorder by Sharna Olfman, Associate Professor of Developmental Psych, Point Park University, in Introduction to Olfman, 2006

'*Individually calibrated chemical solutions to what are really predominantly social problems*' by Daniel Burston, Associate Professor of Psycholgy, Duquesne University, Pittsburgh in 'Diagnosis Drugs and BiPolar Disorder in Children' in Olfman, 2006.

Recommendation re brain scan: see Gurian, 2001

The feel-good factor

Frank Furedi's the fragile self: see Gill, 2007

Carol Craig's arguments about self-esteem: see Craig, 2007

Quote from Sandy MacLean, Scottish education adviser from 'Merit of school of hard knocks' by Henry Hepburn in *Times Educational Supplement Scotland* (1 August 2008)

Laughing it off

Susan Greenfield quote: Greenfield, 2008

CHAPTER 9: BOYS AND MEN

Information on testosterone levels: personal interview with Professor Simon Baron-Cohen, 2007.

Background information on adolescent development: see BBC Science: Human Body and Mind –http://www.bbc.co.uk/science/humanbody/ body/index.shtml?lifecycle

The eternal quest

Michael Perham's achievements: see 'Boy sails into the record books', *BBC News Online* (3 January 2007)

Dale Carter's career described in *Daily Mail* (3 January 2007)

Influence on antisocial behaviour in adolescence: see Parry, Vivienne, 'It's not just the hormones', *Guardian* (3 March 2005) and Craig, Lucy, 'Brakes off for the peer show', *Times Educational Supplement Magazine*(1 August 2008)

'Even "well-brought-up" privileged boys… ' see Messerschmidt, J. 'Schooling, masculinities and youth crime' in Newburn and Stanko, 1994

Code of honour

Male friendship patterns: see Premack, D. and Premack, A.J., 'Origins of human social competence' in Gazzaniga, M.S., 'The Cognitive Neurosciences' (MIT Press, 1995). 'Males appear more prone to form and join groups than females. [Premack and Premack] theorise that a domain-specific module for social competence evolved which includes a predisposition to perceive similar objects that behave reciprocally towards one another as belonging to one group. Males are more predisposed than females to be attracted to a group': quoted in Benenson, J.F., Duggan, V. and Markovits, H., 'Sex Differences in Infants' Attraction to group versus individual stimuli', *Infant Behavior and Development*, Vol. 27, No. 2 (May 2004)

Empire's sons and freedom's orphans

World Organisation of the Scout Movement: www.scout.org; Boys' Brigade: www.boys-brigade.org.uk; Sea Cadets: www.ms-sc.org

Invention of 'teen culture': see Savage, 2007

Quote (by Bob Bibby, television marketing executive) and statistics about marketing: *The Merchants of Cool* (Frontline Productions) broadcast on PBS (27 February 2007) full transcript at www.pbs.org/wgbh/pages/frontline/ shows/cool/etc/script.html

Margo, J., Dixon, M., Pearce, N. and Reed, H., *Freedom's Orphans*, IPPR (2006) http://www.ippr.org.uk/publicationsandreports/publication.asp?id=496

Quote about structured/unstructured activity: see Mahoney, J., Stattin, H. and Lord, H., 'Unstructured youth recreation centre participation and antisocial behaviour development: Selection influences and the moderating role of antisocial peers', *International Journal of Behavioral Development*, Vol. 28, 553 (2004). See also Mahoney, J. and Stattin, H., 'Leisure activities and adolescent antisocial behavior: The role of structure and social context', *Journal of Adolescence*, Vol. 23, No. 2 (2000)

Australian research about compulsion: see Warburton, J. and Smith, J., 'Out of the Generosity of Your Heart: Are We Creating Active Citizens through Compulsory Volunteer Programmes for Young People in Australia?' *Social Policy and Administration*, Vol. 37, No. 7 (December 2003)

Rites and rights

Background to this section: see Graham, 2004 and Epstein, 2007; also Robert Epstein's presentation at *Foundations for Flourishing* conference, Edinburgh (10 March 2008)

'... aimed at skill-building... ' Mahoney, J. and Stattin, H., 'Leisure activities and adolescent antisocial behavior: The role of structure and social context', *Journal of Adolescence*, Vol. 23, No. 2 (2000)

Activities should involve opportunities for adventure and risk: see Neumark-Sztainer, Dianne, Story, Mary French, Simone and

Resnick, Michael, 'Psychosocial correlates of health compromising behaviours among adolescents', *Health Education Research*, Vol. 12, No. 1 (1997) and Davidson, Lee, 'Qualitative research and making meaning from adventure: A case study of boys' experiences of outdoor education at school', *Journal of Adventure Education and Outdoor Learning*, Vol. 1, No. 2 (2001)

Learning to be men

Steve Biddulph: see Biddulph, 2003, 2004
Michael Gurian: see Gurian, 2001
Good Childhood Inquiry research summary 6: Values http://www.childrenssociety.org.uk/resources/documents/good%20childhood/7584_full.pdf

Me Tarzan, you Jane

I asked an interviewee for a recent example of rap music, and he provided the following from Insane Clown Posse's album *The Tempest* (2007):

> 'Bitch, i'm here to tell you i lied
> When i seen that thick-ass it was over
> Nothin else mattered, i ain't even care
> I pulled the rubber off when i stuck it up in there too
> Bitch, i lied, everytime i left town
> I really stayed right here at home
> Dickin hoes down, every penny that you helped my mom
> With went straight to the asian spa, bitch'

Waller Newell quote: Newell, 2003

Sex and drugs and rock and roll

Violence/sexual references etc. in music and music videos: see Roberts, D.F., Christenson, P.G. and Gentile, D.A., 'The effects of violent music on children and adolescents', *Media Violence and Children*, Gentile, D.A. (ed.) (Praeger, 2003). Parents and others are particularly worried by the content of rap music: see Eberstadt, 2004; Giles Hattersley: '*!@**! Where did that come from?' *Sunday Times* (31 July 2005); *Independent* (17 August 2005) and 'Youth and Violent Music', Issue Brief Series (2000)
Susan Greenfield 'loss of mind': see Greenfield, 2008
Brett's story told by himself and his teacher, Alison Mitchell, at the

Foundations for Flourishing conference, run by the Centre for Confidence and Wellbeing in Edinburgh (11 March 2008)

CHAPTER 10: LOST BOYS

'I've been in so much trouble it's unreal... ' from 'You've got to be a bully' by Josh Cole, *Independent on Sunday* (13 April 2008)

'It usually starts outside McDonald's' quote, Prime Minister quote and other details from 'Britain's Mean Streets' by Catherine Mayer, *Time* (26 March 2008)

Britain's mean streets

Chief Constable of the West Midlands Police quote: Gill 2007

UK Children's Commissioners Report to the UN Committee on the Rights of the Child, June 2008: see http://www.11million.org.uk/resource/31f7xsa2gjgfc3l9t8o8qfsi.pdf

Camilla Batmanghelidjh's 'initiators' and 'imitators': see 'Ways to be sure that the kids are all right', *Times* (2 June 2008). There's increasing evidence that the worst initiators may be boys for whom genetic and environmental effects combine: see Caspi et al., 'The role of genotype in the cycle of violencein maltreated children', *Science*, Vol. 297 (2002)

The gang is a surrogate family: quote from Geraldine Gammell of the Princes Trust in Scotland, where one fifth of children surveyed looked to gangs for role models. Reported in Howie, Michael, 'Lack of role models drives young people to join gangs', *The Scotsman* (14 August 2008)

'You've got to be a bully' quote by Cole, Josh, *Independent on Sunday* (13 April 2008)

'If I join a gang I'm 50% safe': see Gabarino, 1995

'knife-wielding, gun-toting, pit-bull-packing hoodies' from 'Street Crime Special: trigger-happy tales from Britain's front line', *Independent on Sunday* (13 April 2008)

Association of Chief Police Officers quote and hospital admissions figures from O'Neill, Sean, 'Unite against knife crime, police chief Alf Hitchcock tells politicians', *Times* (14 July 2008)

29.5% increase in admission to hospital for serious assault: see Bellis et al., *Journal of Epidemiology and Community Health*, quoted in

New Scientist (19 July 2008)

Young people carrying blades for defence: see Leppard, David, 'Knife crime doubles in two years', *Sunday Times* (19 August 2007)

Gun crime figures: see 'Gun crime up by 35%', *BBC News Online* (January, 2003)

Knife crime figures: see Percival, Jenny, 'Knife-carrying down in crime hotspots', *Guardian* (11 December 2008)

Gang membership increasing among younger teens. Researchers in London and Birmingham in 2008 found that the number of under-sixteens involved in gangs had roughly doubled in the past five years: see 'Schools to fight in war against gang culture', *Education*, Vol. 315 (30 May 2008)

Born losers

It's now widely accepted that both genetic and environmental factors are involved in teenage antisocial behaviour, but poverty seems to play a major part both in triggering genetic factors and in creating an environment that leads to poor outcomes (including the sorts of negative peer pressure mentioned notes to Chapter 9, 'The eternal quest' above). For a summary of major research see powerpoint presentation by Professor Barbara Maugham of Kings College, London: *Influences on antisocial behaviour in adolescence*: www.york.ac.uk/inst/cdw/present/ Barbara%20Maughan.ppt#335,45,Slide 45

Educational disadvantage obvious at two years old: see Feinstein, Leon, 'Very early evidence' *Centrepiece* (2003), http://cep.lse.ac.uk/centrepiece/vo8i2/feinstein.pdf

2005 report on mental health: Office of National Statistics survey (31 August 2005), see News Release: http://www.statistics.gov.uk/pdfdir/cmd0805.pdf

70% of young offenders: UNESCO report cited in the Annual Review of the Youth Justice Board, 2001/2: *Building on Success*

The poverty trap

Until the late 1970s, poverty gap narrowed: see Layard, 2005

In 2004–05 the UK had the seventh largest inequalities in incomes of the 27 EU member states. The top 20% of the UK population earned around 5.7 times the income of the lowest 20%, compared with an EU average of 4.9: Commission of the European Commu-

nities, *Joint Report on Social Protection and Social Inclusion: Supporting Document* (2007)
http://ec.europa.eu/employment_social/social_inclusion/docs/2007/joint_report/sec_2007_329_en.pdf

Gap growing year on year: see Elliott, Larry, 'Up Up Up Child poverty, pensioner poverty, inequality', *Guardian* (11 June 2008)

Narrower gap in Nordic countries: including social transfers, Sweden had an 'at risk' of poverty rate of 9% of its population below 60% median income in 2005 before deducting housing costs. This compares with around 12% for Finland, 18% for the UK and 16% for the EU-25 states as a whole:
Central Statistics Office (Ireland), *EU Survey on Income and Living Conditions* (EU-SILC) 2006 (November, 2007),
http://www.cso.ie/releasespublications/documents/eu_silc/current/eusilc.pdf

Finland and Sweden do well in international studies of educational achievement: see
http://news.bbc.co.uk/1/hi/education/7126562.stm

UNICEF report: UNICEF Innocenti Research Centre: *An overview of child well-being in rich countries: a comprehensive assessment of the lives and well-being of children and adolescents in the economically advanced nations*, (UNICEF, 2007) http://www.unicef.org/media/files/ChildPovertyReport.pdf

Comparative crime figures: Walmsly, Roy, *World Prison Population List*, (Home Office, 2003)

Britain has highest rate of incarceration in western Europe: figures released by Howard League for Penal Reform on 18 January 2006, see http://www.howardleague.org/fileadmin/howard_league/user/pdf/international_imprisonment_rates_01.pdf (dated incorrectly on press release)

'New super-prisons to be built', *BBC News Online* (5 December 2007) (three planned at that date),
http://news.bbc.co.uk/1/hi/uk/7128181.stm

Tough on crime

In 2005 the overall reoffending rate of juveniles (those aged ten to nineteen at date of sanction or on release from custody) was 40.8%.Medhurst, Craig and Cunliffe, Jack, *Re-offending in juveniles: results from the 2005 cohort*, Ministry of Justice statistical bulletin

(July, 2007),
http://www.justice.gov.uk/docs/reoffending-juveniles2005.pdf
Youth Justice Board – http://www.yjb.gov.uk/en-gb/
Shaun Bailey: personal interview
Marine story: at conference under Chatham House rules
Ray Lewis: see Griffiths, Sian, 'Ray Lewis: Pied Piper to the Wild
    Boys', *The Times* (10 May 2008). Thanks also to Sian Griffiths for
    personal conversation about this article.
Alf Hitchcock recommendation: see 'Send jobless youths on national
    service, says Britain's new knife crime tsar', *Daily Mail* (14 July
    2008)

Tough on the causes of crime

'The dividend is 12-16%...' in Sinclair, Alan, 0-5: *How Small Children
    Make a Big Difference'*, *Provocation series*, Vol. 3, No. 1 (The Work
    Foundation 2007)
Scientific evidence about good early childcare: for an authoritative
    and up-to-date summary of the state of play re the effects of envi-
    ronment on brain development, see *National Scientific Council on the
    Developing Child* Working Papers 1 to 5 Summer 2004–08, pro-
    duced by the University of Harvard: www.developingchild.net
    More specific info in Rutter M. *The promotion of resilience in the face of
    adversity*. In: Clarke-Stewart, A., Dunn, J. (eds). Families Count:
    Effects on Child Adolescent Development. (Cambridge University
    Press, 2006), pp 26–52 and Widom, C. and McGloin, J., 'Re-
    silience among abused and neglected children grown up', *Dev
    Psychopathol*, Vol. 13, pp. 1021–1038 (2001)
Sure Start: see http://www.surestart.gov.uk/
Nurse Family Partnership programme: see http://www.nursefamily-
    partnership.org/index.cfm?fuseaction=home
A good start is only the start: Professor Leon Feinstein at Baroness
    Greenfield's all-party House of Lords committee: *Well-being in the
    classroom*, Portcullis House (23 October 2008)

Born winners

Good effects of equality: see Wilkinson, 2006 and Layard, 2005
'Human beings will always betray you': see Curtis, 2007
'They get so used to seeing low-level parenting ... 'quote from child
    protection expert in 2008 is Eileen Munro, of the LSE in Purves,

Libby, 'She's starving, but how's her IT?', *The Times* (27 May 2008)

Children 'lifted out of poverty': the conflict between official government figures and reality is outlined in an IPPR press release 'Government must rescue 'forgotten million' in poverty' (3 January 2008), http://www.ippr.org/pressreleases/?id=2965 .

Guardian complaint in 2008: 'Balls' test answer? More of the futile, top-down plans that Labour loves' by Jenni Russell in the *Guardian*, 28 January 2008

Levelling the playing field

'Outbreak of honesty' quote: see Harford (14 August 2008)

OECD quote from *Raising Educational Achievement and Breaking the Cycle of Poverty in the United Kingdom* (2008), www.olis.oecd.org

Colder, sadder, meaner

Report on effects of media violence on children: American Academy of Pediatrics, *Joint Statement on the Impact of Entertainment Violence on Children*, presented at the Congressional Public Health Summit, Washington DC, (26 July 2000), http://www.aap.org/advocacy/releases/jstmtevc.htm

Mark Lawson review: 'Is the Dark Knight suitable for children?', *Guardian* blogs (31 July 2008)

Jenny McCartney comments in 'The Dark Knight Taints Our Children's World View', *Daily Telegraph* (26 July 2008)

Department of Health report: *Working Together to Safeguard Children: a guide for interagency working to safeguard and promote the welfare of children* (Department of Health, 1999)

Layard quote: Layard, 2005

BIBLIOGRAPHY

Abbott, John, *Overschooled but Undereducated: society's failure to understand adolescence* (21st Century Learning Initiative, 2008)

Alliance for Childhood, *Tech Tonic* (Alliance for Childhood, 2004)

Baron-Cohen, Simon, *The Essential Difference: men, women and the extreme male brain* (Allen Lane, 2003)

Bettelheim, Bruno, *A Good Enough Parent: guide to raising your child* (Thames and Hudson, 1995)

Biddulph, Steve, *Raising Boys: why boys are different and how to help them become happy and well-balanced young men* (Thorsens new edition, 2003)

Biddulph, Steve, *Manhood* (Vermilion, revised edition, 2004)

Biddulph, Steve, *Raising Babies: why your love is best* (HarperThorsons, 2006)

Blakemore, Sarah Jayne and Frith, Uta, *The Learning Brain* (Blackwell, 2005)

Boxall, Marjorie, *Nurture Groups in Schools: Principles and Practice* (London: Paul Chapman, 2002)

Brizendine, Louann, *The Female Brain* (Bantam Books 2006)

Bruce, Tina and Spratt, Jenny, *Essentials of Literacy 0 – 7* (Sage Publications, 2008)

Byron, Tanya, *Your Child Your Way: create a positive parenting pattern for life* (Michael Joseph, 2007)

Clark, Eric, *The Real Toy Story* (Black Swan, 2007)

Claxton, Guy, *What's the Point of School?* (One World, 2008)

Coleman, Will, *Brave Tales: developing literacy through storytelling* (Network Continuum, 2007)

Collins, Andrew, *Where Did It All Go Right? Growing up normal in the 70s* (Ebury Press, London 2003)

Craig, Carol, *Creating Confidence: a handbook for professionals working with young people* (Centre for Confidence and Wellbeing, 2007)

Cunningham, Hugh, *The Invention of Childhood* (BBC Books, 2006)

Curtis, Adam, *The Century of the Self* (BBC 2002; available on Google Video)

Curtis, Adam, *The Trap: what's happened to our dream of freedom?* (BBC, 2007; available on Google Video)

Damasio, Antonio, *Descartes Error: emotion, reason and the human brain* (Vintage, 2006)

Damasio, Antonio, *Looking for Spinoza – Joy, Sorrow and the Feeling Brain* (Vintage 2004)

Del Vecchio, Gene: *Creating Evercool: a marketer's guide to a kid's heart* (Pelican 1997)

Dolya, Galina, *Key to Learning: the technology of child development* (GDH Publishing, 2008)

Donald, Merlin, *A Mind So Rare: the evolution of human consciousness* (WW Norton, 2001)

Dowd, Maureen, *Are Men Necessary?* (Headline Review, 2005)

Eberstadt, Mary, *Home Alone America: the hidden toll of daycare, behavioural drugs and other parent substitutes* (Sentinel; Penguin Group USA, 2004)

Elium, Don and Jeanne, *Raising a Son* (Celestial Arts, 2004)

Elkind, David, *The Hurried Child: Growing Up Too Fast Too Soon* (Da Capo Press; Perseus Books Group, 2001)

Epstein, Robert, *The Case Against Adolescence: rediscovering the adult in every teen* (Quill Driver Books, 2007)

Fine, Cordelia, *A Mind of Its Own* (Icon Books 2006)

Frith, Uta, *Autism and Asperger Syndrome* (Cambridge University Press,1991)

Garbarino, James, *Raising Children in a Socially Toxic Environment* (Jossey-Bass, 1995)

Geary, David, *Male, Female: the evolution of human sex differences* (American Psychological Association, 1998)

Gerhardt, Sue, *Why Love Matters: how affection shapes a baby's brain* (Routledge, 2004)

Gilbert, Susan, *A Field Guide to Boys and Girls* (Quill 2000)

Gill, Tim, *No Fear: growing up in a risk-averse society* (Gulbenkian Foundation, 2007)

Goddard Blythe, Sally, *The Well Balanced Child: movement and early learning* (Hawthorne Press, 2004)

Goddard Blythe, Sally, *What Babies and Children Really Need* (Hawthorn Press, 2008)

Goleman, Daniel, *Emotional Intelligence: why it can matter more than IQ* (Bantam Books, 1997)

Goleman, Daniel, *Social Intelligence: the new science of human relationships* (Arrow Books, 2007)

Gopnik A, Meltzoff, A.N. and Kuhl, P., *The Scientist in the Crib: what early learning tells us about the mind* (Perennial, 2001)

Graham, Philip, *EoA: the end of adolescence* (Oxford University Press, 2004)

Greenfield, Susan, *The Human Brain: a guided tour* (London: Phoenix, 1997)

Greenfield, Susan, *Tomorrow's People: how 21st century technology is changing the way we think and feel* (Allen Lane, 2003)

Greenfield, Susan, *ID: the quest for identity in the 21st century* (Sceptre, 2008)

Guest, Tim, *Second Lives: a journey through virtual worlds* (Random House, 2007)

Gurian, Michael, *Boys and Girls Learn Differently: a guide for teachers and parents* (Jossey Bass, 2001)

Harford, Tim, *The Logic of Life: uncovering the new economics of everything* (Little, Brown, 2008)

Harris, Judith Rich, *The Nurture Assumption: why children turn out the way they do* (Pocket Books, 1999)

Harris, Judith Rich, *No Two Alike* (WW Norton and Co, 2007)

Hart, Betty and Risley, Todd R., *Meaningful Differences in the Everyday Experience of Young American Children* (Baltimore: Brookes Publishing, 1995)

Hartley-Brewer, Elizabeth, *Raising Confident Boys: 100 Tips for Parents and Teachers* (Da Capo Press, 2001)

Herschkowitz, Norbert and Herschkowitz, Elinore Chapman, *A Good Start in Life: understanding your child's brain and behaviour from birth to age 6* (Dana Press, 2004)

Hobson, Peter, *The Cradle of Thought* (Macmillan, 2002)

Hoff Somers, Christina, *The War Against Boys* (Simon and Schuster, 2000)

Holland, Penny, *We Don't Play With Guns Here: war, weapons and super-*

hero play in the early years (Open University Press, 2003)

Honoré, Carl, *Under Pressure: rescuing our children from the culture of hyper-parenting* (Orion 2008)

James, Oliver, *They F*** You Up: how to survive family life* (Bloomsbury, 2007)

James, Oliver, *Affluenza* (Vermilion, 2007)

Johnson, Steven, *Everything Bad is Good for You* (Allen Lane, 2005)

Jones, Steve, *Y: The Descent of Men* (Abacus, 2002)

Kagan Jerome, *Galen's Prophecy: temperament in human nature* (Free Association Books, 1994)

Kindlon, Dan and Thomson, Michael, *Raising Cain: protecting the emotional life of boys* (Ballantine Books, 2000)

Lamb, Michael (ed), *The Role of the Father in Child Development*, Fourth Edition (John Wiley and Sons, 2004)

Lane, Christopher, *Shyness: how normal behaviour became a sickness* (Yale University Press, 2007)

Law, Professor James, *Learning to Talk: A practical guide for parents* (Dorling Kindersley, 2004)

Layard, Richard, *Happiness: lessons from a new science* (Penguin, 2005)

Lindstrom, Martin, (with Seybold, Patricia B) *Brand Child* (Revised Edition) (Kogan Page Limited, 2003)

Linn, Susan, *Consuming Kids: the hostile takeover of childhood* (NY New Press, 2005)

Linn, Susan, *The Case for Make Believe: saving play in a commercialised world* (New Press, 2008)

Livingstone, Tessa, *Child of Our Time: how to achieve the best for your child from conception to 5 years* (Bantam Press, 2005)

Louv, Richard, *Last Child in the Woods: saving our kids from nature-deficit disorder* (Algonquin Books, 2005)

Mansell, Warwick, *Education By Numbers* (Politicos, 2007)

Martin, Paul, *Making Happy People: the nature of happiness and its origins in childhood* (Fourth Estate, 2005)

Massey, Alexandra, *Happy Kids: understanding childhood depression and how to nurture a happy, well-balanced child* (Virgin Books, 2007)

Mayo, Ed, *Shopping Generation* (National Consumer Council, 2005)

Mcintyre Christine and McVitty, Kim, *Movement and Learning in the Early Years* (Paul Chapman, 2004)

McLure, Ali, *Making It Better For Boys in Schools, Families and Communities* (Network Continuum, 2008)

McNeal, James U., *Kids as Customers: a handbook of marketing to children* (NY: Lexington Books, 1992)

Moir, Anne and Moir, Bill, *Why Men Don't Iron: the new reality of gender differences* (HarperCollins, 1999)

National Research Council, Institute of Medicine From *Neurons to Neighborhoods – The Science of Early Childhood Development* (National Academy Press 2000)

Neall, Lucinda, *About Our Boys: a practical guide to bringing out the best in boys* (Neall Scott Partnership, 2007)

Neall, Lucinda, *Bringing the Best Out in Boys: communication strategies for teachers* (Paul Chapman, 2003)

Newborn, Tim and Stanko, Elizabeth A., *Just Boys Doing Business: men, masculinities and crime* (Routledge, 1994)

Newell, Waller R., *The Code of Man* (Regan Books, 2003)

Olfman, Sharna (ed.), *No Child Left Different* (Praeger, 2006)

Paley, Vivian Gussin, *A Child's Work* (University of Chicago Press, 2004)

Paley, Vivian Gussin, *Boys and Girls: Superheroes in the Dolls' Corner* (University of Chicago Press, 1986)

Palmer, Sue, *Toxic Childhood* (Orion, 2006)

Palmer, Sue, *Detoxing Childhood* (Orion, 2007)

Palmer, Sue and Bayley, Ros, *Foundations of Literacy: a balanced approach to language, listening and literacy skills in the early years* (Network Continuum, third edition 2008)

Pink, Daniel H., *A Whole New Mind: moving from the information age to the conceptual age* (Riverhead Books, 2005)

Pinker, Steven, *The Blank State* (Penguin Books, 2003)

Pinker, Susan, *The Sexual Paradox* (Atlantic Books, 2008)

Pollack, William S. and Shuster, Todd, *Real Boys' Voices* (Penguin, 2000)

Postman, Neil, *Amusing Ourselves to Death* (Random House, 1985)

Postman, Neil, *The Disappearance of Childhood* (Vintage Books; Random House, 1994)

Restak, Richard, *The New Brain: how the modern age is rewiring your mind* (Rodale, 2004)

Richardson, Alex, *They Are What You Feed Them* (HarperCollins, 2006)

Ridley, Matt, *Nature via Nurture* (HarperCollins, 2004)

Royal College of Paediatrics and Child Health, *Helpful Parenting* (Royal College of Paediatrics and Child Health, 2002)

Salinger, J.D., *The Catcher in the Rye* (Penguin, 1958)

Salzman, Marian, Matathia, Ira and O'Reilly, Ann, *The Future of Men* (Palgrave Macmillan, 2005)

Savage, John, *Teenage: the creation of youth culture* (Viking, 2007)

Sax, Leonard, *Why Gender Matters – What parents and teachers need to know about the emerging science of sex differences* (Doubleday, 2005)

Shor, Juliet, *Born to Buy: the commercialised child and the new consumer culture* (Shribner, 2005)

Shaw, Robert, *The Epidemic: The Rot of American Culture, Absentee and Permissive Parenting, and the Resultant Plague of Joyless, Selfish Children* (ReganBooks, an imprint of HarperCollins Publishers, 2003)

Sheppard, Philip, *Music Makes Your Child Smarter: how music helps every child's development* (Artemis Editions, 2005)

Shonkoff, Jack P. and Phillips, D. (eds.), *From Neurons to Neighbourhoods: the science of early childhood development* (National Academy Press, 2000)

Sigman, Aric, *Remotely Controlled; how television is damaging our lives and what we can do about it* (Vermilion, 2005)

Snowling, Margaret, *Dyslexia* (Blackwell, 2000)

Stone, Wendy L., *Does My Child Have Autism: a parent's guide to early detection and intervention in autism spectrum disorders* (Jossey Bass, 2006)

Sunderland, Margot, *The Science of Parenting: practical guidance on sleep, crying, play and building emotional wellbeing for life* (Dorling Kindersley, 2006)

Thomas, Susan Gregory, *Buy Buy Baby: how big business captures the ultimate consumer – your baby or toddler* (HarperCollins, 2007)

Timimi, Sami, *Naughty Boys: anti-social behaviour, ADHD and the role of culture* (Palgrave Macmillan, 2005)

Ward, Dr Sally, *Babytalk* (Century, 2000)

Weinberger, D, *Everything is Miscellaneous: the power of the new digital disorder* (Times Books, 2007)

Weissbluth, Marc, *Healthy Sleep Habits, Happy Child* (The Random House Publishing Group, 1998)

Wilce, Hilary, *Help Your Child Succeed at School* (Piatkus, 2004)

Wilkinson, Richard, *The Impact of Inequality: how to make sick societies healthier* (New Press, 2006)

Williams, Fiona, *Rethinking Families* (Calouste Gulbenkian Foundation, London, 2004)

Wilson, Gary, *Breaking Through Barriers to Boys' Achievement* (Network Continuum, 2006)

Wilson, Gary, *Raising Boys' Achievement* (Network Continuum Pocket Pal, 2007)

Winn, Marie, *The Plug-in Drug: Television, Computers, and Family Life* (Penguin Books, 2002)